Energy Politics
in Colombia

Energy Politics
in Colombia

René De La Pedraja

Routledge
Taylor & Francis Group

LONDON AND NEW YORK

First published 1989 by Westview Press

Published 2018 by Routledge
52 Vanderbilt Avenue, New York, NY 10017
2 Park Square, Milton Park, Abingdon, Oxon OX14 4RN

Routledge is an imprint of the Taylor & Francis Group, an informa business

Library of Congress Cataloging-in-Publication Data
De La Pedraja Tomán, René.
  Energy politics in Colombia / by René De La Pedraja.
    p. cm.—(Westview special studies on Latin America and the
Caribbean)
  Includes index.
  ISBN 0-8133-7655-6
  1. Energy policy—Colombia. 2. Natural resources—Government
policy—Colombia. I. Title. II. Series.
HD9502.C72D4 1989
333.79′09861—dc19   88-11098
                                                                               CIP

ISBN 13: 978-0-367-01270-0 (hbk)
ISBN 13: 978-0-367-16257-3 (pbk)

To Beatriz

Contents

Epilogue   225

Index   233

Acknowledgments

Only a collective thank-you can go to those institutions and many individuals who at considerable risk have provided much of the information on which this book is based. Anonymity may not be enough protection for them; I still hope for a day in Colombia when they may be mentioned without fear of reprisal and without accelerating the destruction of compromising evidence. I have done everything possible to verify and compare this information with that available in U.S. and British archives as well as in the public record—all sources that contribute valuable dimensions of their own. The referees' comments have contributed to the final shape of this book.

The staffs at the various archives and libraries I consulted were unfailingly helpful. Support from Kansas State University for the final research is greatly appreciated. Nedra Sylvis typed the manuscript with her usual precision. Special thanks go to Helen Toman, as well as to Elvira and Terry Buttler. My son, Jaroslav, helped classify the seemingly endless piles of documents and clippings, while my wife, Beatriz, once again patiently read and improved upon the text, a gigantic effort in itself, and also drew the maps. More important, she provided intelligent support for home and family life during a particularly trying time in our careers, until at last this book could fend for itself.

René De La Pedraja

Introduction

Why has Latin America remained an economically underdeveloped and generally poor area in spite of the abundance of natural resources of the most varied kinds? The example of Colombia, the third most populated country in Latin America, clearly shows that the failure to replace human and animal power with ever-increasing amounts of mechanically derived forms of energy has been one of the causes of poverty among Latin Americans; it has also helped create fertile ground for recurrent political strife.

My previous book, *Historia de la energía en Colombia, 1537–1930*, revealed how the country lagged from the very start in meeting the energy needs of its economy, but one question remained unanswered: Why did Colombia fail to properly utilize its vast reserves of coal, hydroelectricity, and petroleum, not to mention its other mineral resources? This book, covering the period since 1920, attempts to provide an answer to this question by examining Colombia's policies concerning a broad range of representative energy development projects.

The Industrial Revolution in Europe had at its very center the application of iron and coal to produce steam power, yet Colombia during the nineteenth century largely failed to incorporate these new advances, as witnessed by the limited spread of steam navigation in the inland rivers and railroads; no more successful was the use of steam to power the incipient shops and the handful of factories. It was only in 1890, when Europe and the United States were already in the middle of the Second Industrial Revolution, that Colombia began to install small generating plants; by 1910 all the major cities enjoyed regular electricity service, although in limited amounts. Small as it was, this stimulus provided by the gradual spread of electricity was at the very core of the onset of industrialization from 1890.

By 1930, even before the Great Depression struck, this first stage of both industrialization and electrification had run into deep trouble. As the private Colombian utilities increased their capacity to transform a backwards and agrarian country, they faced a rising tide of obstacles. Contemporaries agreed that both the utilities and the factories were starved for capital, disregarding, however, signs that other problems also

1

caused the first stage of industrialization, which had never been very hectic, to peter out by 1930.

Where could additional capital be found? The government and private sectors were both financially strained. By the late 1920s the only remaining source of capital ready at hand was to be found in Colombia's large petroleum fields, whose black liquid flowed on the surface, making unnecessary any prospecting or exploratory drilling. Oil revenues would thus finance a vast expansion of hydroelectricity, as well as of industry. However, since government concessions had already granted the two known main oil fields to U.S. companies, a decisive struggle ensued. This is where the first chapter of this book begins.

PART ONE

Petroleum and Natural Gas

1

The First Nationalistic Campaign

Exxon had adroitly maneuvered during the 1910s to acquire the Barrancabermeja field, and Gulf Oil Co. (owned by Andrew Mellon) did the same to acquire the Barco Concession near Cúcuta (Map 1). These two fields contained the main oil deposits in Colombia, and many members of the Colombian elite expected these acquisitions to produce great rivers of wealth for their country. These hopes were dashed during the first half of the 1920s: Exxon in Barrancabermeja considered the export of crude to be its main concern, and other issues, such as local supply of gasoline, were secondary; Gulf did not even bother to exploit the Barco Concession but merely kept it as a reserve. Exxon was supposed to pay the Colombian government a mere 10 percent crude royalty for extracting the oil that naturally oozed to the surface, and in fact it normally paid even less by recourse to numerous subterfuges. By the mid 1920s, Colombia, rather than swimming in wealth, was instead drained by the practices of the U.S. oil companies.[1] A faction within the Colombian elite felt that this situation was unacceptable, and during the presidency of Miguel Abadía Méndez (1926–1930), Minister of Development José Antonio Montalvo led the dissatisfied elements in a campaign to reverse Colombia's petroleum policy and rescue the Barco Concession.

Petroleum and the Great Game of Empire

The presidency of Abadía Méndez witnessed the gradual shift of power from the ruling Conservative Party, dominant in Colombia since the end of the nineteenth century, to the revitalized opposition Liberal Party. Conservative leaders were not unaware of their crumbling position, and to gain a new lease on life, the faction around Montalvo decided to start a nationalistic campaign over petroleum. Their two related goals were to regain popularity, and hence votes, and to increase the revenue received from the Barrancabermeja oil field. The government needed the

MAP 1

N

ATLANTIC OCEAN

GUAJIRA

Santa Marta
Barranquilla

El Cerrejón

Cartagena

El Difícil

PANAMA

Cicuco

VENEZUELA

Jobo

Tibú

Cerromatoso

Zulia

Cúcuta

Casabe Barrancabermeja

Caño Limón

Medellín

Cantimploras

LLANOS

La Dorada Puerto Salgar

Cartago

BOGOTÁ

Buenaventura

Guamo

Cali

PACIFIC OCEAN

COLOMBIA

● Oil Fields
○ Natural Gas Fields
▧ Refineries
— Crude Oil Pipeline
···· Natural Gas Pipeline
–x–x– Refined Products Pipeline

0   100 Kms

Tumaco

Orito

ECUADOR

extra revenue to finance public works and other spending projects designed to keep the Conservative Party in power. However, the government had signed a contract with Exxon in 1916 stipulating that the crude royalty rate would be 10 percent for 30 years starting in 1921.[2] How could the rate be revised in the face of this contract?

Exxon had imposed on Colombia the standard practice shared by other oil companies of never giving up even the smallest acquired privilege, so that when Montalvo sounded out Exxon about increasing the crude royalty rate from 10 to 15 percent, he received an indignant rejection. This refusal forced the Minister of Development to study events in Mexico more closely, and he soon learned that U.S. oil companies became more conciliatory when the state played them off against rival British companies. After preliminary soundings, Montalvo discovered that the English company most interested in Colombia was British Petroleum, which controlled the rich oilfields in Iran but wished to diversify. British Petroleum had the added advantage of partial ownership by His Majesty's Government, thus assuring strong diplomatic support from London to counter the pressures from the State Department. A minor irritant was Colombian law, which, in order to prevent another Panama, forbade granting oil concessions to companies having foreign states as major stockholders.

To temporarily bypass this obstacle, British Petroleum commissioned an agent, Colonel H.I.F. Yates, to carry out the preliminary negotiations on behalf of a dummy corporation; once an agreement had been reached, the Colombian executive would legalize it with congressional approval so that British Petroleum could operate freely. Colonel Yates fully understood the sensitive nature of his mission: He arrived secretly in Bogotá in October 1926, went out only at night, wore false whiskers, and frequently changed residence. In spite of his disguises, agents of the U.S. oil companies were soon hot on his trail and a veritable cloak-and-dagger spy operation ensued. Unable to discover Yates's intentions, an agent of the U.S. oil companies tried another angle and hired an informant for $10,000 to report on the conversations in the Colombian cabinet. Yates expected the move, and he instructed Montalvo to keep their agreement, which they had signed late in June 1927, out of the cabinet until the last moment; the final cabinet approval came on 15 July 1927. The informant (most likely Esteban Jaramillo, the treasury minister), did his best to make up for lost time by obtaining a copy of the Yates contract, which the U.S. oil companies decided to leak prematurely to the press in the first round of the campaign to impede legislative approval.

At first glance the Yates contract seemed quite harmless: The dummy corporation that Yates headed would receive a fifty-year grant over a vast tract of jungle in Urabá in exchange for a 20 percent crude royalty. But the choice of Urabá backfired on Montalvo and the nationalists. Because of its location right next to Panama, only minutes' flying time away from the Panama Canal, the Urabá concession had a strategic value eagerly played up by the U.S. oil companies. Second, the very presence of an English firm in what had traditionally been considered a preserve for U.S. oil companies constituted a direct challenge, irrespective of whether petroleum was even found in Urabá.[3]

The U.S. oil companies were sorely disappointed with both the State Department and U.S. Ambassador to Colombia Samuel Piles, in particular with the latter. Piles had accurately reported that the Colombian government was fully within its rights to assign the Urabá concession to a British concern and had also stated that the defense of the United States was in no way threatened, a position the State Department had come to support. Exxon took the lead in the campaign to block congressional approval of the Yates contract and sent a number of high officials from New York to work against its passage. One of these officials was Mr. Thomas W. Palmer, who came with "a blank check" as an indication that "the Americans will go to any extreme to prevent it from passing."[4]

Lacking State Department support, the U.S. oil companies had two main tools to block the Yates contract: First, they could bribe a significant number of Colombian officials and politicians, and second, they could exert pressure on the whole Colombian government by threatening to cut off loans from New York banks. Colonel Yates, endowed with funds by British Petroleum, enjoyed the challenge of bribing the Colombian officials as good sport, but when the Americans kept raising the stakes, he soon ran out of funds and could not buy the support of the last official whose compliance was needed to secure congressional passage—the influential Treasury Minister Esteban Jaramillo, who was on the side of the United States. Colonel Yates decided that consultations with London were now necessary, and in August 1927 he departed Bogotá as secretly as he had arrived, fully confident that he would return with the winning hand to finish the great game of empire.[5]

In London there was no problem with replenishing the bribe funds, as the sums involved were infinitesimal by oil company standards. The probable lack of oil in Urabá was not a matter for concern either, since Montalvo had repeatedly pressed British Petroleum to take charge of the Barco Concession, emphasizing that Urabá was just the opening gambit. The real barrier was the grip held over Colombia by New York banks: To take Colombia out of the U.S. orbit and into the British sphere, the price tag could go up as high as $75 million in foreign loans. If British financial institutions were ready and willing to make up this difference, then the favorable legislation could be secured in Colombia.

Yet it was precisely the transfer of the international financial center from London to New York during World War I that had allowed U.S. banks to assume such a controlling position over Colombia. How could the powerful economic forces that had produced U.S. economic supremacy be reversed to favor a waning British Empire? Only by the intervention of the English government, but it did not judge imperial interests sufficiently important to risk a confrontation with the United States. The stakes were too high for England in Colombia, and British Petroleum, rather than sending back Colonel Yates, replaced him in 1928 with Arnold Wilson, whose primary task was to reassure the U.S. oil companies as well as to negotiate a British withdrawal on favorable terms. British Petroleum had gotten a good run for its money with the Yates episode, and Exxon, which had never before been so scared in Colombia, was more than glad to enter into lengthy negotiations to settle the issue.[6]

For Colombia, the strategy of playing off the British against the U.S. companies had failed, and Minister of Development Montalvo now had to try to salvage his nationalistic petroleum policy by relying upon whatever internal support he could muster to challenge the united opposition of the U.S. oil companies.

Montalvo's Last Chance

By the end of 1927 Montalvo had begun to realize that the English were not going to challenge the U.S. oil companies. If he was to get the increase in the royalty crude that the Abadía Méndez administration needed to perpetuate Conservative Party rule, the only alternative left was for the government to establish "semi-official" companies for exploration as well as a state refinery for processing the royalty crude. Such intervention was outside the scope of previous laws, and new enabling legislation was needed to implement a policy of state participation in petroleum operations. In a surprise move in November 1927, Montalvo presented an Emergency Oil Bill that gave the government sweeping powers until a definitive oil bill could be studied and drafted. In a flurry of flag-waving rhetoric in the chambers, Montalvo exposed some congressmen who were on the pay of the oil companies, whereupon all was forgiven and the bill rapidly passed into law.[7]

Montalvo had won a first round, and not wishing to lose momentum, in February 1928 he issued a decree that specified the implementation of the Emergency Oil Bill of November 1927. From this moment things did not go smoothly: The oil companies countered with a battery of lawsuits challenging the legality as well as the constitutionality of the Emergency Oil Law and the corresponding decree, effectively hamstringing the Ministry of Development from utilizing its clauses. The legal avenue of attack could easily backfire on the oil companies, and this in fact is what happened when Montalvo fired the government inspector at Barrancabermeja for not enforcing the existing oil legislation. Exxon, accustomed to having the official in the payroll of the company, was shocked to have a new government inspector unearthing incriminating evidence. This evidence confirmed how Exxon had violated provisions in order to give a smaller amount of crude to the government than it was entitled to by law.[8]

Whipping up nationalistic sentiments whenever necessary in order to push home the attack, Montalvo convened a congressional committee to investigate the circumstances surrounding the granting of the Barrancabermeja concession to Exxon in the late 1910s. Without too much difficulty, the congressional committee dredged up a monotonous series of illegal actions, frauds, and misrepresentations in connection with the acquisition. Montalvo's goal was the same as always: to get Exxon to increase the royalty crude from 10 to 20 percent, but he would settle for 15 percent. The existing contract stood in the way because it could not legally be cancelled. But if it could be declared null and void, the road would be open to renegotiate a new contract so that at last the Conservative Party would have the revenues to perpetuate itself in power.[9]

The attempt to declare the Barrancabermeja concession null and void was the last straw for Exxon, which, along with other U.S. oil companies, had been pressuring the State Department in vain for a stronger policy. As one oilman said, "It is time a showdown was called on all this anti-American propaganda. The only way to get anything down here is to make a firm stand and when necessary use economic pressure."[10] Agents of the U.S. oil companies had been spreading false reports about Colombia to New York banks, and in 1928 the interlocking directorates between the oil companies and many banks started to dry up the flow of loans to Colombia. The raw power play was too crass an approach for public relations purposes, however, and the oil companies needed a neutral government pronouncement to be made to supply justification for such actions. The pro-business Department of Commerce was all too willing to oblige, and on 29 September 1928 it issued a Special Circular that alerted investors about the risks of buying bonds from Colombia. The sale value of Colombian bonds, which had already begun to drop, now plummeted, and the government slowly started to face the prospect of a bankruptcy that could not but destroy the chances of the Conservative Party.[11]

Cracking the whip had ended the danger for the U.S. oil companies, but there were still several loose ends in need of tying up. First of all, the U.S. ambassador, Samuel Piles, a kindly and proper diplomat who had consistently argued against pressuring the Colombian government, was replaced by Jefferson Caffery, a politician who understood more than anyone else the fine art of defusing a nationalistic campaign without provoking a confrontation. He needed all his skills to lay to rest the mounting legislative momentum generated by the Emergency Oil Bill of 1927.[12]

The Colombian government had decided to bring in a panel of foreign experts to draft a new oil bill. The oil companies won over to their side all the foreign experts except two—the representatives from Mexico and the United States—and Caffery took care of them. The Mexican, Santiago González Cordero, who at first was preaching a strong nationalistic line, soon had to change his tune. In a temporary aberration, the Mexican government of 1929 was following a strong pro–U.S. oil company line, and Caffery made sure González Cordero received a reprimand from the Mexican government. The U.S. expert, H. Foster Bain, was intractable: As a professional civil servant of the highest character and with thirty years of experience in the U.S. Bureau of Mines, he refuted the oil companies' arguments and wanted no part of their money. Ambassador Caffery assumed the task of discrediting Bain in Washington. Unable to attack his impressive professional credentials, Caffery indirectly but repeatedly questioned Bain's ability to offer the right advice because of lack of familiarity with "local conditions."[13]

Caffery and the oil companies also strongly influenced an opinion survey that Montalvo was carrying out among leading members of the Colombian elite. As Montalvo discovered, most members of the Colombian elite refused to drastically alter oil policy, and quite a few even declined to answer the questionnaire. Although they were sympathetic to the idea of receiving another 5 percent of crude as a royalty, these elite members did not want to provoke any confrontation with the oil companies, whom they felt were doing a good job in extracting the oil and sending it abroad. And since the only way Montalvo could negotiate better terms with the U.S. oil companies was by threatening them, the Colombian elite had in effect pulled the rug out from under him.[14]

Without oil revenue to smooth out ruffled feelings, the edifice of Conservative Party rule continued to crumble and the growing number of disaffected elements eased the Liberal Party's return to power in 1930. Yet Montalvo's campaign had not been wholly without results: Not only had he created—for the first time, in the minds of some Colombians— an awareness of the great wealth represented by the country's oil deposits, but he had also managed to keep the Barco Concession out of the grip of the oil companies.

Venezuela and the Barco Concession

The Colombian government granted the Barco Concession in 1905. This concession, which was next to Venezuela and close to the city of Cúcuta, henceforth was the object of frauds, embezzlement, and bribery. In the early 1920s the situation had narrowed down to a rivalry between two oil companies, Shell and Gulf, with the latter emerging in full control of the concession by 1925. No work had begun on the concession, since Gulf intended to keep the fields in reserve, but when the Colombian government declared the concession null and void on 2 February 1926, the question of who would have final control over fields so rich that the oil oozed out on the surface again came to the fore. Whatever the exact motives for the cancellation, it came as a surprise because the Pedro Nel Ospina administration (1922–1926) had shown excessive deference to U.S. oil companies, in particular Exxon. At any rate, the decision on the Barco Concession was then passed on to the incoming Miguel Abadía Méndez administration, which took office in August 1926.[15]

Gulf's strategy was simple: First, petition the Ministry of Development to reverse the February revocation, and then appeal through the judicial system all the way up to the Colombian supreme court. These procedures would take years, but Gulf was in no rush, and the lawsuits served as the perfect excuse to keep the oil fields in reserve and out of the hands of third parties. For its part, the Abadía Méndez administration offered repeatedly to settle out of court, on the two conditions that Gulf raise the crude royalty to 15 percent and that the oil company build a pipeline as well as a paved road from Cúcuta as far as the Magdalena river. No agreement was reached, however, and there matters rested until Gulf started to worry during 1927 about the gathering momentum of Montalvo's nationalistic campaign.[16]

During Colonel Yates's stay in Bogotá, Montalvo had offered the Barco Concession to British Petroleum, an offer subsequently repeated in 1928. The appearance of a powerful English company meant that Gulf would have to abandon its strategy of just letting matters drift, and so Gulf embarked upon action on various fronts. It hired the law firm of Sullivan and Cromwell to orchestrate activities; William Cromwell, who had masterminded the separation of Panama in 1903, was not up to another big assignment and left the task for a younger man, the no less competent Allen Dulles, who later became famous as director of the Central Intelligence Agency (CIA). Other equally interesting personalities were actors in Gulf's plan. Jordan Stabler, from Gulf's Venezuelan subsidiary, was selected as a special emissary to the Colombian government. Prior to his arrival in Bogotá in May 1928, other persons, including Assistant

Secretary of State Francis White, had carefully prepared the ground by raising the issue of the boundary settlement with Venezuela. The President of Switzerland had given the lands to Colombia in his arbitration award, but now Gulf was goading Venezuela to try to claim the Barco Concession as Venezuelan territory. Border wars were a specialty of the oil companies, and Gulf was playing this card to the hilt.

In his first meeting, Stabler confronted President Abadía Méndez with an ultimatum; he then remained in Bogotá, waiting for his next meeting with the president so that he could deliver another ultimatum. Stabler blustered about cutting off foreign loans if the Barco Concession was not returned to Gulf, and not stopping at such blunt language, he alluded to "difficulties for Colombia" and also mentioned that the "U.S. government will have to seriously consider further steps."[17] Stabler finally left Bogotá in July 1928, his mission having served only to antagonize Colombians; as a direct outcome, on 4 August 1928 the Colombian government rejected Gulf's petition to repeal the 2 February 1926 cancellation.

Stabler's way of raising a storm was well known in oil circles, and the added complications he had created provided a useful pretext to take stronger action against Colombia. By the middle of 1928 British Petroleum was no longer interested in the Barco Concession, and even Montalvo's offer to form an international consortium of both Gulf and British Petroleum failed to attract the English. The first blow came on 29 September 1928 when the pro-business U.S. Department of Commerce issued the Special Circular that effectively dried up foreign credit for Colombia in New York and, incidentally, confirmed Stabler's threats. This measure was instrumental in stopping Montalvo's oil policy in its tracks. But Gulf concluded that a more specific remedy was also needed and asked Allen Dulles to draw up the appropriate plans.[18]

In October 1928 the Colombian government began to receive reports from its agents in Venezuela and elsewhere that a plot was under way to create the "Republic of Zulia" in the province where the Barco Concession was located, with Cúcuta as the capital. Rumors circulated that a large number of U.S. "geologists" and workers were gathering on the Venezuelan frontier and at a given signal would cross the border to defend the newly proclaimed Republic of Zulia, which would promptly be recognized by the U.S. government. Since Venezuela also claimed those lands, Colombia, without allies, faced tremendous international complications; rather than risk another shameful humiliation like the one in Panama in 1903, the Colombian government decided this time to heed the warning signals while there was still time. The garrison in Cúcuta was reinforced, but more important, Montalvo offered more favorable terms to Gulf in the hope that the oil company would accept the Barco Concession.[19]

Gulf showed interest in the offer but held out for even more categorical assurances. These were forthcoming on 5 December 1928, when President Abadía Méndez himself told an oil company representative that he wanted to settle the Barco Concession quickly, even to the point of calling a special session of congress to approve the new contract with Gulf. These guarantees convinced Gulf that neither the British nor a rival oil company now threatened its control, but it was still in no rush to sign a contract that specified the duration of the Barco Concession. Gulf's real goal all along had been "to keep the Barco territory *in reserve* in view of the present over-production of petroleum."[20] To prevent a settlement out of court, Gulf demanded harsher terms, thus allowing litigation to proceed.

In effect, Gulf officials were happy to see the Barco question bogged down and preferred to wait until the right opportunity appeared. Colombia was left at a dead end: Whether the concession was awarded or not, Gulf would exploit the field only when its own interests so demanded, an attitude which bode ill for the country.

Notes

1. For the earlier history of petroleum in Colombia, see René De La Pedraja, *Historia de la energía en Colombia, 1537–1930* (Bogotá: El Ancora, 1985), chap. 6; Stephen J. Randall, *The Diplomacy of Modernization: Colombian-American Relations, 1920–1940* (Toronto: University of Toronto Press, 1977), pp. 90–94; Jorge Villegas, *Petróleo, oligarquía e imperio* (Bogotá: Tercer Mundo, 1975), chap. 1.

2. This and the next paragraph are based on A. T. Wilson Report, 29 June 1927, FO (Foreign Office) 371/11984, PRO (Public Record Office), London, England; Samuel Piles Report, 6 July 1927 Report, and 22 Sept. 1928 Memorandum, 821.6363/316, 463, RG (Record Group) 59, National Archives, Washington, D.C.; Anthony Sampson, *The Seven Sisters* (New York: The Viking Press, 1975), pp. 52–57.

3. Memorandum 12 June 1927, FO 371/11984, PRO; Piles Reports, 25 June, 10, 26 Sept., 9 Nov. 1927, 821.6363/315, 330, 339, 345; and "The Yates-Montalvo Contract," 821.6363/867, RG 59; *Mundo al día,* 22 June, 9 Sept. 1927; *El Tiempo,* 5, 8 Sept. 1927; Villegas, *Petróleo,* pp. 138–140; Ludwell Denny, *We Fight for Oil* (New York: Alfred A. Knopf, 1928), pp. 121–122, 136–137.

4. Naval Intelligence Report, 13 Oct. 1927, FO 371/12753, PRO; Piles Reports, 6 July, 26 Sept. 1927, 821.6363/316, 319, RG 59; *El Tiempo,* 6 July, 26 Sept. 1927.

5. Report of British Petroleum official, 11 July 1927, FO 371/11984, PRO; Piles Report, postscript, 19 Aug. 1927, 821.6363, RG 59.

6. E. Monson Report, 29 March 1928, FO 371/12753, PRO; *Mundo al día*, 6 Aug. 1928; Piles Report, 15 Aug. 1928, Matthews Report, 5 Oct. 1928, Telephone conversation, 28 Dec. 1927, 821.6363/353, 458, 517, RG 59.

7. Piles Report, 9 Nov. 1927, 821. 6363/345, RG 59; Villegas, *Petróleo*, pp. 127–129.

8. José Antonio Montalvo to Alberto Arenas, 25 June 1928, 821.6363/563, RG 59; *El Espectador*, 29 June 1928; U.S. Department of State, *Foreign Relations of the United States, 1928*, 2:588–591; *New York Times*, 20, 22 Feb. 1928.

9. Piles Report, 24 Aug. 1928, Matthews Report, 26 Sept. 1928, Caffery Reports, 26 Sept. 1928, and 12 Aug. 1929, 821.6363/443, 477, 679, RG 59; *Foreign Relations, 1928*, 2:596–600.

10. C. S. Smith Report, 30 Nov. 1927, 821.6363/349, RG 59.

11. E. Monson Report, 29 March 1928, FO 371/12754, PRO; Piles Report, 15 Aug. 1928, 821.6363/458, RG 59; *Foreign Relations, 1928*, 2:599–603; Randall, *The Diplomacy of Modernization*, pp. 60, 104, 105.

12. Francis B. Loomis to Secretary of State, 22 Oct. 1927, 821.6363/334, RG 59. Loomis, undersecretary of state during the Panama episode in 1903, knew well the importance of the "immediate and pressing need for a strong, efficient, and discreet man as the head of our legation" (ibid.); Piles Report, 24 Feb. 1928, 821.6363/366, RG 59; Randall, *The Diplomacy of Modernization*, p. 97.

13. Ministerio de Industrias, *Memoria 1929* (Bogotá: Tip. Romana, 1929), pp. 6–7; Dwight Morrow letter, 9 Aug. 1929, Texaco Report of Samuel Haskell, 821.6363/671, 701, RG 59; Ministerio de Industrias, *Documentos referentes al proyecto de ley del petróleo*, 4 vols. (Bogotá: Imprenta Nacional, 1929–1934), 2:165–331.

14. A. C. Hearn Report, 4 Jan. 1929, FO 371/13471, PRO; Ministerio de Industrias, *Documentos referentes al proyecto de ley del petróleo*, 1:1–336; Caffery letter, 10 Oct. 1929, Records of Francis White, Box 9, RG 59.

15. Report 21 April 1921 of E. Soule, Piles Report 25 Feb. 1926, 821.6363 Barco 20, 48, RG 59; *El Espectador*, 17 Dec. 1926; *El Tiempo*, 21 Feb. 1926; *Foreign Relations, 1928*, 2:603–610; Villegas, *Petróleo*, pp. 118–119; B. S. McBeth, *Juan Vicente Gómez and the Oil Companies in Venezuela, 1908–1935* (Cambridge: Cambridge University Press, 1983), pp. 95–96.

16. This and the next two paragraphs are based on William Wallace Report, 30 June 1928, 821.6363 Barco/103, RG 59; Matthews Report, 25 Sept. 1928, Piles Report, 6 July 1927, 821.6363/316, 472, RG 59; *Foreign Relations, 1928*, 2:610–612; Enrique Olaya Herrera to Miguel Abadía Méndez, 23 Jan. 1928, Academia Colombiana de Historia; *New York Times*, 28 Feb., 7 Aug. 1928. President Abadía Méndez even offered to settle before Montalvo returned from an inspection trip, but Gulf still declined, per Piles Report, 1 April 1928, 821.6363 Barco/86, RG 59.

17. Stabler to Wallace, 27 June 1928, 821.6363 Barco/103, RG 59.

18. E. Monson Report, 10 Aug. 1928, FO 731/12756, PRO; Wallace letters, 13, 28 June 1928, Records of White, Box 31, RG 59; *Foreign Relations, 1928*, 2:614–617; Randall, *The Diplomacy of Modernization*, pp. 98, 99–100.

19. E. Monson Report, 20 Aug. 1928, FO 371/12756, PRO; Telephone conversation, 7 Aug. 1928, Telegram, 28 Aug. 1928, Matthews Report, 19 Oct.

1928, 821.6363 Barco/127, 158, 201, RG 59; Colombian consul to Montalvo, 9 Jan. 1930, Academia Colombiana de Historia.

20. Caffery to secretary of state, 7 Dec. 1928 (emphasis in original), 821.6363 Barco/226, RG 59; Allen Dulles to White, 7 March 1929, and Caffery Report, 22 May 1929, 821.6363/582, RG 59; *Foreign Relations, 1928,* 2:619–635.

2

The Alliance with
the Foreign Oil Companies

The return of the Liberal Party to power for the first time in the twentieth century marked a turning point both in Colombia's history and in petroleum policy. A wave of popular support swept Enrique Olaya Herrera into the presidency in August 1930, and as long as the Liberal Party could sustain the illusion of social reforms for the lower class of Colombia, petroleum royalties remained of secondary importance for the survival of the Liberal government. With this freedom to maneuver, Olaya Herrera gave full rein to his pro–United States sentiments in forging between the Colombian elite and the U.S. oil companies an alliance that, with modifications, has survived down to the present. Olaya Herrera also settled the Barco question to the satisfaction of U.S. interests. In spite of attempts to secure adjustments during 1932–1940, the alliance with the foreign oil companies remained firm.

Enrique Olaya Herrera

By December 1929 the British ambassador at Bogotá had already predicted that the next Colombian administration "may be actively unfriendly, perhaps corrupt, or so much under the influence of United States interests that British firms could hope for little,"[1] and he urged British firms to act quickly while the friendly Abadía Méndez administration was still in office. Shell took the hint and moved quickly to apply for storage tank facilities in the port of Buenaventura, with the aim of flanking Exxon out of the distribution of gasoline and fuel oil in the Pacific coast provinces of Colombia. Minister of Development Montalvo backed Shell but the minister of public works believed that Exxon was better prepared to supply the fuel oil needed to replace the coal used by the locomotives in the Buenaventura-Cali region. A bitter battle ensued, and the British embassy, which had strongly backed

Shell's application, was startled when Shell's London office telegraphed "is not now interested" in January 1930.[2]

The Foreign Office explained the reason for this sudden reversal: "no doubt in this case the Shell company compounded with Exxon on terms possibly satisfactory to both parties," yet Shell remained "quite unconscious of the impropriety of their action in using the Legation as a pawn in the game of humbugging a friendly government."[3] The other English company, British Petroleum, had been urged by the embassy in Bogotá to secure fields even though the legal prohibition against granting oil concessions to firms partially owned by foreign governments was still in force. This English company, which had so actively pressed for a concession in 1927, appeared to follow the embassy's suggestions, but the final result was not too different from that of the Shell case: In 1930, British Petroleum and Exxon reached an agreement whereby the former backed out of Colombia in exchange for unnamed privileges in other parts of the world. In the great game of empire, Colombia, like many other Third World countries, was simply assigned to its respective sphere of influence by the rival oil companies. Shell and British Petroleum considered the election in February 1930 of Enrique Olaya Herrera to the presidency as a clear confirmation of U.S. supremacy.[4]

The negotiated withdrawal of the English firms removed the last bargaining chip left to the Colombian government, yet this did not dismay the new Liberal president, Enrique Olaya Herrera, when he took office in August 1930. Elected on a platform of promises to take Colombia out of the Great Depression, he raised expectations that the Liberal Party, in control of the executive branch for the first time in the twentieth century, would inaugurate a period of prosperity and usher in social reforms for the lower class. Olaya Herrera was not fooled by the campaign charges blaming the Conservatives for having caused the Great Depression, and he knew that the cure had to be sought where the depression had started, namely in the United States. Because of his eight years' residence as Colombian ambassador to the United States, he was deeply and completely pro-American. He believed that the key to remaking Colombia in the U.S. image as well as to bringing it out of the Great Depression was to restore U.S. investment, which would come in the form of renewed loans from New York banks and direct investment by U.S. oil companies.

The foreign loans were foremost in his mind because they would allow the Colombian government to build a state refinery to process the royalty crude. Montalvo had suggested this possibility as far back as 1927, but Olaya Herrera went a step further. In his last months in the United States, Olaya Herrera contacted Bethlehem Steel and Foster Wheeler about the cost of constructing the refinery and asked the brothers

Avnatamoff, who had directed Tsarist oil fields, whether they would agree to run the refinery in Colombia until local native personnel could be trained. The price tag on the refinery of 10,000 barrels was $5 million. A bankrupt Colombian treasury whose revenues were decreasing because of the world depression clearly could not afford such outlays, making the foreign loans indispensable. In politely declining Olaya Herrera's requests, the banks had a ready-made excuse in the "hostile" environment created by the previous nationalistic campaign and the lack of the right investment "climate." Wall Street bankers conditioned the granting of new loans both on the passage of oil legislation acceptable to the oil companies and on a favorable settlement of the Barco Concession— terms spelled out in detail to president-elect Olaya Herrera when he visited New York City prior to his departure for Colombia to assume office.[5]

At this point, Undersecretary of State Joseph P. Cotton stepped into the picture with a proposal. Cotton was dissatisfied with the one-sided reporting of Ambassador Jefferson Caffery, who was a passionate advocate of the U.S. oil companies. To find where the truth lay, Cotton suggested sending an independent adviser who would report both to him and to Olaya Herrera. The undersecretary proposed sending George Rublee, who had previous experience under Dwight Morrow with Mexican oil. Olaya Herrera at first did not like the idea, but upon his return to Colombia he realized that Rublee could be an important tool to secure passage of the oil legislation that he hoped to propose. Rublee, who arrived in Bogotá in November 1930, gradually gravitated to the position of Ambassador Caffery and the U.S. oil companies, although he did try to avoid their most extreme demands. Once Undersecretary Cotton became ill in January 1931 (and died the next month), Rublee abandoned all pretense of independent opinion and instead strongly backed the demands of the oil companies.[6]

Olaya Herrera presented the oil bill to the Colombian congress at the end of September 1930. As the bill advanced through the normal legislative process, different amendments appeared and the legislators did not attempt to hide their repugnance. It was clear that a bitter fight was in the wings to secure passage. Disturbing reports had gradually weakened Olaya Herrera's resolve for the fight. Since January 1930 Exxon had been contemplating wage reductions for its workers, and although this move was in line with the practices of Colombian companies, which were likewise lowering wages in reaction to the Great Depression, it belied the repeated promises made by Exxon and the other oil companies about an impending expansion in activities as soon as the bill was passed. A more direct warning came from the Colombian broker Alfredo Esparza Rosas, who until recently had been the local representative of a foreign company. According to Esparza, oil companies were winding down their operations and pulling out of Colombia because the Great Depression had produced a glut of oil in the world market.[7]

Olaya Herrera could not accept that his American friends had lied to him, and confused by this contradictory information, he gradually lost interest and allowed matters to drift in late 1930. The oil companies and Ambassador Caffery were unrelenting in lobbying for the oil bill, but they knew that the president would have to push the bill through a hostile congress. The decisive argument did not come from the local U.S. representatives but from New York. The Wall Street firm of Baker, Kellogg & Co., which had made previous loans to Colombia and served informally as financial adviser to the Olaya Herrera administration, spelled out the "facts of life" in surprisingly frank terms, which still remain valid today:

> Everybody who is interested in Colombia is awaiting with keenest interest the passage of an oil law satisfactory both to the oil companies and to the Colombian government. The feeling is general in banking circles that upon this foundation stone the future credit of the country may have to rest.
>
> The chief reason for the recent depreciation of Colombian bond prices in this market has been the coffee situation and the recognition that Colombia is so largely dependent upon coffee for its future prosperity. All good friends of Colombia, even such as are entirely disinterested and dissociated from the oil interests, are hoping fervently that this oil law will pass before a disastrous break in coffee prices occurs.
>
> It is much more to Colombia's interest that oil should be allowed to flow out of the country than that the country gets the highest possible royalty upon the production. It might be just as well, instead of obtaining the highest possible royalty on a small production, to have half the royalty on twice that production. This would produce as much for the national treasury, while at the same time it would involve very much larger investments of foreign money in oil development, give employment to more labor, and aid generally in the internal economy of the country.[8]

This last point about overcoming the Great Depression struck a particularly receptive chord in Olaya Herrera, who now responded to the incessant demands from Ambassador Caffery and the U.S. companies to push the oil bill through congress with renewed interest. The Colombian congress approved the bill by banging on the desks (*pupitrazos*)—the usual way of expressing an unrecorded voice vote in response to a presidential command—and Olaya Herrera duly signed the bill on 4 March 1931.[9]

Law 37 of 1931 not only showered the oil companies with an impressive list of privileges and benefits but also excluded the nationalistic clauses contained in Montalvo's earlier bills. Royalties were reduced on new discoveries and taxes slashed on both old and new fields. Requirements upon the companies were largely eliminated, so that among many other things they no longer had to file regular reports to the government, nor did they have to hire native Colombians for executive positions. Ambassador Caffery and Rublee considered it "a good, practical, workable law," an opinion shared by Exxon but not by all U.S. oil companies.[10]

Although these new incentives to find oil were generous indeed, companies like Texaco, which at the time did not have fields in production, felt that give-away legislation was still needed. They did not hesitate to express their dissatisfaction to the Colombian government and even worse to New York banking circles. Their requests were so outrageous that Caffery considered them counterproductive and refused to forward them. Still, Baker, Kellogg & Co. reported from New York in March 1931 "that the oil companies had not been left completely satisfied" but only "in good part," and since "the commercial banks and the banking firms have to base themselves upon the opinions expressed by the oil companies," the 1931 law was only "the beginning of a long road" if Colombia was to escape a "dark future."[11]

What tangible benefits did Colombia receive in exchange for the passage of Law 37 of 1931? The news of the law produced a brief rally in the New York stock market, and Colombian state bonds, which had dropped to 66 percent of face value, climbed to 72—only to resume a downward plunge in subsequent months. Needless to say, not a single new loan was forthcoming to Colombia, so that the country could not escape from its "dark future." Texaco's response was swift: In June 1931 it withdrew its geologic teams with fanfare, and other companies soon followed suit.

Exxon, which had a monopoly on Colombian production, refining, and distribution, had postponed the wage cuts until after the passage of the oil law in March 1931, but with that hurdle cleared, the company now fully exploited its new tax advantages without any fear of reprisals. Olaya Herrera could not claim surprise, as he had been personally warned about these impending actions and had also been informed that independent oilmen had been lobbying for bills in the U.S. Congress since January 1931 to restrict Colombian oil imports into the United States. Those companies with large foreign oil holdings had managed to block those bills temporarily, but knowing that the pressure of the independent oilmen was very strong, they had sought other ways to avoid restrictive legislation. In early May, at the suggestion of the secretary of commerce, U.S. oil companies made an informal agreement to reduce foreign oil imports by 25 percent. Exxon, the only producer in Colombia, sent two-thirds of its crude to the United States, so that when New York headquarters mandated a 12 percent reduction in Colombian output, slashes in wages as well as layoffs in workers were inevitable. So powerful was Exxon that it did not even bother to give prior notice to the Colombian government but just sent a statement after the fact. No less striking was Minister of Development Francisco José Chaux's unconditional acceptance of Exxon's explanations for this sudden and swift reversal, which at one blow had negated all the previous promises about the prosperity the oil legislation would bring to Colombia.[12] Before analyzing Colombia's reaction to this unexpected turn of events, there still remains the question of how a settlement for the Barco Concession was found, the subject of the next section.

The Settlement of the Barco Question

The revocation of the Barco Concession in 1926 had given the Colombian government a significant alternative; here were important fields overflowing with oil ready to be pumped without requiring any expenses for exploration. Incoming president Olaya Herrera could have relied on these proven oil fields to take Colombia out of the Great Depression, yet he was more concerned with earning a good reputation in the United States. Thus Olaya Herrera ignored Montalvo's earlier proposal to establish a semi-official company to exploit the field, and at most he only briefly toyed with dividing the Barco Concession between Gulf and Shell. At the insistence of the U.S. oil companies he dropped the idea.[13]

Olaya Herrera knew that if the country was to come out of the Great Depression, foreign money would have to flow into Colombia again. The president-elect held talks personally in New York in April 1930 to negotiate a $20 million loan from the National City Bank. The first one granted to Colombia since the Special Circular was released in 1928, this loan imposed harsh conditions upon Colombia; among the most stringent was the requirement that Gulf's title to the Barco Concession be recognized as valid. This condition reportedly was stated by Andrew Mellon himself when, as secretary of the treasury, he met Olaya Herrera at a banquet. In any case the Mellon interests (the owners of Gulf) fully expected the Colombian government to live up to this promise as a quid pro quo for the $20 million loan, which was to be paid out in installments. The State Department was particularly accommodating in bringing together New York financiers with the Colombian president and in exchange expected favorable and swift consideration for the Barco Concession.[14]

Nationalistic sentiment against granting the Barco Concession to Gulf was so strong in the country that Olaya Herrera reluctantly concluded that an out-of-court settlement would face legal difficulties and that instead, to prevent a series of crippling lawsuits, congressional approval was needed. He circulated Gulf's proposal for a settlement, but even politicians normally loyal to Olaya Herrera rejected it; in particular, they cited the demand for a concession without any time limit as unacceptable. A fifty-year period for the concession eliminated that objection. Olaya Herrera called upon George Rublee in January 1931 to take up the Barco matter as soon as possible. Rublee prepared another draft, but Gulf Oil continued to make extreme demands, so the company and Minister of Development Chaux engaged in another round of negotiations. Gulf wanted to pay only a 5.5 percent royalty on crude delivered at the export port, but after extended discussions finally accepted the 6 percent Colombia wanted. The company gave way on a few other minor points but refused to accept a specific term for beginning oil exploitation. This requirement was crucial to obtaining congressional approval because "the congress [was] obsessed with the idea that the oil companies seek concessions in Colombia not for the purpose of production but for the purpose of creating reserves."[15] Olaya Herrera appealed in February to the U.S. State Department for reconsideration on this point, but to no avail.

Olaya Herrera had by now lost all enthusiasm for the settlement of the Barco Concession, especially when Gulf would not even accept a ten-year limit to begin operations or else forfeit the concession. He duly signed the contract on 4 March 1931, but as expected, massive opposition in the congress bogged the bill down. The State Department did not want to press the president any further, and although Jefferson Caffery continued to prod Olaya Herrera (the ambassador afterwards immodestly claimed the credit for the bill's success), it was clear that something more was needed to secure passage of the bill ratifying the Barco contract. However, before anything else could be tried, the position of Olaya Herrera would first have to be made impregnable. The nationalistic leader Suárez Castillo was organizing a militia with arms he had received from the previous minister of war and was threatening to march on Bogotá to keep the government from granting the Barco Concession to Gulf. Government troops were short of ammunition, but the U.S. government responded positively to requests to send munitions on short notice from the Canal Zone by plane if any trouble materialized.[16]

The planned revolt was aborted, but another complication arose. Gulf made sure that Olaya Herrera received information about previous attempts to create the Republic of Zulia on the border with Venezuela where the Barco Concession was located. The shadow of the loss of

Panama in 1903 loomed large over Colombian public life, and Olaya Herrera knew that he could not survive the loss of an inch of Colombian territory. He began to receive "friendly" warnings in May 1931 that "national sovereignty" was at stake and soon was feeling the heat about another Panama-type coup to create the Republic of Zulia. Congress was recalcitrant, just as it had been in 1903 over Panama, and rather than risk a defeat of the bill granting Gulf the Barco Concession, Olaya Herrera was on the point of postponing the issue until he could muster support in the next session of congress. It was at this juncture that outside intervention convinced the wavering president that a delay would be equally dangerous: The National City Bank announced that it would hold up the last $4 million payment of the $20 million loan granted in April 1930 on a technicality until the Barco Concession bill was approved. The president, now panicking, went into action, and he used all his powers of persuasion to convince a reluctant congress into approving the law, which he signed on 26 June 1931.[17]

The Colombian government sent a very patriotic officer to take command of the garrison at the Venezuelan border, and with the removal of the real cause of the separatist movement, local feeling for the Republic of Zulia waned. Colombia and other Latin American countries had no choice but to accept the dictates of Wall Street banks, but so great had been the abuse of power and the official connivance of the U.S. government that an outcry finally forced the Senate Finance Committee of the U.S. Congress to investigate the whole issue of foreign lending. Highly questionable as were some of the actions of the State Department, and in particular those of Ambassador Jefferson Caffery, the real censure fell upon the dealings of the oil companies and the New York banks. But rather than allowing the disclosures, the probusiness administration of Herbert Hoover decided upon a cover-up scheme to protect the private companies. Files were destroyed, slanted testimony was presented before the Senate Finance Committee, and in short, everything possible was done to cover up the misdeeds of the banks and the oil companies. The strategy backfired, however, and the spectacle of powerful private companies as well as the Mellon interests hiding behind the mantle of diplomatic privilege deeply impressed the people of the United States. In fact, this scandal was one of the factors that, along with the Great Depression, triggered a move away from business-oriented Republican administrations in the United States and influenced the election of the Democratic candidate Franklin D. Roosevelt in 1932.[18]

The United States could confidently look forward to the New Deal to take it out of the Great Depression, but for Colombia no redress was possible and the country continued to suffer the worst effects of the Great Depression. Now that Gulf Oil had the Barco Concession, the fields became just another reserve to be exploited only when it was in the interest of the company rather than of Colombia. For Gulf itself the whole affair had just been a gigantic speculation: In October 1935 Gulf offered to sell the Barco Concession to a French group backed by the Paris government. Texaco found out about the deal, and its chairman, Torkild Rieber, preempted the sale and acquired the Barco Concession in early 1936. To secure more political backing for the operation, Rieber wanted an associate; Mobil agreed to participate in April 1936, with each company holding a 50 percent share. Even then there was no rush to begin production, and not until 1939 would the crude flow out of the concession via the pipeline constructed to the Caribbean coast.[19] Since the Colombian government received only a 6 percent royalty, the rest was pure profit for Texaco-Mobil; this was one of the most lucrative operations for U.S. companies in Colombia, and as will be explained in Chapter 5, it was little more than looting the fields.

Trying to Cope: 1932-1940

Exxon remained with a monopoly on oil production, refining, and distribution that included the contract privilege of charging Colombia the gasoline prices of New York City, then among the highest in the world. Even members of the Colombian elite started to feel that the U.S. company was abusing its monopoly position, but Exxon was unperturbed and relentlessly advanced to tighten its grip upon the Colombian government. The U.S. company had bought Colombian foreign bonds for practically nothing in 1933 when the value of the bonds collapsed after the country suspended payment on the foreign debt. As owner of so many of these worthless bonds, Exxon took the lead in organizing the Colombian committee of the Foreign Bondholders' Council. This Colombian committee suggested such measures as impounding the 5 percent crude royalty from the Barrancabermeja concession to pay off the foreign bonds, thus in effect depriving Colombia of all of its oil. The Colombian government was helpless to act, but to its good luck this maneuver with the bonds as well as other tricks were foiled in the United States when the newly created Securities and Exchange Commission made partial exposures.

The New Deal had temporarily saved Colombia from the still powerful oil giant, and already in 1936 talk was heard about extending the Barrancabermeja concession, which was scheduled to expire in 1946. The threat of Exxon dominance was so real that even its most fervent admirer, President Olaya Herrera, realized that he had been duped and that Colombia had to take steps to escape Exxon's iron grip.[20] The concern was shared by the next president, Alfonso López Pumarejo

(1934–1938), and in succession they tried to cope with the adverse situation by addressing the issues of: (1) the refinery; (2) the French; and (3) the English.

The Refinery

Assessing the value of the crude royalty from Exxon had always been a sore point for controversy; if delivered at the export bay of Cartagena, the government received only 5 percent instead of the 10 percent it received if the crude was delivered in Barrancabermeja, and in the latter case the government had no choice but to accept whatever price Exxon set for the purchase of the crude. Montalvo had advocated building a refinery in front of Barrancabermeja since 1928, not only so the government would receive the 10 percent crude but so the gasoline and other refined products would break Exxon's monopoly over refining and distribution. Olaya Herrera had toyed with the idea in 1930 and again in 1933, but he could not risk antagonizing the oil companies because he needed their support for the war against Peru (1932–1934). López Pumarejo (1934–1938) did present a bill to the Colombian congress in October 1934 calling for the establishment of a state refinery. Immediate opposition came from Exxon and the U.S. ambassador, so that by the time the bill became Law 160 of 1936, its original purpose had been transformed into a series of incentives and further privileges to the foreign oil companies, including tax benefits for the establishment of more refineries in the country.[21]

Henceforth, anyone could build and operate a refinery, an opportunity that Exxon itself utilized to immense benefit during the 1950s and 1960s. In the mid-1930s only the Colombian state was interested in building a second refinery, and late in 1936 it conducted feasibility studies that conclusively proved that the construction of a refinery to handle the 10 percent royalty crude was a very profitable undertaking. One of Colombia's first petroleum engineers, Eduardo Ospina Racines, took the lead in drafting and promoting the proposals. Ospina Racines faced massive opposition from Exxon and its many allies, including Minister of Development Antonio Rocha, yet the soundness of the proposal convinced Ospina Racines to return from the United States, where he had studied oil and refinery operations, to fight for the state refinery as an official of the petroleum bureau of the Ministry of Development. Upon his arrival, he discovered that both the position and the salary were way below his qualifications, and the oil companies used the opportunity to convince him to change sides. From 1939 until his retirement in the early 1960s, he was the most important Colombian advocate of the oil companies, constantly lobbying and pressuring the Colombian government in every way possible. He wrote articles, gave conferences, and published a book that was distributed for free (with printing and other expenses of the two editions covered by the oil companies). This book for many years remained the vade mecum of petroleum for the Colombian elite. The first order of business was to give a proper burial to the idea of building a state refinery, and Ospina Racines effectively lobbied until the government dropped the proposal. Thus, at least with regard to refining and distribution, Exxon retained its monopoly position in Colombia.[22]

The French

President Olaya Herrera faithfully reflected the new elite attitudes when he placed the state refinery proposal within a larger policy to bring competition against Exxon. Olaya Herrera had antagonized the English by his pro–United States bias, and as offended British sensibilities could not be expected to forget nor forgive, all he could do was to spread the word that the English were welcome to come back. In the case of the French, whom he had not previously antagonized, he could immediately start work: Colombian diplomats and officials began a long and quiet campaign to interest the Paris government and French investors in the possibilities of Colombian oil, a policy which bore first fruits when representatives of the Société Européenne des Pétroles arrived in Colombia in June 1931.

Three French business groups were the majority stockholders in the Société, with Spanish and Italian investors holding minority interests. The primary asset of the company was a well in French Morocco, and it was now diversifying into the Colombian venture in response to the welcome extended by the Olaya Herrera administration. However, the Société Européenne des Pétroles was more concerned from the start with speculation. The U.S. embassy in Bogotá reported: "The frog sucker public is being framed for a big ride in European Petroleum Company."[23] Rather than look for oil in Colombia, the French company engaged in a lawsuit to acquire lands that supposedly had oil; even when the lawsuit was won, the company still did nothing, and the Colombian government felt obliged to cancel its concession in 1935.

France had already discovered that Colombia had oil potential, and other offers were forthcoming. The most important came in 1935 when the Paris government backed another French business group that wanted to buy the Barco Concession from Gulf. The French initially had leverage over the Colombian government because the business group was able to tie the negotiations to the repayment of Colombian foreign bonds held by French investors. But when the Colombian government settled the bond issue, the two issues were divorced. Texaco was able to outmaneuver the French group and bought the rights to the Barco Concession. Thus, the two known oil reserves in Colombia, the Barco Concession and the Barrancabermeja field, both had remained under U.S. companies. When representatives from Compagnie Française des Pétroles appeared in 1938 to sound out Colombian prospects, they soon realized that massive exploration and drilling throughout the country would be needed to find fields of comparable wealth. The French, on the eve of World War II, desisted from such a vast undertaking, partly on the understanding that the English would take the lead in any new oil operations in Colombia.[24]

The English

Playing the French card had failed to counter the Exxon monopoly, and the Colombian government now renewed the efforts to bring back the English. Olaya Herrera started mending the fences with the English through Alfonso López Pumarejo, then Colombian ambassador to the United Kingdom. As a noted Anglophile, and as the person chosen by the Liberal Party to succeed Olaya Herrera in the presidency, López Pumarejo was particularly suitable for the task of contacting British investors through his friends in the London set.

The Colombian government's first choice was British Petroleum, the company that Montalvo had tried to bring into the country in the 1920s. To extend the welcome mat, Law 160 of 1936 recognized the right of companies partially owned by foreign governments to operate in Colombia, thus removing the legal obstacle that had hindered approval of the 1927 Yates contract. López Pumarejo, personally in London and later as president, sounded out British Petroleum, and the company sent high-level delegations to visit Colombia during the 1930s, but no firm arrangement was concluded. British Petroleum had other priorities, in part because of new oil discoveries in Iran but mostly as a result of the British government's decision to concentrate the company's activities in the Middle East and leave the defense of British oil interests in Latin America primarily to Shell.[25]

Both British Petroleum and Shell had signed agreements recognizing Exxon's control over Colombia, but by the mid-1930s Shell felt that those agreements had been overtaken by later events. Exxon had stepped up its meddling in the Middle East, traditionally in the British sphere of influence, and to ease the pressure on British Petroleum, Shell and the London government decided to open a rival front in Colombia against Exxon. So when López Pumarejo went into London circles to seek support, he found ready listeners in Shell officials—who, however, hid their overeagerness to begin explorations. Like other foreign oil companies, Shell could not resist the temptation to ask for more incentives, which the Colombian government granted in Law 160 of 1936. Promptly after its signature, the entry of Shell employees and equipment began on a large scale, but all was carried out in complete secrecy so as not to alert Exxon until it was too late for the U.S. company to take counter-measures to block the British.

Surveys and drilling soon began in various parts of the country, and at last Colombia seemed to have found a force to balance the overwhelming U.S. control over oil. The chief of the Shell geologists was Daniel Trompy, a Swiss citizen who had uncanny abilities to discover oil, as later in his career he would again reveal with the discovery of sub-Saharan fields in Africa. Trompy arrived in Colombia in November 1936, and from the study of the general geologic structures, he quickly confirmed the existence of major oil deposits outside the two largest known fields in the Barco Concession and in Barrancabermeja. Pinpointing the exact location and determining the size of the reserves proved a longer and more costly undertaking, but gradually results began to appear—beginning with the discovery of a number of small fields widely scattered along the Magdalena river valley.[26]

By 1938 the world situation had become very dangerous, and Shell was no longer interested just in making profits or in serving as a counterpoise to Exxon in Colombia. The events leading to the outbreak of World War II in September 1939 were unfolding with an ominous inevitability, and since 80 percent of England's refined products came from Curazao, an offshore island which by then refined most of Colombia's as well as Venezuela's crude, the British government worried that an attack on that refinery would wipe out its supply of gasoline. The United States could not be counted upon to defend Curazao, which was a Dutch colony, but U.S. help for strategic Colombia, its staunchest ally in South America, was a foregone conclusion. To safeguard imperial fuel needs, Shell had to build a refinery in Colombia. But in order to avoid unduly antagonizing Venezuela, with its larger crude output, adequate deposits had to be found in Colombia to justify building the refinery there. Shell now pumped large sums into exploration, and among many lesser finds, two larger ones clearly stood out.[27]

The first was the Casabe field in the Magdalena river valley. This field was across the Magdalena river in front of Barrancabermeja; Exxon had ruled out this area as worthless and had not bothered to obtain a concession, much less to drill for oil. Now Trompy directed Shell to drill, and a large pool of oil was found right under the noses of Exxon. This discovery rocked both the local Exxon subsidiary as well as New York headquarters and caused numerous shake-ups in personnel. Sensational as the Casabe field was, its output was not large enough to justify a refinery to supply England's needs, but this difficulty was soon remedied by Trompy's most spectacular find: oil in the Colombian Llanos. The existence of oil under the Venezuelan Llanos was a closely guarded secret, but nobody knew how far these underground lakes extended into Colombia. Trompy correctly calculated that major deposits existed on the Colombian side, and drilling soon bore him out. To find the boundaries of the underground pools, he had picked the least promising areas in the Colombian Llanos to start the drilling; not only were the wells more than satisfactory, but they allowed him to pinpoint the exact location of the really huge deposits.

Before large-scale exploitation of the Llanos oil could begin, international strategic realignments upset earlier assumptions. By 1940 the United States had committed itself to defending the Curazao refinery against foreign attack, thus eliminating the need to construct a separate refinery in Colombia, and the entry of the United States into World War II on 7 December 1941 put to rest any British fears over their fuel supply. Other oil sources were now more readily available, including U.S. production, so that the urgency to bring the oil of the Colombian Llanos into the market disappeared. Shell quietly buried the reports with the secrecy that has traditionally characterized oil company operations.

In the case of the Casabe field, this discovery had been such a propaganda coup that it could not be hidden, and this field entered into production in the mid-1940s. Now Colombia had an important active field outside the control of U.S. companies, but earlier hopes of receiving a greater benefit from the oil wealth were soon dashed. The Colombian government received a paltry amount of royalty crude, while the rest of the Casabe oil flowed out for export without leaving anything in return for Colombia. The end result was not too different from the previous dominance under the U.S. companies, and moreover, oil was exported that Colombia later sorely missed during the 1970s. Yet the Colombian elite largely agreed with this policy, since taking the oil out of the country was considered a fundamental means of consolidating the existing social structure. Oil flowed out of the country, the people remained poor and backwards, and the elite retained its commanding position, with their only complaint being that they had to pay gasoline prices that were among the highest in the world. As far as rational exploitation of Colombia's oil resources for the benefit of its population, the prospects were very bleak and no alternative was in sight for a helpless government. Yet beginning in the late 1930s, new winds were already blowing from abroad that would open another dimension.

Notes

1. Report of 20 Dec. 1929, Foreign Office (FO) 371/14220, Public Record Office (PRO), London, England.
2. Report of 14 Jan. 1930, FO 371/14220, PRO; Tropical Oil Company to Minister of Industries, 28 June 1929, 821.6363/659, Record Group (RG) 59, National Archives, Washington, D.C.
3. Memorandum of 11 March 1930, FO 371/14220, PRO.
4. Telegram of 2 Jan. 1931, FO 371/15054, PRO; Caffery Report, 21 Feb. 1931, 821.6363/1078, RG 59.
5. Bethlehem Steel Co. to Enrique Olaya Herrera, 27 May 1930, Baker, Kellogg & Co. to ibid., 28 May 1930, Alfonso Palau to ibid., 19 June 1930, Academia Colombiana de Historia; Stephen J. Randall, *The Diplomacy of Modernization: Colombian-American Relations, 1920–1940* (Toronto: University of Toronto Press, 1977), p. 108; Jorge Villegas, *Petróleo, oligarquía e imperio* (Bogotá: Tercer Mundo, 1975), pp. 153–154.
6. Francis White to Jefferson Caffery, 1 Aug. 1930, and Caffery's reply, Records of Francis White, Box 9, RG 59; George Rublee Oral History, Columbia University, pp. 229, 245–246, 250–252; U.S. Department of State, *Foreign Relations of the United States, 1931*, 2:1–4, 16–18.
7. Alfredo Esparza Rojas to Olaya Herrera, 25 Aug. 1930, Academia Colombiana de Historia; *Foreign Relations, 1931*, 2:8–10.
8. Baker, Kellogg & Co. to Olaya Herrera, 17 Nov. 1930, Academia Colombiana de Historia.
9. *Foreign Relations, 1931*, 2:15.
10. *Foreign Relations, 1931*, 2:12, 15.
11. Baker, Kellogg & Co. to Olaya Herrera, 6 March 1931, Academia Colombiana de Historia; Randall, *The Diplomacy of Modernization*, pp. 111–112; Villegas, *Petróleo*, pp. 157–159; *New York Times*, 30 Jan., 7 April 1931.
12. Francisco José Chaux to Exxon, 19 May 1931, Academia Colombiana de Historia; *Foreign Relations, 1933*, 2:243–245; Randall, *The Diplomacy of Modernization*, pp. 116, 118–120; *New York Times*, 23 April 1931.
13. H. Freeman Matthews and Caffery Reports, 9 Jan. 1930, 4 March 1930, 821.6363 Barco/265 and 273, RG 59; *Foreign Relations, 1931*, 2:21.
14. British embassy to Foreign Office, 21 Jan. 1932, FO 371/15869, PRO; Memorandum for Francis White, 24 April 1930, Records of Francis White, Box 31, RG 59; U.S. Senate Finance Committee, *Sale of Foreign Bonds or Securities in the U.S.*, 3 parts (Washington, D.C.: GPO, 1932), parts 2–3.
15. *Foreign Relations, 1931*, 2:18–22; Randall, *The Diplomacy of Modernization*, pp. 112–113.
16. Telegram from Caffery, 10 April 1931, 821.6363 Barco/487, RG 59; George Rublee Oral History, Columbia University, pp. 253–255; *Foreign Relations, 1931*, 2:25; *New York Times*, 5 March 1931.
17. Colombian consul to José Antonio Montalvo, 9 Jan. 1930, Camilo C. Restrepo to Carlos E. Restrepo, 21 May 1931, Academia Colombiana de Historia; *Foreign Relations, 1931*, 2:26–28; *New York Times*, 18 June 1931, 13 Jan. 1932.

18. British embassy to Foreign Office, Washington, D.C., 21 Jan. 1932, FO 371/15869, PRO; Senate Finance Committee, *Sale of Foreign Bonds*, parts 2–3; Randall, *The Diplomacy of Modernization*, pp. 115–116; *New York Times*, 13, 15, 21 June 1931.

19. Spencer R. Dickson to Foreign Office, 3 Oct. 1935, FO 371/18673, PRO; *Time*, 4 May 1936; *New York Times*, 1, 5 May, 9 Oct. 1936, 26 Feb. 1939.

20. "Memorandum sobre el problema de los petróleos," Academia Colombiana de Historia; Randall, *The Diplomacy of Modernization*, pp. 82–83; *New York Times*, 23, 29 June 1934, 29 March 1936, 4, 5, 18 March 1937.

21. Report of Petroleum Department, 5 Feb. 1936, FO 371/19777, PRO; S. Walter Washington Report, 6 Oct. 1934, 821.6363/1232, RG 59; Ministerio de Industrias, *Memoria 1929* (Bogotá: Tip. Romana, 1929), pp. 14–28; Villegas, *Petróleo*, pp. 127–128; Randall, *The Diplomacy of Modernization*, pp. 124–125; *El Espectador*, 2 Oct. 1931.

22. *El Tiempo*, 14, 22 Dec. 1937; Eduardo Ospina Racines, *La economía del petróleo en Colombia: Compilación de estudios sobre diversos aspectos jurídicos, técnicos y económicos de la industria*, 2nd ed. (Bogotá: Artes Gráficas, 1947).

23. Report of 31 July 1931 and Dawson to Secretary of State, 821.6363/1158 and 1227, RG 59; *New York Times*, 18 Nov. 1935.

24. Winthrop S. Greene to Secretary of State, 16 Dec. 1938, 821.6363/1298, RG 59.

25. M. Paske-Smith to Foreign Office, 11 May 1938, FO 371/21446, PRO.

26. Paske-Smith to Anthony Eden, 24 Aug. 1936, FO 371/19777, PRO; William Dawson Report, 821.6363/1249, RG 59; *New York Times*, 23 Dec. 1936.

27. This paragraph and the rest of the section draws on correspondence of the Board of Trade, May–June 1938, FO 371/21439, PRO; Spruille Braden Report, 14 Aug. 1939, 821.6363/Royal Dutch Shell/1, RG 59; David Bushnell, *Eduardo Santos and the Good Neighbor, 1938–1942* (Gainesville: University of Florida Press, 1967), p. 106.

3

New Winds

The alliance between the foreign oil companies and the Colombian elite confronted its greatest challenge during the 1940s. Would state enterprises make the presence of foreign oil companies unnecessary in Latin America? When Mexico proved that nationalization and a state petroleum company were feasible alternatives, the Colombian elite had to rethink many assumptions. As a first step, the dispute over the expiration date of Exxon's Barrancabermeja concession required immediate attention. The Colombian elite could then ponder at leisure the alternatives that best suited their own interests. By 1946 the debate gave way to clashes, and a ferocious struggle ensued between competing factions within the elite and their respective allies as to what institution was best to harness the country's petroleum.

The Nationalization of Oil in Mexico

The one event that reversed the downward trend in Colombia's oil plight was the nationalization of Mexican Oil in 1938.[1] Prior to that event, Colombia's elite was undecided as to the merits of pursuing a state enterprise for petroleum, in part because of doubts about existing state enterprises in other countries. His Majesty's Government was the principal stockholder in British Petroleum, but since that company's primary task was the colonial exploitation of Iran's oil resources, it hardly provided an appropriate example to follow. Much closer to the Colombian experience was the example of the Soviet Union. Tsarist Russia had been an underdeveloped agrarian country but from the 1917 Revolution had embarked upon a rapid expansion, which transformed the country into a major power by World War II. The Soviet Union had shown for the first time in the twentieth century that expropriation without compensation for foreign oil companies was possible and also that the latter were not indispensable for the effective development of the Russian fields to benefit the whole population. In spite of these successes, the

33

Colombian elite dismissed the Soviet state enterprises as too far removed from them and even "Asiatic," and at most the exception to the rule. Ignoring the largest country in the world was a major but necessary feat for the Colombian elite if it wanted to continue dismissing state enterprises as a real alternative for Latin America.

A rude awakening came when Mexico nationalized its oil and directly challenged the foreign oil companies; in reprisal, England immediately broke diplomatic relations. Although the Soviet example had shown Mexico that nationalization could be accomplished, the procedure did not exactly parallel the Soviet experience. First of all, the Mexican government of Lázaro Cárdenas had not seriously considered the possibility of expropriation until the foreign oil companies flaunted their open defiance against a decision of the Mexican Supreme Court. In accordance with their standard practice in Latin America, the foreign companies in Mexico were just as outraged over minor modifications as they were over major challenges to their dictatorial positions. Steps were readily available to avoid the nationalization, and yet the foreign companies refused to bend, even over the minor issue of a wage settlement. Mexican president Cárdenas ably judged the international situation and concluded that on the eve of World War II the United States could not afford to have a hostile Mexico on its borders. He announced the nationalization by radio on 18 March 1938, and just to be on the safe side, he did not follow the Soviet model of expropriation without compensation but instead proceeded to initiate negotiations with the U.S. government over the amount of compensation the foreign oil companies were entitled to claim for their installations, but not a single cent was to be given to the companies for the petroleum deposits, which belonged to the state according to Mexican law.

The Colombian elite watched the events in Mexico with keen interest, and gradually, two positions emerged. The first predicted that Mexico would be crushed by the foreign oil companies, thus not only serving as a warning to those who dared repeat such an act of rebellion, but at the same time also confirming the wisdom of the Colombian policy of total submission to the dictates of the oil companies. A second, more opportunistic position, expressed even by president López Pumarejo in private, held that the oil companies, now driven out of Mexico, could not but invest heavily in a risk-free Colombia. The Colombian government made no direct statements about Mexico, although official pronouncements reaffirmed the country's commitment to scrupulously honoring the contracts in force with the oil companies.[2]

Meanwhile, Mexico single-handedly battled against the oil companies, which had imposed financial and economic sanctions as well as declared a boycott on Mexican crude; an oil executive told Colombians in private that the Mexicans would have to eat their oil. The public watched with attention, and the climax came in September 1939 at a press conference: Although the oil companies had expected a capitulation, the Mexican Minister of Develoment explained that Mexico could not take any more orders for export because all of its crude had been sold. This was no bluff; the foreign oil companies had totally miscalculated the unsettled market conditions on the eve of World War II. Nazi Germany, which lacked oil deposits of its own, had been buying crude cargoes since 1938 to stockpile strategic reserves. Germany's purchases then triggered a buying spree on the part of neutrals, who feared they could be left short of fuel when war broke out. As a matter of fact, huge profits were waiting to be made, and even U.S. companies such as Texaco sold oil to Nazi Germany from the Barco Concession in 1940.

Not only had the campaign against Mexico failed, but the oil sales abroad had reaped windfall profits for the country. More help was on the way for Mexico, since the Roosevelt administration gradually moved toward accepting Mexico's position as valid, overcoming the initial hostility of the State Department. The U.S. government decided to pursue its negotiations with Mexico even over the opposition of the oil companies, and the Mexican government, for its part, was trying to whip up support in Latin American countries. Mexicans contacted labor unions and members of the elite, but the latter were unenthusiastic. Colombia had been handed leverage to pry a few more percentage points of royalty crude out of the U.S. companies, but the Colombian government refused to budge from its pro–oil company policy. Mexican agents even planted a story in the media claiming that Colombia was about to nationalize the holdings of Exxon, whereupon the Eduardo Santos administration (1938–1942) speedily issued a disclaimer.

Mexico pressed ahead without Colombian support. It secured a major victory in the November 1941 agreement that limited compensation to the value of the installations owned by the oil companies and definitely excluded compensation for the value of the underground reserves. With this hurdle cleared, there only remained to set a value, and this figure was decided upon by a joint U.S.-Mexican commission whose verdict of April 1942 was very favorable to Mexico.

This outcome was watched very carefully by the Colombian elite, whose members reluctantly admitted that Mexico had won a decisive victory in the struggle over nationalization. They drew three main lessons from the experience. The first was that the oil companies were not as omnipotent as in their arrogance they had boasted, and that individual countries could successfully defy their financial and economic grip. A second lesson was that state enterprises could effectively run oil operations, as was proved by the Mexican National Petroleum Company

(PEMEX) that ran the nationalized oil fields and refineries. Lastly, the most important lesson that the Colombian elite learned was that the existence of a state oil enterprise, even in a monopoly position like PEMEX, did not mean the nationalization of the entire private sector, and more crucially, did not pose a threat to the control held by the elite. Not only was a state enterprise compatible with control by the private sector, but a state enterprise could even bolster the position as well as the profits of the privileged minority. These were intriguing possibilities that made some members of the Colombian elite think hard and long.

Storm over the Barrancabermeja Fields

Mexico's nationalization of oil awoke considerable interest in petroleum throughout Latin America. In response to this revived concern the Colombian government created the Ministry of Mines and Petroleum on 18 May 1940. Up to this point jurisdiction over oil had remained within the Ministry of Development, but since 1940 (except for a brief interlude in 1951–1952) this separate cabinet-level ministry has handled petroleum policy as its primary occupation, since mining policy has never wandered beyond filing and shuffling permits for exploiting mineral and metal deposits. The sleepy atmosphere of the mining bureau within the ministry contrasted with the dynamism of the petroleum office, the latter almost immediately involving itself in the dispute over whether the Barrancabermeja concession expired in 1946 or 1951.[3]

To forestall the whole controversy, the Santos administration had offered Exxon a timely alternative. The Colombian government, short of money, wanted three things: a lump payment of at least $10 million, an increase of 1 or 2 percent in crude royalties, and the return of a symbolic part of the untouched area in the concession (Exxon had developed only 10,000 hectares of the more than 500,000 in the concession). In exchange for the above, the Santos administration offered to renew the contract for twenty-five years, and even longer if Exxon wished because the president did not care about the time limit. This alternative was not made casually but was reiterated on numerous occasions to no avail. Exxon refused to accept the proposals, either because it was holding out for better terms, or more likely (as Ambassador Spruille Braden charged), because of the incompetence of the local Exxon manager, R. I. Dodson, who was later demoted. Santos held the offer open as long as possible, but Exxon's refusal exposed him to pressure by the nationalists, who finally forced his hand. Early in 1941 the Colombian president, with great regret, took the first steps toward bringing a lawsuit before the Colombian Supreme Court claiming that the Barrancabermeja concession expired in 1946 and not in 1951.[4]

Exxon officials were outraged and felt betrayed at this turn of events, and in full haste they turned to the U.S. embassy for complete diplomatic protection of their interests, which they felt were being violated. The initial reaction of Ambassador Braden was to the point: "I question both the wisdom and the ethics of the oil companies so continually ignoring our advice, only later to put their sick babies in the Department's lap, simultaneously crying to high heaven against the iniquities of the other American Republics."[5] These and other complaints did not change the minds of State Department officials who strongly defended Exxon in the dispute over the expiration date of the concession.

The merits of the company's case were very weak at best: The trail of contracts by which Exxon had obtained the Barrancabermeja concession was so muddled that, as one embassy official put it, the whole title to the concession was either null and void or at the very most lasted only until 1946. Company lawyers felt that Exxon would have a better chance at winning if they relied on the traditional ways to influence the courts: It always paid to know the judge before the trial. This strategy, however, could backfire, because no matter how many Supreme Court judges could be bribed or otherwise influenced, additional safeguards were needed: This was no petty case involving smuggling, but rather, it would deeply affect the most important economic activity in the whole country.

Besides, so much popular feeling had poured out on this issue, and the petroleum worker's union was so restless, that only a high-level political decision could guarantee not only a favorable verdict by the Supreme Court but also that it would be enforced. Eduardo Santos saw all these complications coming, and to avoid them he repeated one last time at the end of 1941 his earlier offer of a long-term renewal in exchange for cash to the government. Rebuffed again by Exxon, he washed himself of the whole matter. The issue now fell to the next president, Alfonso López Pumarejo, who began his second term in office in 1942. For Ambassador Braden, López Pumarejo was the key to the solution. Prior to becoming president, he received monthly payments from Texaco and Gulf, and almost certainly from Exxon as well, to sustain his high style of living. Braden directed all the companies to focus their efforts on López Pumarejo as the best way to secure a verdict from the Supreme Court that would be favorable to Exxon's claims.[6]

After the final arguments were filed in 1942, president López Pumarejo had plenty of time to convince the judges to see the big picture, and finally on 20 October 1944 the Supreme Court handed down its verdict. To the surprise of the Colombian public, which had been kept in the dark about the negotiations, the Supreme Court overlooked the fraudulent evidence behind the concession contract and ratified the expiration date as 25 August 1951. This decision inflicted tremendous loss upon Colombia, since Exxon now would have five more years to drain the deposits in the Barrancabermeja concession, depriving the country later of revenue as well as of much needed crude. As Exxon increased its pumping, rather than dropping, as expected, output continued to rise, and the realization slowly started to spread among company executives that the reserves were many times larger than originally believed. The Supreme Court verdict postponing the reversion until 1951 turned into a bittersweet victory for the company, which now regretted not having accepted Eduardo Santos's reiterated offers to extend the concession for another twenty-five years.[7] Now it was too late, and the issue was back in the hands of the Colombian elite, which confronted its most momentous decision yet: what to do with the Barrancabermeja fields when the concession expired on 25 August 1951?

Initial Proposals for a National Petroleum Company

As far as the Colombian elite was concerned, Exxon had failed the test of supplying gasoline in minimal amounts during World War II. The members of the upper class considered an adequate supply of gasoline to keep their automobiles running to be indispensable to their style of life. It was not really a matter of price; resentful as they were about the high gasoline prices Exxon charged, the elite was willing to pay them as a mechanism to keep the Colombian masses from climbing in the social hierarchy. The wartime gasoline shortage came from Exxon's decision not to enlarge the Barrancabermeja refinery, whose output remained too small to cover domestic needs, thus requiring a reliance on imported gasoline since the 1920s. Submarine sinkings and other wartime dislocations necessarily interrupted tanker movements, and there was still the question of whether Exxon manipulated the whole situation to reap even higher wartime profits, for which there was considerable circumstantial evidence.[8]

The standard oil company practice of exporting huge amounts of crude without returning any foreign currency was not under question per se, except as it might need to be modified to assure a supply of gasoline. From the start, any nationalization of oil was excluded because it was a measure that could backfire against private properties, thus reducing the debate to the fate of the Barrancabermeja fields, now scheduled to revert to the state in 1951. The Colombian elite had to decide among three alternatives: a purely private company, a mixed company with some private and state capital, or a state enterprise.

Closest to the hearts of the Colombian businessmen was a private petroleum company, yet several attempts to establish oil exploration companies by private capital had all ended in failure, in part because the mainly mercantile experience of Colombians was not directly applicable to oil operations. Furthermore, even during the 1940s the refinery process seemed incredibly complex and simply beyond the technical reach of the country. In actual fact, however, the failures of the private companies, such as Colombian Royalties and National Company of Carare, had resulted from infiltration and undermining activities perpetrated by the foreign oil companies. In spite of the foreign companies' inevitable gloating over these failures for publicity purposes, the Colombian elite pursued the possibility of having a private Colombian company run the Barracanbermeja fields vigorously to the end.[9]

One way to avoid the risks inherent in private Colombian control was to combine it with foreign capital, the state, or both. This "mixed" company was very attractive for Exxon because it would secure a de facto extension of its monopoly contract over the Barracanbermeja fields. As early as 1944 Exxon acquiesced in accepting the idea of a mixed company with private Colombian investors, but it did not push very strongly for its acceptance. The proverbial shortage of private funds inevitably led to the inclusion of the state as another "partner" in this mixed company. Determining the exact percentage share for each private investor had been hard enough, and now that a quota had to be reserved for the state, the task of negotiating a workable agreement became extremely trying and time consuming.

In contrast, the state enterprise had a simplicity that made it an attractive proposal from the start. The Ministry of Mines and Petroleum, created in 1940, had raised—parallel to the Barrancabermeja lawsuit—the issue of what institution could replace Exxon in running the concession. The Mexican example was a powerful stimulus to bolster confidence in state enterprise, but the ministry went further and studied relevant cases in Latin America, such as Argentina, as well as in other parts of the world, like Rumania. The feasibility studies left no doubt that even under the least favorable circumstances, a national petroleum company was not only viable but also highly profitable. Now fully convinced, the Ministry of Mines and Petroleum, led by a group of young and idealistic engineers, began in 1942 to press relentlessly for the creation of a national petroleum company fully owned by the Colombian state.[10]

International support for a state enterprise came from various quarters. Venezuela was in the midst of a reexamination of both its petroleum and economic policies and concluded by 1944 that greater state intervention was necessary. This meant challenging the privileges of the foreign oil companies, and to secure support for such a move, Venezuela sounded out Colombia repeatedly starting in 1946 about the possibility of adopting common legislation toward the foreign oil companies. Just the very idea of challenging the oil companies was too drastic for the Colombian elite, however, and the Venezuela proposals only fostered an endless round of trips and reciprocal visits.

Another international example could not be ignored so easily. The United States was not satisfied with the way the oil companies had performed during World War II, and in 1944 it signed agreements with England making their respective governments, at least briefly, partners in foreign oil matters. Such a policy had far-reaching implications and was closely watched in Colombia as well as in other countries of Latin America. For the Colombian elite, the Anglo-American oil agreements of 1944 paved the way for a realization that state intervention in petroleum was an acceptable formula that could be pursued if other alternatives had failed to materialize.[11]

In August 1946 the Conservative Party returned to power after a sixteen-year interlude of Liberal Party rule. Yet there was no break in oil policy, as the statist traditions of the Conservative Party allowed the Ministry of Mines and Petroleum to continue with its proposals for an official National Petroleum Company.

The Mariano Ospina Pérez Administration: 1946–1950

The First Phase: 1946–1948

When the Conservative Party president Mariano Ospina Pérez took office in August 1946, he received from the previous Liberal government two oil problems that had to be disposed of before his administration could devote full attention to the proposed National Petroleum Company.

Early in 1946 the Colombian congress had passed Law 31 creating a National Petroleum Council with wide-ranging attributes and even power to run any future National Petroleum Company. The outgoing Liberal government had not been able to organize the Council because of oil company opposition. As an autonomous board within the Ministry of Mines and Petroleum, the National Petroleum Council, two of whose five members were to be appointed by congress, was supposed to provide independent judgment to the Colombian government. The council replaced the previous Advisory Commission on Petroleum, which, without the same broad powers, had largely restricted itself to offering advice on narrow legal aspects of concession contracts. Several cabinet ministers as well as the minister of mines and petroleum resented the new Council as an invasion of their powers, but the firm determination of President Ospina Pérez overcame the opposition and at last, on 6 February 1947, the Council's first session was held under the presidency of Félix Mendoza; another of the founding members was Juan José Turbay, who with Mendoza played a very important role in determining the ultimate shape of the National Petroleum Company.[12]

The second problem concerned the proposal by the independent Texas oilman D. D. Feldman to refine the royalty crude in a 2,000-barrel-a-day refinery that he promised to construct. Feldman had made his proposal late in 1945 under the Liberal government, and a contract was ready for signature in April 1946, but the issue remained unresolved. The Ospina Pérez administration postponed any action until the National Petroleum Council could study the matter. Upon closer examination, some curious aspects came to light; for example, no contract was needed to establish a refinery in Colombia, and the size of the proposed refinery was too small, yet the Council still recommended approval. Even the U.S. embassy was suspicious of the Feldman proposal and considered it a ploy to break into the profitable distribution that Exxon operated. In spite of the mounting skepticism, the Feldman refinery project continued to take up time and effort for several years until at last in 1948 President Ospina Pérez personally took action to kill the proposal because it was in conflict with the proposed National Petroleum Company.[13]

The National Petroleum Council, even after its first session in February 1947, was slow to start working. Again, a presidential decision by Ospina Pérez was needed to assign the necessary personnel and budget to the new council. These delays allowed the Colombian congress to take the lead, and congressman Arturo E. Márquez in September 1947 presented a bill to create a state petroleum company. The bill quickly passed the house, and passage in the senate was assured. Congress had become a redoubt for nationalistic sentiments, with legislators openly sympathizing with the petroleum unions that challenged the foreign companies. The mood was such that no renewal of the Barrancabermeja concession stood any chance of passage.

President Osina Pérez personally welcomed the Márquez bill in spite of the haste with which it had been drafted; yet once again the oil companies intervened with a threefold counterattack. First of all, they presented a rival oil bill, which, even though it had no chance of passage, at least gained time by invoking the normal legislative procedures to determine which was the best of the two bills. Secondly, Eduardo López Pumarejo, the brother of former President López Pumarejo, presented a proposal to the government to exploit the Barrancabermeja fields after 1951 in association with unnamed U.S. companies, possibly Sinclair or more likely Exxon itself. The strategy was to bypass the congress and instead use the executive branch to transfer the concession to a private Colombian citizen who would then hand control back to the U.S. company. Lastly, and to flex its muscles, Exxon began to lay off 500 workers at Barrancabermeja, a move that provoked a bitter protest from the petroleum union and soon culminated in a crippling strike in January 1948.[14]

Emergency measures settled the strike, with favorable concessions granted to the petroleum workers. Yet the hard political fact remained that labor sentiment was passionate in demanding a state enterprise and that the union would not hesitate to declare further strikes. Ospina Pérez now galvanized the National Petroleum Council into action and prodded for the drafting of a bill that would go to the congress with the full backing of the presidency. The Council debated the three alternatives of a private, mixed, or state company but could reach no final agreement; at one point the Council considered presenting the alternatives before the congress so that the latter could make up its mind, but the Council's members were afraid that the legislators might choose the worst alternative. Instead, a consensus started to develop around Council member Juan José Turbay's argument in favor of a state company. The Council's acceptance of his report also signified that Turbay's star in the Council was on the rise, and he gradually started to eclipse Félix Mendoza, the Council president, who in spite of constant talking, debating, and bustling could point to very few accomplishments. President Ospina Pérez accepted a bill based on Turbay's report, and the bill became law at the end of 1948. This bill called for the creation of a state company but allowed private or foreign investors to provide no more than 49 percent of the capital.

The oilmen who had been clamoring for ten years to obtain more favorable legislation were furious at the speedy passage of Law 165 of 1948, yet they could find comfort in one provision of the law that authorized the Colombian government to contract out the refinery operations. Authorship of this idea rested with Félix Mendoza—indeed, this was one of his few contributions to the whole process, although his true motives were still not known. Since January 1948 Mendoza had urgently argued for the enlargement of the Barrancabermeja refinery, in effect entangling the debate over the precise nature of the National Petroleum Company with the separate issue of refinery expansion.[15]

The Second Phase: 1949–1950

After the passage of Law 165 at the end of 1948, oil matters entered into a temporary recess. To establish the National Petroleum Company, the leadership of a dynamic oil minister was indispensable, but from January 1949 no one who was willing to hold the post could be found. One minister resigned after forty days, other individuals declined to serve, and with acting appointees matters drifted. Normally in Colombia a crowd of aspirants craved to hold any cabinet position, but when word had spread that the López family was opposed to a state enterprise, nobody would even come near the ministry out of fear of reprisals from the powerful López family or the oil companies. Even capitulating to the demands of the López family was political suicide, since no incumbent minister could survive the massive outcry from the public and from the worker's unions. At last, in May 1949, President Ospina Pérez reached as far away as the frontier province of Pasto next to the border with Ecuador to find José Elías del Hierro. Followers of López Pumarejo had already burned down the newspaper office of Elías del Hierro, who was no longer afraid of reprisals and, furthermore, saw in the cabinet post a great opportunity to put his convictions on the need for state involvement in petroleum into practice.

The first order of business for the new oil minister was to decide once and for all whether Exxon would participate in the new petroleum company. The National Petroleum Council had previously sent a study mission to Mexico; it now decided to send Félix Mendoza to New York and Toronto to talk directly to Exxon executives because the local company officials had taken such extremist positions that they even misled U.S. Ambassador Willard L. Beaulac. Hostile as New York headquarters was to a partnership with the state, the company did not reject the proposal out of hand and was willing to accept it provided Exxon had a 50 percent share and complete management control. The Colombian executive could grant the latter but not the former, since Law 165 of 1948 had specified a maximum of 49 percent for the foreign companies.[16]

Exxon was not used to taking "no" for an answer, so it promptly launched a campaign to have the Colombian government change Law 165 to allow the 50 percent share. The year 1949 coincided with a previously planned shift by a few small oil companies out of Colombia and into the Middle East, yet Exxon contrived to make this expected departure appear as an exodus of all oil companies to protest the unfavorable terms afforded to foreign capital. The Export-Import Bank was willing to bring pressure to bear through restricting loans to Colombia. But Exxon realized that an even more appropriate instrument was the recently founded World Bank, which, because of its claims to adhere to "objective" economic principles, could more effectively make the "pitch" that favorable consideration of loans depended upon Colombia's acceptance of the terms Exxon demanded for the Barrancabermeja fields. Ambassador Beaulac, a worthy successor to Braden, eagerly backed the oil companies to the hilt, but the State Department, whose Latin American policy was under the control of Assistant Secretary of State Edward Miller, refused to harass or blackmail the Colombian government.

Without clearance from Miller, both the Export-Import Bank and the World Bank were hesitant to try punitive tactics, so that on 22 July 1949 President Ospina Pérez could tell the U.S. ambassador in very polite language but with an air of finality that about changing Law 165, there was nothing he could do.[17]

Exxon meanwhile orchestrated one last attempt to bring private Colombian capital into the new National Petroleum Company. The only private investors who showed any sustained interest were the factory owners of Antioquia in the National Association of Industrialists—of which Exxon was also a member. The industrialists came to the endless discussions with a bundle of inquiries but without funds to invest. In a frank revelation of elite attitudes, the Medellín factory owners from the start demanded as preconditions that the Colombian government crush the petroleum workers' union, expel the squatters from the fields, and abolish the workers' pension and severance funds.[18]

To remove the entanglements and delays that Exxon continued to pile up, the nationalists in May 1950 leaked evidence to the Bogotá newspapers proving that the president of the National Petroleum Council, Félix Mendoza, had been an agent of the foreign oil companies for many years. Mendoza tried to hang on to his position, but the overwhelming public outcry finally forced him to present his resignation, which was accepted on 22 May 1950. Released from the brake of Mendoza, oil minister Elías del Hierro now surged ahead. He immediately confronted the Medellín industrialists with the demand that they either "put up or shut up"; needless to say they faded into the background. Time was running against Elías del Hierro, however, and in August 1950 the four-year term of the Ospina Pérez administration ended, leaving the final decision about the National Petroleum Company, or Ecopetrol, in the hands of the next Conservative president and his new oil minister.[19]

The Birth of Ecopetrol
(National Petroleum Company)

President Laureano Gómez, even before he took office in August 1950, was firmly committed to the state enterprise. He chose Manuel Carvajal to replace José Elías del Hierro as oil minister. Carvajal, a wealthy industrialist from Cali, believed that any private Colombian company was doomed to failure and that the only way to stimulate competition against the foreign oil companies was through state involvement. Furthermore, the idea that the creation of a state petroleum company was in the interest of the Colombian elite had started to gain momentum. Political leaders like ex-president Alberto Lleras Camargo advocated the viewpoint that the oil companies had enjoyed too good a deal for too

long. Undaunted, in late August 1950 Exxon made another offer to run
the Barrancabermeja fields, but by 6 September the National Petroleum
Council (now under the influence of Juan José Turbay) rejected the
proposal as a subterfuge to renew the concession for an indefinite time
in clear violation of the intent of Law 165 of 1948.[20]

Exxon, however, still would not give up, and in one last burst of
effort managed to escape complete defeat by convincing the Conservative
administration that some form of foreign participation was needed to
assure the success of Ecopetrol. By the terms of the contract signed on
1 December 1950, Exxon agreed to operate the refinery for ten years
past the reversion date of 25 August 1951 and also to secure foreign
financing for the expansion of the refinery; in this form the earlier idea
planted by the oil company agent Félix Mendoza now bore fruit. Rather
than letting Ecopetrol begin to function and then decide for itself what
was the best method of expanding the insufficient refinery capacity, the
administration saddled the company from the start with a huge debt
as well as conditions imposed by Exxon. The easy acceptance of the
refinery expansion plan on Exxon's terms was an indication that even
from the very beginning, the Colombian elite, although accepting the
creation of Ecopetrol, did not want to see it grow into a giant that
would totally displace the foreign oil companies. In a separate contract,
Exxon pledged itself to providing technical assistance and other forms
of expertise for oil field operations, but as soon as Ecopetrol began
operations in August 1951, officials of the state company were counting
the days until they could cancel the technical assistance contract, which
had turned out not only to be useless but also to present a downright
hindrance to operating the fields.[21]

The agreement of 1 December 1950 had decided the fate of a National
Petroleum Company that still had not been formally created. A formal
decree was released at the end of December, but final approval was not
forthcoming until January of 1951. Laureano Gómez sensed that he was
making a momentous decision, and his firm determination to rapidly
overcome the obstacles that continued to appear was decisive for the
creation of Ecopetrol. Rumors about the possible candidates for the top
jobs in Ecopetrol began to circulate as early as December 1950—a sure
sign that its creation could now be taken for granted. A rudimentary
staff began to function during the first months of 1951, and gradually
a team of engineers and experts was patiently gathered from all corners
of Colombia to assume the task of running the Barrancabermeja fields
beginning on 25 August 1951.[22]

In spite of the rear-guard action by Exxon securing a ten-year lease
on life for the refinery concession, nothing could hide the fact that the
largest oil field in Colombia to date had passed out of the control of

U.S. companies. This was the first permanent setback the foreign oil companies had ever experienced in Colombia, and it was the first time in Latin America that a concession had returned to a host government as a result of nonrenewal of an existing contract. To disguise the bungling of the renewal, local Exxon officials played up the public relations angle of a peaceful and legal reversion to the maximum.

New York headquarters had left final solution of the matter to local Exxon officials and had also agreed to play the game of bluffing by demanding no less than a 50 percent share. But when the Colombian government had called the bluff, officials at the company headquarters were infuriated at the failure of the local subsidiary to take the 49 percent share (with a management contract), since this option would be infinitely better than having no control over the oil fields at all. There was no hiding the fact that Exxon had suffered a real defeat, and remedial measures were not long in appearing. Henceforth, greater direct supervision from New York headquarters became the rule in foreign subsidiary operations. At the same time, the Canadians and older U.S. officials were phased out, to be replaced by a new breed of hard talking and fast dealing U.S. oilmen who gradually rose to prominence. The best representative of this new breed in Colombia for Exxon was Francisco Espinosa.[23] The challenge these new oilmen faced was real: A rising nationalistic tide and setbacks throughout the continent boded ill for the survival of foreign oil companies in Latin America. Could the trend toward a monopoly by state enterprises be reversed? This was the question the oil companies had to answer during the 1950s, as the next chapter shows.

Notes

1. For the discussion of events in Mexico, this section is based on Lorenzo Meyer, *Mexico and the United States in the Oil Controversy, 1917–1942* (Austin: University of Texas Press, 1977); George W. Grayson, *The Politics of Mexican Oil* (Pittsburgh: University of Pittsburgh Press, 1980); George Philip, *Oil and Politics in Latin America* (Cambridge: Cambridge University Press, 1982); Stephen J. Randall, *United States Foreign Oil Policy, 1919–1948: For Profits and Security* (Montreal: McGill-Queens Universty Press, 1985); and the papers (forthcoming) presented at the Mexican Petroleum Nationalization Conference held at the University of Texas at Austin, February 1988.

2. M. Paske-Smith Reports, 1 April, 4 June 1938, Foreign Office (FO) 371/ 21446, Public Record Office (PRO), London, England; Greene Report, June 1938, 821.6363/1290, Record Group (RG) 59, National Archives, Washington, D.C.; *El Tiempo*, 14 June 1938.

3. David Bushnell, *Eduardo Santos and the Good Neighbor, 1938–1942* (Gaines-ville: University of Florida Press, 1967), p. 100; Spruille Braden, *Diplomats and*

Demagogues (New Rochelle, N.Y.: Arlington House, 1971), p. 218; Bogotá embassy report, 821.6363/1335, RG 59.

4. *New York Times*, 1 June 1941; 17 June 1941, 821.6363 Tropical Oil Company/ 164, RG 59; Jorge Villegas, *Petróleo, oligarquía e imperio* (Bogotá: Tercer Mundo, 1975), pp. 220–221; Braden, *Diplomats and Demagogues*, pp. 218–219.

5. Braden to Laurence Duggan, 11 July 1941, Spruille Braden Papers, Rare Book and Manuscript Library, Columbia University, Box 7.

6. Memorandum, 821.6363 Tropical Oil Company/164 and 21 Sept. 1944, 821.6363/9-2144, RG 59; Braden to Wright, 24 Nov. 1941, and Braden to Duggan, 18 July 1939, Braden Papers, Box 7, Columbia University.

7. W. E. Dunn Report, 21 Sept. 1944, Roy W. Merritt Report, 11 Sept. 1943, 821.6363/9-2144, 1499, RG 59; Villegas, *Petróleo*, pp. 227–230; *New York Times*, 24 Sept. 1944.

8. Bushnell, *Eduardo Santos*, pp. 103–120; *El Siglo*, 26 Feb., 20 March 1941; *New York Times*, 25 Nov. 1943; Jon V. Kofas, *Dependence and Underdevelopment in Colombia* (Tempe, Ariz.: Center for Latin American Studies, 1986), p. 109.

9. Eduardo Ospina Racines, *La economía del petróleo en Colombia*, 2d ed. (Bogotá: Artes Gráficas, 1947), pp. 128–130; *El Siglo*, 1 June 1939; *El Tiempo*, 5 March 1937, 3 Sept. 1940.

10. Merrit to Ambassador, 19 Sept. 1942 and 1 June 1944, 821.6363, RG 59.

11. U.S. Senate, Committee on Foreign Relations, *Documentary History of the Petroleum Reserves Corporation, 1943–1944* (Washington, D.C.: GPO, 1974); Randall, *U.S. Foreign Oil Policy*, chap. 6.

12. Kofas, *Underdevelopment in Colombia*, p. 111; *El Espectador*, 19 April 1947; *El Tiempo*, 7 Feb. 1947.

13. R. M. Connell to Ambassador, 16 July 1946, 21 Feb., 5 March 1947, 821.6363/7-1646, 2-2147, RG 59; *El Tiempo*, 28 April 1947; *New York Times*, 14 May 1946.

14. Memorandum, 18 April 1947, Memorandum of Conversation, 17 April 1947, Petroleum Division, Box 18, RG 59; *El Tiempo*, 30 April, 25, 27 Oct., 28 Nov. 1947, 30 Nov., 14 Dec. 1948; *El Siglo*, 28 Nov. 1947, 14 Sept., 20 Oct., 19 Nov. 1948; Kofas, *Underdevelopment in Colombia*, pp. 133–138.

15. *El Tiempo*, 29 Aug. 1947, 5 March 1949; Henrietta M. Larson, Evelyn H. Knowlton, and Charles S. Popple, *New Horizons* (New York: Harper & Row, 1971), p. 370; Kofas, *Underdevelopment in Colombia*, pp. 138–142.

16. Willard L. Beaulac Report, 29 April 1949, 821.6363/4-2949, RG 59; Larson et al., *New Horizons*, p. 371; *El Tiempo*, 23, 27 Jan. 1949; *Boletín de Minas y Petróleo*, no. 154 (1950), p. 195.

17. U.S. Department of State, *Foreign Relations, 1949*, p. 612; Ibid., *1951*, p. 825; Beaulac Report, 4 June, 31 Aug., 26 Oct. 1948, 821.51/6-448, 8-3148, 10-2648, and Beaulac Memorandum, 1, 25 July 1949, 821.6363/7-149, 7-2549; *El Tiempo*, 17, 22 March 1949; *El Siglo*, 4 Oct. 1948; Kofas, *Underdevelopment in Colombia*, pp. 111–112.

18. *El Siglo*, 24 April 1950; R. M. Connell Report, 17 Oct. 1946, 821.6363/ 10-1746, and Beaulac Reports, 10 Feb., 24 Aug. 1949, 821.6363/2-1049, 8/2449, RG 59.

19. *El Espectador*, 26 Aug., 7 Sept. 1950, and Bogotá press of May 1950; *Boletín de Minas y Petróleo*, no. 153 (1950), pp. 97–99; *El Tiempo*, 4 Aug. 1950.

20. *El Siglo*, 20, 30 Aug., 26 Oct. 1950.

21. *New York Times*, 9 Dec. 1950, 3 Jan. 1951; *El Tiempo*, 5, 18 Dec. 1950; *Colombia económica*, no. 103 (1950), pp. 1259–1264; *El Espectador*, 15 Dec. 1950; *El Siglo*, 11 Nov., 8, 15 Dec. 1950; Larson et al., *New Horizons*, p. 731.

22. Office Memorandum by Edward Miller, 4 Sept. 1951, 821.2553/9-451, RG 59; Larson et al., *New Horizons*, pp. 731–732; *New York Times*, 13 July, 27 Aug. 1951.

23. Larson et al., *New Horizons*, pp. 116, 726–727.

4

The Oil Companies Counterattack

From the nationalization of Mexican oil in 1938 until the late 1940s the oil companies were on the defensive, reeling constantly from one blow after another. Beginning in the late 1940s, however, even as the National Petroleum Company was on the verge of becoming reality, the oil companies were organizing a determined counterattack that formed part of a worldwide offensive, which had its best known success in Iran in 1954. The first order of business was to attempt to capture the oil of the Colombian Llanos. Another concentrated campaign involved trying to destroy or at least neutralize Ecopetrol; at the same time a parallel movement sought powerful allies among Colombia's elite. As the offensive rolled on during the 1950s, all that remained was to collect the fruits of victory in the shape of giveaway oil legislation.

Venezuela and Oil in the Llanos

Exxon could reconcile itself to the loss of the Barrancabermeja oil fields not only because of the rising flood of Middle East oil,[1] but also because of the discoveries in the Colombian Llanos next to the Venezuelan frontier. Shell had started drilling in the 1930s and had soon been joined by Mobil and Exxon. All the oil companies guarded every scrap of information jealously and duly reported to the Colombian government that they were discovering only an unbroken and ever growing number of dry holes. In reality, they were making spectacular finds. The oil companies were able to confirm that the pools of oil in the Venezuelan Llanos under the Orinoco river basin (also a tightly kept secret) extended far into the Colombian Llanos. The lakes of oil under the Llanos were certainly bigger than the Barco Concession, over which such ferocious controversy had raged, and they formed with Barrancabermeja and the Amazon the trio of the largest oil deposits in Colombia.

Upon discovery of the fabulous Llanos deposits, the oil companies had independently reached the conclusion not to exploit these fields but to keep them in reserve for a better opportunity. This occasion came in the late 1940s when Middle East oil was flooding the world markets and pushing prices down to the floor. The operation of most Western Hemisphere deposits had been undercut by Middle East oil, so that only wells with the lowest operating expenses could compete. This situation presented a perfect opportunity for taking advantage of Llanos oil, since with its very low cost of extraction it could still reap a very high rate of profits for the companies.

There was one hitch, however: A pipeline had to be built to the seacoast, but the cost of such a project would drive up the price of Llanos oil—unless, of course, the Colombian government could be convinced to build it for free. The Colombian government, seeing that the pipeline issue had silenced oil company opposition to the passage of the 1948 law on Ecopetrol, agreed to the project without carefully studying the details. By 1949, when government officials discovered that the planned 625-mile pipeline from the Llanos to the Caribbean coast of Colombia would cost at least $100 million, they were dumbfounded; they had not the slightest idea of where such a sum of money could be found.

To try to get out of this bind, Colombia's leaders now remembered Venezuela, a bordering country that for more than four years had been seeking cooperation for a joint binational policy toward the oil companies. The polite neglect that Colombia had shown to the Venezuelan suggestions was now transformed into a bold 1949 proposal to construct a pipeline from the Colombian Llanos to the nearest deep water port in Venezuela. Not only was the distance of the pipeline reduced to one fourth of the original distance, or 156 miles, with the natural savings on pumping and maintenance expenses, but the construction costs dropped even more dramatically without mountain ranges to cross.

Venezuela, which was rapidly acquiring experience about oil matters, saw right through this issue and refused from late 1949 to be dragged into the maneuver hatched by the oil companies. Venezuela did not have an export crop as important as coffee in Colombia and desperately needed to export oil to earn foreign exchange, but with prices dropping so low because of the Middle East glut, Venezuela faced having to curtail production. Bringing the Colombian Llanos into the picture meant protracting the period of low world prices, and this Venezuela simply could not allow.

The Colombian government brought up the pipeline over and over again until early 1951 in the vain hope that Venezuela might reconsider, but to no avail. The oil companies were furious at the outcome, and they blamed the Colombian government for dragging its feet in the negotiations with Venezuela. The oil companies' whole plan for Colombia had now been upset, and the perfectly measured exchange of the Llanos deposits for the Barrancabermeja zone had collapsed. The oil companies demanded immediate compensatory oil legislation, but still not satisfied, they lashed out with a vengeance at the newest actor on the scene—Ecopetrol.

Ecopetrol Under Siege

As least as early as 1949 the Exxon manager at Barrancabermeja was "pushing the wells on the De Mares concession as hard as he [could]" in preparation for turning over the fields to the newly created National Petroleum Company.[2] Trying to drain the fields was not enough for Exxon, which did not overlook even the last day's oil pumped from the ground, so that on the day of the transfer, 25 August 1951, the storage tanks were empty.

The condition of the physical installations could well be imagined. The 1936 Combined Distillation Unit formed the core of the refinery, but by now its pumps were worn out and had been discontinued by the manufacturer, while the instrument panels had reached the end of useful service. The Combined Distillation Unit had an electrical system that not only had been badly installed in 1936 and was in disastrous condition, but its technology was obsolete. The old power plant for the whole refinery gave way to constant outages and needed urgent replacement. Cannibalization was rampant among the rest of the equipment: As machinery broke down, the still usable parts were removed and taken to keep the other units limping along even though they were already ten years past their maximum service life.

Most of the equipment was old even when it had first arrived in the 1930s, because Exxon had taken maximum advantage of U.S. tax depreciation deductions to write off and then ship this equipment to countries like Colombia. Polished and then glamorized by public relations, the discontinued equipment fascinated the elite of an agrarian society with the wonders of modern technology. Any good quality machinery, like the crucial drilling rigs, had vanished mysteriously before the transfer to Ecopetrol took place on 25 August 1951.

Ecopetrol consoled itself with the thought that it would at least soon be the proud owner of Exxon's impressive "White Fleet" of steamers, tugs, and barges that plied the Magdalena river. No concealment of the vessels was possible, since the oil company needed them until the last minute to distribute the products of the refinery. However, a hitch soon developed: Exxon lawyers claimed that in spite of the very explicit language in the Supreme Court decision of 1944, the White Fleet was not included in the list of items to be reverted to the state in 1951.

Flabbergasted at this blatantly illegal interpretation, the Ministry of Mines and Petroleum sought opinions from three lawyers who specialized in predicting how judges would react to the surrounding political pressures. To the government's surprise, all three replied that another Supreme Court decision would uphold Exxon's right to the White Fleet. Ecopetrol, not wishing to risk judgments that might take away even more things, resigned itself to see the White Fleet sail away into hostile hands.[3]

An alternative to the White Fleet was to make use of an old network of pipelines. These pipelines (as well as a railroad) cross the Barrancabermeja zone, and as a result of a long-forgotten power play by Exxon in 1948, one pipeline went as far south as Cantimploras. Exxon had gladly turned over these pipelines to Ecopetrol, but the reason for this willingness soon became apparent: The deteriorated 1920s pipelines were breaking down from old age, while the Cantimploras segment could explode at any moment because it had been built out of World War II tubes not intended for pipelines. In any case, the Cantimploras pipeline emptied its products at a river terminal for further transport by the White Fleet; Ecopetrol could truly claim to have received a pipeline that went from nowhere to nowhere.[4]

Barrancabermeja had striking similarities with the desolated Ploesti oil fields in Rumania, but in 1951 the Colombian goverment, which had previously been so impressed by Rumanian oil legislation, refused to seek assistance from Rumania. From the moment in 1945 when the country had nationalized all her oil properties, Rumania ceased to exist for the Colombian elite—not as hard a task as might seem for people who had before easily blocked out of their minds the largest country in the world, the Soviet Union. However, the Rumanian influence was not totally absent: One Colombian who had worked for fifteen years in the Rumanian oil fields now served as a high executive for Ecopetrol and worked tirelessly day and night to rebuild the operation, but the past finally caught up with him and he was purged from the National Petroleum Company during the dictatorship of Gustavo Rojas Pinilla.

Not even purges could stop the wave of nationalistic feeling that swept the workers and most of the officials who took up the challenge at Barrancabermeja with passion and dedication. The immense pressures that Exxon and the other oil companies mobilized to attempt to destroy the National Petroleum Company merely served to evoke in these dedicated Colombians almost superhuman feats of sacrifice to save the idea of the state enterprise at all costs. These workers, engineers, clerks, and most executives (all of whose names must be protected to avoid reprisals) were constantly hamstrung by a generally hostile Colombian elite yet somehow managed to concentrate their efforts in three areas: (1) the refinery; (2) pipelines; and (3) drilling.

The Refinery

Negotiations to enlarge the Barrancabermeja refinery, which then supplied only half of Colombia's needs, had taken place for years. Once the reversion took place in August 1951, Exxon rushed to conclude the arrangements before the report of the first year's earnings in August 1952 could convince Ecopetrol that it really did not need foreign loans. Exxon, which continued to manage the refinery for a ten-year period, quickly imposed most of its viewpoints on what type of expansion was needed, and in December 1951 brought a Colombian official to New York City to finish the loan negotiations. Appearances had to be maintained, however, and Exxon claimed to have only $10 million; the only hope of getting the remaining $8 million rested in the hands of the Chemical Bank. Exxon pledged its maximum effort to secure a favorable hearing at Chemical Bank, so that when the loan was approved, a very gullible Colombian government, which did not know about interlocking directorates and similar practices, was doubly grateful to Exxon for its generous and "spontaneous" efforts.[5]

Construction began in April 1952 and the new refinery was completed in August 1954. The capacity of the refinery now rose from the previous 16,000 to 35,000 barrels a day. For the first time Barrancabermeja produced aviation fuel (meeting 100 percent of the domestic demand), and it now refined 77 percent of the gasoline sold in Colombia. However, rising consumption quickly showed that the expansion had been too small; only slowly did the Colombian government realize that Exxon had deliberately recommended a reduced expansion for Barrancabermeja in order to justify the construction of a separate refinery in Cartagena. After the 1952 and 1953 earnings reports came in, Ecopetrol had the funds to build a new refinery by itself, but instead it was locked into interest payments on these outstanding loans, thus slowing down capital accumulation.[6]

Pipelines

The most important market for fuels and lubricants was Bogotá, the capital city, and to counter the National Petroleum Company's expected push in that direction, Exxon devised a twofold plan. First of all, for the construction of the 92-mile pipeline south from Cantimploras to Puerto Salgar (Map 1), Ecopetrol was saddled with, and had to give thanks for, a $3 million loan that Exxon "generously" granted. Since the National Petroleum Company also had to reconstruct the existing 60-mile section between Barrancabermeja and Cantimploras, Ecopetrol was kept tied down for some time using up profits to pay for the construction of the pipeline as well as the interest on the loan.[7]

Second, the last link to the capital required an 87-mile pipeline over the mountains from Puerto Salgar to Puente Aranda on the outskirts of Bogotá. The provincial government of Cundinamarca, always jealous to defend its powers from encroachments by the central government, would operate the pipeline. As was usual with provincial governments, Cundinamarca lacked funds, so that an eager Exxon lent the whole amount. The Puerto Salgar–Bogotá pipeline was completed in July 1952, but even before then the provincial government could not find the funds to meet the first payments on the loan. Exxon then spontaneously offered to negotiate longer terms in exchange for making the pipeline a de facto dependency of the oil company in both operations and rates, but still cloaked under the mantle of the provincial government.

Exxon had pulled off a wonderful coup and was more than ready to meet the challenge from the new pipelines Ecopetrol had completed to Puerto Salgar in January 1954. That same month, the Rojas Pinilla dictatorship issued a decree that, under the guise of codifying the principles of "public use," not only favored the oil companies but also penalized Ecopetrol for using its own pipeline. The National Petroleum Company protested these abuses. In addition, in 1958 the state company began to plan the purchase of the Puerto Salgar–Bogotá pipeline from the provincial government of Cundinamarca.[8]

Drilling

Prior to the reversion in 1951 Exxon had constantly emphasized the high cost and the extreme difficulty of extracting oil and had also spread the idea that the Barrancabermeja fields were nearly exhausted, a belief given credence by the company's frantic attempt to pump the fields dry. For the National Petroleum Council, "secondary recovery" of the oil fields by means of injecting water or gas appeared a necessity to rescue the state enterprise from certain failure. Finding a company willing to try secondary recovery methods took some years, and not until 1955 and after much prodding did the Forest Oil Corporation agree to do some preliminary tests. Only in 1956 did it sign a contract with Ecopetrol to begin operations the next year. Secondary recovery was a complete success, but long before then, Ecopetrol had decided upon a more direct approach.[9]

The first task at hand was to spend more than $1 million on new drilling equipment, since Exxon had left no rigs behind in August 1951. In front of the Barrancabermeja zone and across the Magdalena river stretched the Casabe concession held by Shell: Exxon had never bothered to drill a slanted well under the Magdalena river, something that Ecopetrol now successfully did. Shell protested bitterly, but to no avail since a clause in the 1948 law that created Ecopetrol had authorized the National Petroleum Company to drill in any lands bordering on the Barranca-bermeja zone right up to the limits of whatever concessions were still in private hands. Shell was now joined by other oil companies in an attempt to surround the Barrancabermeja zone with their own concessions, thus trying to strangle the newly formed National Petroleum Company. Most of these lands had once been included in concessions held by the oil companies, but they had forfeited their rights to them when after many years they had refused to drill or claimed that the lands contained no oil. Now that Ecopetrol showed interest in exploring these supposedly worthless lands, the oil companies feverishly maneuvered to block the state from entering. For the first and only time, the dictator Rojas Pinilla refused to favor the oil companies—something for which they never forgave him. The oil companies now took the law into their own hands and fabricated evidence to keep three concessions—El Roble, Conchal, and El Limon—out of Ecopetrol's grasp, thus initiating a long lawsuit that was not decided until 1972.

The best investment Ecopetrol ever made was in drilling equipment. The Colombian crews began drilling wells with a vengeance, discovering oil as well as proving that these fields were not on the verge of exhaustion. While holding the zone, Exxon had only skimmed the cream, called "horizon A," which held only the shallowest wells. So abundant was the production that Exxon had neglected to explore even all of horizon A. Furthermore, Exxon had refused to drill very deeply (except on paper for public relations purposes), so that when Ecopetrol sank a few deep wells, it was surprised to discover an entirely unknown level, "horizon C." Secondary recovery of some parts of horizon A was advisable, but even more important was the discovery of the rest of horizon A and the exploration of the newly discovered horizon C.[10]

When rumors of these fabulous oil discoveries under what had been considered the worthless Barrancabermeja zone began to reach Exxon, infuriated company executives decided to make one last attempt to destroy the state enterprise. The strategy was simple: If Ecopetrol had gone broke, the red ink would have permanently discredited state activity; but its success in piling up huge profits year after year made it an ideal target for a hostile takeover by the private sector. Stories began to appear in the press about all the corruption that had taken place in Ecopetrol under the Rojas Pinilla regime and playing up the inherent "inefficiency" of state-run enterprises. The ensuing outcry for moralizing reforms paved the way for proposals to turn the Barrancabermeja fields over to private investors (who could also be foreign oil companies).

The strategy did not work because Ecopetrol was rapidly on the way to becoming the richest enterprise in all of Colombia, the whole private sector could not gather enough funds to buy a controlling interest. The oil companies, joined by the merchant-brokers, now pushed the alternate formula of having Ecopetrol contract the operation of the oil fields out to another company. But with this formula the enemies of the state enterprise had revealed their true intentions, the defenders of the National Petroleum Company counterattacked, and Ecopetrol was saved.[11]

Refinery in Cartagena

The pipeline that had carried oil for export from Barrancabermeja since 1926 ended at the seaport terminal of Mamonal in the bay south of Cartagena. As discussed in previous chapters, when Exxon had the Barrancabermeja concession it was under contract to meet Colombia's refining needs, an obligation the company ignored because it was so much more profitable to export petroleum and sell imported gasoline and lubricants. By 1948, when imports accounted for half of Colombia's gasoline consumption, the company offered to build a second refinery in Cartagena as proof of "good faith," but the harsh terms led the government to reject the offer. Exxon partly went ahead anyway and in 1950 enlarged the terminal at Cartagena by adding storage facilities to help in the distribution of gasoline and lubricants through the Caribbean provinces.[12]

The National Petroleum Council dumped the problem on the newly created Ecopetrol, which, on economic grounds, quickly discarded any idea of spreading itself thin across two refineries and instead concentrated on enlarging the refinery at Barrancabermeja. Moreover, it did not make sense to have a refinery at Cartagena, where it would be exposed to both air and sea attack; Barrancabermeja was inland and therefore was a wiser choice both economically and strategically. Exxon rushed into this opening left by Ecopetrol to realize its long-standing goal of operating a refinery in the coast. In early 1952 the oil firm began to wage a quiet campaign to mobilize support in the Caribbean coast provinces. This task was complicated by Exxon's determination to have the refinery conveniently located near its existing installations at Cartagena, a small city then without industry and with very little economic activity. Without revealing the planned location, company agents concentrated on Barranquilla, which, as the largest city in the Caribbean region, did have considerable political influence on the Colombian government.[13]

Ecopetrol, astounded by the magnitude of the first year's profits, now belatedly realized that it had the capital to build a second refinery. A deadlock ensued within the Colombian government; in an effort to find a solution, the Ministry of Mines and Petroleum appointed a special four-member commission to make an "independent" report. Chaired by the minister of mines and petroleum, the commission was actually stacked in favor of the oil companies, which, besides their own representative, also had a firm ally in Jorge Mejía Salazar, the delegate of the National Association of Industrialists, who had been and again would be an oil company executive. The delegate from Ecopetrol, who should have argued strongly and forcefully for the state's position, was hamstrung by strong pressure from the president of Ecopetrol, Santiago Trujillo Gómez, an unconditional supporter of the oil companies. Not unexpectedly, the minister of mines and petroleum, a veteran politician, easily found himself siding with the majority; the report delivered in February 1953 not only gave highest priority to a refinery on the Caribbean coast and a "Pipeline to the Pacific" but also stressed that projects of this type should be undertaken by private capital, preferably with a mix of foreign and domestic sources. The report went on to lay the "technical" bases for what Exxon wanted: subsidies to import crude oil for the refinery, high prices for the sale of the refined products either abroad or in Colombia, and the right to export the crude from the company's oil fields in Colombia.[14]

When Pedro Nel Rueda became the new minister of mines and petroleum, he tried one last gambit to halt the Exxon takeover of the Cartagena refinery. Ecopetrol proposed a partnership with Exxon to build and run the Cartagena refinery in the hope that the U.S. company would back away in horror, just as it had done in 1950 when the National Petroleum Company was being organized. But the oilmen knew well what cards they were playing and instead defiantly announced that they would not accept Ecopetrol in the new venture. Pedro Nel Rueda on his own authority entrusted the whole matter to Ecopetrol, but he was overruled by the dictator Rojas Pinilla, who, fearful of losing the political support of the Caribbean provinces, told Ecopetrol to participate only if voluntarily accepted by Exxon.[15]

Exxon had ably pulled political strings to win the prize from a ruler who also had other considerations in mind. Europe, then in the process of rapidly reconstructing its industries, was offering cut-rate financing and giveaway prices to push sales abroad of industrial equipment. Colombian state agencies received tempting offers even without having called for bids, and with so much money floating around there was no doubt that Exxon made an excellent business deal on new equipment to fortify its position in Colombia. Exxon later repeatedly claimed that it deserved "gratitude" for having acceded to set up the refinery.

One last hurdle remained in the way: Barranquilla, which had already celebrated its selection as the site for the refinery, now had to be gradually dissuaded. An intense public relations campaign (including many high-level delegations) was on the point of success when an executive of

Exxon in Colombia, Francisco Espinosa, known as "Espi" in petroleum circles, blew this mopping-up operation. The old strategic arguments had been revived taking the slant that Cartagena had a decided advantage over Barranquilla because it was the site of a major naval base. But Espi could not resist saying—in front of a gathering of people—how decrepit were the World War I vessels of the Colombian navy that were supposed to protect the Cartagena refinery. This comment created needless resentment among Barranquilla's elite, which now realized only too late that it had been duped.

Although the feelings of the Barranquilla elite were badly hurt, the damage done to Colombia by turning the Cartagena refinery over to Exxon was immensely greater. Inaugurated on 1 December 1957, from July 1958 the refinery enjoyed the privilege of a subsidy paid by Ecopetrol to purchase crude oil abroad. Furthermore, Exxon sold the refined products at such high prices that, in a bizarre twist, the small National Petroleum Company ended up subsidizing the largest private oil company in the world.[16]

Forging Links with the Elite

Exxon reasoned that the favorable disposition among the Colombian elite needed reinforcement with additional direct links. Wonderful results had already been obtained by letting local merchants handle gasoline stations, and in the 1950s this strategy was widened to other areas, in particular the Pipeline to the Pacific and natural gas.

Gasoline Stations

Gasoline stations provided the oldest form of direct cooperation with members of the Colombian elite, yet because of the emphasis Exxon placed on exports, the gasoline stations had taken a very low priority in spite of the fact that the operations were profitable. Exxon opened gasoline stations across the country very slowly, and the usual way to buy gasoline outside of the few main cities was in a general store where the gasoline tin can, and only rarely a pump, were mixed next to general goods and even foodstuffs—clearly an unsafe practice.

By the late 1940s Exxon decided to give more attention to distribution and created a new subsidiary in December 1949 to handle the project. Profits were not lost sight of, but only as a part of the general policy of developing closer links with the Colombian elite. Exxon bought lots and built gasoline stations that it subsequently rented out to local merchants, thus creating a propertied class with a strong vested interest in the fate of the oil company. In this way, Exxon was moving to cancel the adverse criticisms generated during the 1930s and 1940s when the company had abused its monopoly position to the neglect of consumers.[17]

Exxon's gasoline station expansion was, however, misinterpreted by most members of the Colombian elite, who feared a consolidation of the previous gasoline monopoly even though the Exxon subsidiary had offered 40 percent of its shares to Colombians. Soon both Ecopetrol and the Ministry of Mines and Petroleum began to fear the political consequences of having a compact block of gasoline station managers solidly behind Exxon, but there was little the government could do. Ecopetrol was reluctant to enter into the retail business, not only because of legal complications but also because it feared accusations of state monopoly. Again, as in 1936, the Colombian government had no choice but to turn to Shell, the English oil company, to counter the U.S. monopoly. Negotiations with Shell in 1952 led to the creation of a subsidiary distinct from the company which handled the Casabe oil fields in front of Barrancabermeja. Shell took the opportunity to challenge its worldwide rival Exxon in another area with great gusto, and by 1954 Shell had inaugurated a chain of gasoline stations throughout the country, most of them bigger, better equipped, and more modern than those of Exxon.[18]

Shell's success triggered an imitative effect among other oil companies, and soon Mobil and Texaco were also retailing gasoline and lubricants, always under the system of renting out either the gasoline stations or the franchise to local merchants, thus assuring a widening political base of support for the oil companies. To try to break this bond, official encouragement (but not capital) was given in the mid-1950s to a private Colombian company called Codi, but without the backing of Ecopetrol or of a foreign oil company, this Colombian chain of gasoline stations had a hard time surviving. In 1958 Mobil invested heavily in Codi shares and by 1962 was a majority stockholder, whereupon the Colombian gasoline stations were gradually merged into Mobil's own growing chain.[19]

The merger of Codi with Mobil still had not stabilized gasoline retailing, which had rapidly degenerated into cutthroat competition. All four distributors (Exxon, Mobil, Texaco, and Shell) were losing money. For the first and only time, the oil companies faced a situation where the Colombian government, more by accident than by careful design, had outmaneuvered them. However, careful studies revealed that excellent service and adequate profits would be possible if only three gasoline retailers were operating. Exxon and Texaco declared that their other dealings in Colombia required that they keep their stations open for the sake of publicity, even if it meant losing money, but Shell and Mobil were not so categorical. In 1972 a secret contract was signed in London between Shell and Mobil whereby each agreed to sell its holdings to the one that had made the highest sealed bid. The envelopes were opened and Mobil won, thus taking over the gasoline stations of Shell, but Shell retained the right to sell lubricants through retail stores, a business that has turned out to be vastly more profitable than the gasoline itself. In any case, Exxon, Mobil, and Texaco have remained in the gasoline retailing business until the present, and this practice has succeeded in keeping important members of the Colombian elite safely on their side, thus forging an invaluable link.

Pipeline to the Pacific

Supplying Cali with fuel oil, gasoline, and other petroleum products— a problem that dated as far back as the 1920s and had never been adequately solved—came to the fore again in the 1950s. A dirt road and an underequipped railroad over a mountain range allowed only an irregular supply of fuel to be delivered to Cali from the port town of Buenaventura 40 miles away.[20] Raised on a tradition of looking to the Pacific Ocean to meet their fuel needs, the inhabitants of this region could not be expected to accept proposals that regarded Colombia's own petroleum as the best solution for Cali. In any case, by 1950 the Cali elite had repeatedly asked the central government to build a Pipeline to the Pacific. The fact that the minister of mines and petroleum (and then of development) during the first year of Ecopetrol's existence was Manuel Carvajal, a native of Cali, gave a strong boost to the proposal. The Colombian government was on the point of issuing bids for con- struction contracts when Carvajal left the Ministry. The new officials did not follow up on the project. For Exxon, the Pipeline to the Pacific was the necessary complement to the Cartagena refinery: From Cartagena, tankers shipped refined products via the Panama Canal to Buenaventura, thus assuring almost a monopoly situation for Exxon in distribution over all of Colombia's Pacific coast; as a matter of fact, Central America was also included in the larger global strategy of the parent company.[21]

The local allies most amenable to the project, Cali factory owners, were conveniently gathered in the branch office of the National Association of Industrialists. Negotiations advanced quickly, thanks to Manuel Car- vajal, who felt he had to make good on his earlier promise as minister of mines and petroleum. By February 1954 an agreement had been reached whereby Exxon put up 40 percent of the capital for a new company called Pipeline to the Pacific, while local private investors provided the remainder.[22]

One complication appeared to threaten Exxon's maneuver. The Cali factory owners were slow to provide their share of the capital; like most Colombian industrialists, they needed rather than had extra cash. The central government had graciously granted an ample postponement, but something more than time was needed. Exxon now secretly intervened with the saving formula: The company lent the missing sums to merchant-brokers, who then bought the shares that the industrialists had been unable to purchase, until the 60 percent was covered. This proposal sent the merchant-brokers scurrying frantically to obtain any part of the juicy transaction, which did not even require collateral, since pledging future dividends was enough for Exxon.[23]

The news soon reached Ecopetrol officials and Minister of Mines and Petroleum Pedro Nel Rueda, who were outraged not only at the tactics but at the whole power play by Exxon, which had thus gained majority control from its minority position. Nel Rueda decided to defy Exxon and on 5 July 1954 wrote to the Cali promoters that the unsold shares would be acquired by Ecopetrol. Nel Rueda's action caught Exxon by surprise, but it quickly reacted and decided to make a lesson out of the Pipeline to the Pacific issue that would long be remembered in Colombia. The probusiness Eisenhower administration was mobilized, and the next month, in August 1954, Henry F. Holland, assistant secretary of state, did not wait for formal embassy reporting but quickly intervened. Chastising Colombia harshly, he asked, "Does this indicate either a new trend in government thinking or is it merely perhaps empire building on the part of the National Petroleum Company?"[24] Both Holland and Exxon threatened the Colombian government with two reprisals: Exxon would not build the Cartagena refinery, and the Export-Import Bank would halt consideration of all pending loan applications from Colombia.

These threats sounded like bluffing to Pedro Nel Rueda. In the first place, Ecopetrol wanted to build the Cartagena refinery to escape the burdensome conditions that Exxon had imposed, and second, the pending Export-Import Bank loans were so small that Ecopetrol, which was proving every day to be incredibly rich in funds, could easily make up the difference. Calling the bluff would have meant victory for Colombia, but once again Exxon knew what cards it was playing. When Pedro Nel Rueda went to tell the good news to dictator Rojas Pinilla, the minister of mines and petroleum found himself without a job. No sooner had a new minister taken office than he rushed to praise the original terms as worthy of total acceptance. The new minister furthermore extended his warmest congratulations, on behalf of the government, to the promoters of the pipeline project, which was completed in 1956.[25]

Natural Gas

Up to the mid-1940s, Colombia's vast natural gas resources evoked very little interest. The oil companies generally considered gas to be a nuisance that got in the way of the more valuable oil. Lucky was the gas well plugged upon discovery, for the normal wasteful practice was to burn off the gas that flowed up in an oil-gas mixture. Incalculable amounts of natural gas were destroyed in this way, although, in partial justification, these same wasteful practices were prevalent in many U.S. oil fields as well. At least the United States, as an immensely wealthy country, could afford such luxuries, but that was not the case for poverty-stricken Colombia. Even when Exxon pioneered the installation of equipment to convert part of the gas found in Barrancabermeja to gasoline, the leftover gas was still burned away.

The initiative to derive some advantage for Colombia from natural gas came from the Bogotá Light and Power Company. The private utility had concluded that its high rate of internal savings had simply been outstripped by the rapidly rising demand for electricity in Bogotá. The available capital barely financed sufficient capacity for electric power and light, so that the private utility had no choice but to abandon the plans to supply current for electric stoves, since the required investment surpassed the total assets of the private company several times over. In 1944 the Bogotá Light and Power Company decided to distribute gas for cooking, in the manner of many utilities in the United States. Exxon initially demanded to distribute the gas itself but finally agreed in early 1946 to organize the Colombian Gas Company to bottle and distribute gas throughout the country. Capital was nominally divided in equal parts between Exxon and Colombian investors, but many of the latter had trouble finding enough money. To save the project, Exxon extended secret loans, bringing this "Colombian" gas distributor under its own control. The Bogotá Light and Power Company, which had originally proposed the idea of bringing gas to the capital city, felt compelled to buy a small number of shares but soon lost interest, so absorbed was the utility with expropriation negotiations.[26] In the long run, this failure to have a single company handle electricity and gas (and later white gasoline) became the fundamental structural weakness that blocked any attempt to solve Bogotá's chronic energy problems.

For Exxon, the creation of the Colombian Gas Company was an instant and outstanding success. The gas that had previously been burned off was now sold for a nice profit in Barranquilla, Bucaramanga, and Bogotá, allowing the company to use the idle capacity of its transportation and storage networks. The new subsidiary, the Colombian Gas Company, also turned in a tidy profit. Stoves, hot water heaters, and refrigerators all powered by gas began to appear in the homes of a grateful Colombian elite, thus earning considerable good will for the oil company.[27]

The struggle to create the National Petroleum Company had been a close call, and although the private gas interests still had not developed to the point where they could have a decisive influence on the outcome, they now could help the oil companies to better cope with what they all considered a problem: Ecopetrol. Behind all this was the real fear, which has never disappeared, that Ecopetrol would enter the distribution of gas and operate in the same cities and towns as the Colombian Gas Company, and even in areas not served by the latter, thus putting the private gas companies out of business at one stroke. The fear turned to panic late in 1951 when the Colombian Gas Company discovered that a sizable shipment of new gas bottles (prized possessions during the Korean war scarcity) had been left behind among the equipment turned over to Ecopetrol, possibly out of carelessness or because Exxon had to leave behind something new to maintain appearances. In any case, Ecopetrol refused to hand over these scarce bottles, but undaunted, the Colombian Gas Company used its powerful influence in the now "reconstituted" Ministry of Mines and Petroleum to secure their retrieval in 1952.

Furthermore, Ecopetrol had to sell the gas at cheap prices to Exxon or else "would have to eat it," in the expression of an oilman. In October 1953 Ecopetrol tried to raise the prices of gas, but Exxon quickly lobbied with the compliant Rojas Pinilla to secure a prompt reversal. Exxon and the other private gas companies continued to buy gas at a very low price from Ecopetrol for resale to consumers at a higher rate. Since the consumers still paid less for gas than for coal or electricity—the other cooking fuels—demand for bottled gas rose rapidly. All involved profited except for Ecopetrol, and to cut its losses, the National Petroleum Company decided to acquire its own distribution facilities before further enlarging its gas production capacity. Shortages in the supply of gas appeared for the first time in 1958, thus inaugurating the recurrent cycles of scarcity and abundance that have characterized Colombia's natural gas supply until the present.[28]

In conclusion, there was no denying that the oil companies had ably manipulated issues like the Pipeline to the Pacific and the retailing of gasoline and natural gas in order to secure much needed support among the elite for the central purpose of extracting oil from the ground for export, as the next section shows.

Rewards for the Oil Companies

The oil companies had been clamoring since 1940 for a new oil law that would vastly improve the very generous clauses in the 1931 and 1936 laws. The disruptions of World War II and the marked hostility of the Colombian congress had blocked the oil bills; one company executive charged that Colombia was eight years behind in approving "modern" legislation. When the Colombian congress quickly approved the law creating Ecopetrol in 1948, the oil companies were furious over what they considered discriminatory treatment, and to placate them the Colombian government acceded to their exploitation of the Llanos oil fields. When the Llanos alternative collapsed, this was the last straw for the oilmen, who then threw down the gauntlet: the state would have to choose between favorable oil legislation or Ecopetrol; it could not have both.

Congress still would not budge, and to save the Ecopetrol project, which President Mariano Ospina Pérez deeply wanted, he had no choice but to resort to emergency powers early in 1950 to issue Executive Decree no. 10, which for the first time in Colombia's history introduced the oil depletion allowance. Up to 10 percent of the oil extracted could be deducted provided it did not exceed 20 percent of the taxable income of the oil company. Colombia thus joined a very exclusive club composed of the United States and a handful of other countries that have oil depletion allowances. In spite of such an extraordinary privilege, the oil companies pressed incoming president Laureano Gómez (who took office in August 1950) to issue Legislative Decree 3419 in November 1950, again by recourse to emergency powers. The new decree (among other benefits) declared that the zones for national reserves would henceforth be limited to the concessions that had already reverted to the state (essentially Barrancabermeja), thus handing over the previously existing national reserves to the oil companies.[29]

The oil companies now had received much more than they had asked for, but they still had one grudge to settle. The existence of an independent body of engineers in the Ministry of Mines and Petroleum and the constant labors of its advisory body, the National Petroleum Council, had rankled the oilmen, who would never forgive those government agencies for the role they had played in the creation of Ecopetrol. In a complex power play, the oil companies argued that now that the National Petroleum Company had been decided upon, the Ministry of Mines and Petroleum had become useless and should be abolished as an economy measure. The Colombian government agreed, and on 28 February 1951 the Ministry of Development assumed oil policy. Most employees who had fought for Ecopetrol now found themselves without jobs because their positions had been abolished, and the National Petroleum Council was deprived of staff and salaries. The memory of these cutbacks lingered permanently among the employees, who henceforth were most reluctant to ever again antagonize the oil companies. Even later in February 1952 when the government realized its mistake and recreated the Ministry of Mines and Petroleum, the former aggressiveness never returned.[30]

The two key pieces of legislation, decrees no. 10 and 3419 of 1950, had been passed under emergency powers, and the oil companies wanted the more formal congressional sanction. In 1952 the government repeatedly presented bills, but they were either rejected or died in one of the two houses. So much work had gone into the bills that the acting president, Roberto Urdaneta (1952–1953), himself a former agent of the oil companies, did not want to see it all go to waste. Thus, he issued the massive compilation as Colombia's first Petroleum Code, again under emergency powers. This Petroleum Code (Decree 2270 of 1952) extended the life of concessions in the Llanos and the Amazon for another ten years (for a total of fifty years), thus postponing their exploitation, since none were producing. Pipeline regulation in the code favored the private companies and penalized Ecopetrol for using its own lines. Furthermore, the Petroleum Code granted duty-free entry for all drilling, production, and pipeline equipment in such broad terms that the oil companies used the privilege to bring anything into the country, from clothes to foodstuffs and even whiskey to console the lonely work crews, thus depriving the state of massive customs revenues.[31]

The Rojas Pinilla regime (1953–1957), by the very fact that it was a dictatorship, could not provide the normal congressional approval that the oil companies wanted, yet to avoid charges of hostility toward private enterprise, Rojas Pinilla asked the oil companies to draft a bill for another executive decree. The oilmen huddled to make a long list of requests. Exxon, the company that had been in Colombia the longest, wanted special exemptions to attract new companies into the country, but so defined that Exxon qualified as a "new" company. This was too much for Shell. After many heated sessions and on the verge of breaking up their united front with the other oil companies, Exxon reluctantly withdrew its proposal but told the other companies they were taking a risk.

Rojas Pinilla delivered Decree 2140 of August 1955, which, among other provisions, increased the time for exploiting concessions in the Llanos and the Amazon by another twenty years for a total of seventy years. The oil depletion allowance remained at 10 percent, but now up to 35 percent of taxable income could be deducted rather than just the previous 20 percent. However, some unknown conscientious official at the Ministry of Mines and Petroleum had waited until the last minute to slip in a clause that effectively limited other special tax privileges. These privileges, involving Colombian oil refined for internal consumption, had been abused by the oil companies in the past by the practice of declaring for internal consumption oil that was really exported abroad. The last-minute clause limited the privileges to the oil actually refined and thus ended this abuse. Exxon, which refined all its crude in the

Cartagena refinery, was untouched, but not the other oil companies, and for months afterward Exxon officials gloated in pointing out to them that because of their earlier opposition they now found themselves in this small bind.[32]

Since the 1920s a cardinal policy of the oil companies had been to maintain freedom from foreign exchange controls. In 1958 this freedom was threatened, but not because of any pressure on the part of the Colombian government. On the eve of the 1958 devaluation of the peso, the International Monetary Fund (IMF) imposed very harsh conditions on Colombia; among these was the demand that the government control the foreign exchange transactions of the oil companies. The Colombian government washed its hands of the whole matter, since it knew from experience that in negotiations with the IMF, unlike those with the World Bank, no amount of argument or discussion had any effect on what was essentially a master-slave relationship. The oil companies, however, knew where to turn, and John Foster Dulles, in one of his very rare direct interventions in Colombian affairs, made a phone call to the U.S. Executive Director of the IMF. The IMF's objections to dropping the controls vanished, and in the decrees adopted in 1958, the oil companies retained their traditional freedom from foreign exchange controls.[33]

The old hurdle of congressional approval still remained, and the oil companies impatiently waited for this final ratification. The presidency of the Liberal Alberto Lleras Camargo (1958-1962), the first popularly elected president after the fall of Rojas Pinilla, provided the opportunity. The Alberto Lleras administration, the first of four that alternated the presidency until 1974 between the Conservative and the Liberal parties, enjoyed an overwhelming majority in congress. Passage of the legislation proved very difficult, however, because many members of both parties sensed that this would be the last chance to express their voice; in effect, what was being asked from congress was an abdication of authority. The oil companies had to mobilize their powerful allies in the natural gas companies, in the Pipeline to the Pacific, and in the gasoline stations, but this support was not enough. The issue was back in the hands of the elite, who had to decide whether the presence of the oil companies was in its own interest. Calling upon discipline in both parties to secure the votes, in 1961 after bitter opposition congress finally approved Law 10, which essentially ratified the previous decrees issued under emergency powers by the presidents. The decade-long battle over oil legislation was over, since there was nothing else left for congress to give to the oil companies.[34]

Notes

1. This section relies on Anthony Sampson, *The Seven Sisters* (New York: Viking Press, 1975), pp. 87–105; Stephen J. Randall, *United States Foreign Oil Policy, 1919–1948: For Profits and Security* (Montreal: McGill-Queens University Press, 1985), pp. 224–236; Rómulo Betancourt, *Venezuela: Oil and Politics* (Boston: Houghton Mifflin Co., 1979), pp. 124–151, 320–332; Franklin Tugwell, *The Politics of Oil in Venezuela* (Stanford: Stanford University Press, 1975), pp. 38–48; Gustavo Coronel, *The Nationalization of the Venezuelan Oil Industry* (Lexington, Mass.: Lexington Books, 1983), pp. 19–23; Stephen G. Rabe, *The Road to OPEC: United States Relations with Venezuela, 1919–1976* (Austin: University of Texas Press, 1982), pp. 103–107, 122–126.

2. Memorandum of 1 March 1950, 821.2553/3-150, Record Group (RG) 59, National Archives, Washington, D.C.

3. *El Tiempo*, 28 Feb., 5 Dec. 1950; Report, 821.6363/1-749, RG 59.

4. World Bank, *The Basis of a Development Program for Colombia* (Baltimore: Johns Hopkins Press, 1950), pp. 140, 459–460.

5. Jon V. Kofas, *Dependence and Underdevelopment in Colombia* (Tempe, Ariz.: Center for Latin American Studies, 1986), p. 114; Norman Medvin, *The Energy Cartel* (New York: Vintage Books, 1974), pp. 183, 201; *New York Times*, 7 Jan. 1953.

6. 6 June 1951, 821.2553/6-651, RG 59; *El Tiempo*, 10 Jan., 13 Feb. 1950, 25 Aug. 1954; *New York Times*, 29 Aug. 1954.

7. 14 July 1951, 821.2553/7-1151, and Report, 821.6363/1-749, RG 59.

8. This and the following paragraphs are based on World Bank, *The Basis of a Development Program*, pp. 459–460; *El Tiempo*, 5 Feb. 1950, 20 Feb., 6, 10 July 1952; *Industria colombiana*, nos. 52–53 (1958), p. 11.

9. *New York Times*, 4 Jan. 1952; Memorandum of conversation, 9 March 1955, 821.2553/3-955, RG 59; *El Intermedio*, 25 Jan. 1951.

10. *El Tiempo*, 25 Aug. 1954; *Industria colombiana*, nos. 52–53 (1958), pp. 10–11.

11. 21 Aug. 1957, 821.2553/8-2157, RG 59; *El Tiempo*, January to March 1958.

12. World Bank, *The Basis of a Development Program*, pp. 432–433; *El Tiempo*, 4 Jan. 1950, 15 July 1951. The 1949 World Bank mission came out strongly against the Cartagena refinery, and its arguments later formed the basis for Ecopetrol's initial opposition.

13. *El Siglo*, 22 May 1952, 4 Feb. 1953.

14. 18 Feb., 8 June 1953, 821.2553, RG 59.

15. Pedro Nel Rueda to E. C. Borrego, 15 Dec. 1953, 821.2553/12-2153, RG 59; *New York Times*, 7 Feb. 1953, 6 Jan. 1954.

16. 8 Aug. 1958, 821.2553/8-858, RG 59; *New York Times*, 2 June 1954.

17. Kofas, *Underdevelopment in Colombia*, p. 114; *Industria colombiana*, no. 22 (1955), p. 25; *El Tiempo*, 15 June 1950.

18. 7 Jan. 1952, 821.2553/1-752, RG 59; *El Tiempo,* 12 June 1952, 10 Nov. 1954.

19. *El Tiempo,* 6 July 1958.

20. René De La Pedraja, *Historia de la energía en Colombia, 1537–1930* (Bogotá: El Ancora, 1985), pp. 216–217.

21. *El Espectador,* 1 Aug. 1950; *El Tiempo,* 5 April 1952.

22. Report from U.S. embassy, 15 Feb. 1954, 821.2553/2-1554, RG 59; *New York Times,* 5 Jan. 1955.

23. Letter, 25 Aug. 1954, Henry F. Holland Files, Box 3, RG 59.

24. Letter, 18 Aug. 1954, Henry F. Holland Files, Box 3, RG 59.

25. *New York Times,* 5 March 1956.

26. *El Tiempo,* 16 Dec. 1944; Report of Petroleum attaché, 16 July 1946, 821.6363/7-1646, RG 59; *Liberal,* 25 April 1946.

27. *El Siglo,* 2 Feb. 1948; *El Espectador,* 8 March 1947; *El Tiempo,* 18 Jan., 23 Dec. 1947.

28. *El Tiempo,* 11 March, 30 April, 2 Dec. 1958.

29. Kofas, *Underdevelopment in Colombia,* pp. 112, 114; *New York Times,* 26 April 1945, 17 Nov. 1950; Jorge Villegas, *Petróleo oligarquía e imperio* (Bogotá: Tercer Mundo, 1975), pp. 241, 243, 247.

30. 27 May 1952, 821.2553/5-2752, RG 59; *El Tiempo,* 4 Feb. 1951, 21 Feb. 1952.

31. *New York Times,* 7 Jan. 1953; Villegas, *Petróleo,* pp. 255–258; *El Tiempo,* 12 July, 19 Nov. 1952.

32. Villegas, *Petróleo,* p. 271; *El Tiempo,* 8 Oct. 1954.

33. Kofas, *Underdevelopment in Colombia,* p. 114; *New York Times,* 7 Jan. 1953; U.S. embassy report, 6 May 1958, and John Foster Dulles reply, 821.2553/5-658, RG 59.

34. Villegas, *Petróleo,* pp. 281–286.

5

The Last Nationalistic Backlash

The counterattack of the oil companies discussed in the previous chapter had advanced so far and so fast that it outran its supply lines and left flanks exposed; at the same time, its deep penetrations had necessarily awakened new opposition. Thus, as the oil companies rolled on to their last victories in the late 1950s, the nationalistic opposition was already laying the groundwork for a campaign to nationalize the entire oil sector. The nationalization campaign kept the oil companies tied down until 1963, but it scored its only permanent success in the Barco Concession. Unfortunately, the nationalization campaign was not properly coordinated with the struggles over the refineries and the pipelines, so that precious opportunities to strike blows against the oil companies escaped forever.

The Nationalization Campaign: Pardo Parra

The attempted sale of Ecopetrol in 1958 triggered a nationalistic reaction that soon reached major proportions. A growing number of officials and even members of the Colombian elite concluded that since the oil companies were drilling less and less, Ecopetrol should take over the private concessions and assume the task of searching for deposits in other parts of the country. The labor unions eagerly backed the nationalization campaign, and their support turned to wild enthusiasm in 1960 when Cuba, by a somewhat convoluted process, expropriated the oil refineries on the island.

Such an extreme measure seemed too drastic to the Colombian government, which even ordered a sympathetic Ecopetrol not to sell crude to Cuba in 1960, thus tightening the blockade against the island and forcing it to turn to the Soviet Union to meet its supply needs. There was general agreement in Colombia that any expropriation would have to include payment for the equipment and machinery the oil companies held in their concessions; after all, even Mexico had granted this much in 1938, and the sums involved were really very small. If compensation was also given for the value of the oil in the ground— a step Mexico had successfully refused to take in 1938—the sums became astronomical. As much as many members of the Colombian elite wanted to end the nationalization campaign, the issue would not go away, and demonstrations, speeches, and meetings kept the debate alive from 1960 to 1963.[1]

A crucial clash took place in April 1963. Minister of Labor Belisario Betancur came out strongly in favor of Ecopetrol and stated that unnamed dangers threatened the National Petroleum Company. He thus tacitly put himself in opposition to the private companies, in a sense balancing out the minister of mines and petroleum, who was bitterly opposed to nationalizing the oil industry. Out of the blue, Cali elite member Manuel Carvajal, who had distinguished himself in the creation of Ecopetrol, issued a letter dated 19 April 1963. Carvajal, in one of the frankest public expressions of elite attitudes, denied that any threat existed against Ecopetrol, in spite of overwhelming evidence to the contrary. Furthermore, he stressed that he was opposed to nationalizing petroleum because "what is advisable for Colombia is competition in all aspects of the petroleum sector,"[2] but he did not detail how a handicapped state company could successfully compete against the largest multinational oil corporations in the world. Perhaps more because of the personal prestige of the signer than the logic in the arguments, the Carvajal letter put the proponents of nationalization, who over the next year gradually dwindled to the labor unions, into disarray.

In early 1963 the momentum of the nationalization movement was still so strong that the position of the oil minister who defended the private companies became untenable. He was replaced in May 1963 by a new and dynamic figure, Enrique Pardo Parra, who immediately instilled into the Ministry of Mines and Petroleum a vitality that had not been seen since the creation of Ecopetrol in 1951. Pardo Parra was diligent, honest, and above all, he was determined to save Colombia's oil resources. However, in his first month in office, he made a crucial mistake that turned his ministry of two years into a long, desperate struggle against overwhelming odds. Overawed by the $10 billion the companies were demanding for the crude in their concessions, he dropped the effort to nationalize oil. The companies, up to this point kept on the defensive by the nationalization campaign, were now free to block not only Pardo Parra's enforcement of petroleum laws but also his attempts to find alternate ways to tap Colombia's oil potential.[3]

In effect, Pardo Parra learned only when it was too late, in 1965, that it took the same amount of effort to challenge the oil companies over a clause in a contract as over nationalization, and that if a country wants redress of the former, it must threaten the latter. The local manager of Exxon, Francisco "Espi" Espinosa, took command of the campaign against Pardo Parra. An endless stream of publications, declarations, and messages constantly denounced the oil minister's attempts to eliminate the many abuses that had crept into oil policy. In late May 1963 Espi went so far as to revive the old idea of selling Ecopetrol to private investors, and although the proposal had no chance of success, it was a good enough tactical diversion to distract the new oil minister.[4]

Exxon, which had pioneered the tried and proven policy of joining individual elite members to the oil companies, widened its reach significantly in 1963 by the establishment of a financial subsidiary to invest in private Colombian business distinct from oil or petrochemicals, such as commerce and factories. These new allies now joined the private gas companies and the gasoline station managers to form one vast group of influential individuals whose fate depended on their absolute loyalty to the oil companies. The noose started tightening slowly around the oil minister's neck, yet he was not able to counter the threat until late 1964, when he at last unveiled his proposals for new oil legislation. Among other things, he proposed abolishing the foreign exchange privileges and the oil depletion allowance. Such a bill indirectly moved closer to the original idea of the nationalization campaign: If the oil companies found the bill unbearable, then they could carry out their threat to abandon the country once and for all.[5] By 1965 a major legislative battle over the bill was in the air. Nothing like this had been seen in the Colombian congress since Montalvo's proposals of the late 1920s.

To overcome the solid opposition the oil companies were marshaling from their many allies in the Colombian elite, the oil minister counted on a good performance by Ecopetrol. Not since Pedro Nel Rueda's ministry in 1953–1954 had another oil minister backed the National Petroleum Company so strongly. The oil companies had decreed a halt to private exploratory activity as a reprisal against Colombia, but Ecopetrol had easily covered the sudden shortage and had even managed to increase national oil output, proving that the presence of the oil companies was not quite as indispensable as they had claimed. Encouraged by Ecopetrol's success, Pardo Parra decided to take bolder moves to counter the oil company hostility and to place the National Petroleum Company in a commanding position far ahead of its rivals.

In late 1964 General Charles de Gaulle, the president of France, paid a state visit to Colombia that had as its main goal promoting economic links between the two countries. Pardo Parra suggested that cooperation on petroleum matters be included in the agenda, and after preliminary discussions during and after de Gaulle's trip, the French agreed to cooperate. In 1966 a loan and technical assistance for a petrochemical plant were approved. On the side of oil exploration, events came to a head much more rapidly.

The French replied by early 1965 that they were interested in prospecting only in the Llanos. When word of this reached the oil companies, utter panic set in, because the French state petroleum company now employed Trompy, the Shell geologist fired by the English who later went on to discover the sub-Saharan oil fields for the French. By 1965 he had already acquired worldwide fame, and furthermore, since he had already discovered the Llanos oil in the early 1940s, he had only to point where the oil lay. This development was simply too much for the oil company officials, who now desperately contacted their headquarters asking for help. Fortunately for the oil companies, Colombia happened to be in the middle of one of its recurrent foreign exchange crises. Negotiations with the IMF were bogged down as usual, but soon the paralyzing effect spread to the World Bank, to private banks, and even to U.S. agencies like AID, each of which cut off all loans; only the Inter-American Development Bank with its limited funds remained sympathetic to Colombia's plight.

The freeze imposed by the foreign financial institutions had left Colombia without foreign credits for nearly a year, and into this already tense situation the New York headquarters of the oil companies intervened to bring even more pressure against the Colombian government. Powerful influences were moved in financial circles until finally the right hint was dropped: To ease the acceptance of "softer" credit terms, Colombia should create a more favorable investment climate for private companies. Needless to say, oil minister Pardo Parra was dismissed in October 1965.[6] Now that foreign credits flowed again to Colombia, the next oil minister bent over backwards to please the private companies. With the fall of Pardo Parra, the campaign for the nationalization of Colombian oil came to an end.

The End of the Barco Concession

The campaign for the nationalization of oil had managed to take up the issue of the Barco Concession in 1962. This revived public interest caught Texaco and Mobil by surprise, and they did not have time to abandon two highly questionable practices before they were discovered. Starting in 1958, and alleging needs in other fields, the two oil companies had begun to slowly remove equipment from the Barco Concession that under the terms of the original 1931 law was supposed to revert to the Colombian state in 1981. Second, Texaco and Mobil, which paid a 10 percent royalty to the Colombian state in crude, had decided to dump the unsalable residual fuels from their small local refinery into the royalty crude. This senseless fraud, which saved only a total of $55,000 over a four-year period, was immediately detected by Ecopetrol in 1962 when the National Petroleum Company started directly handling the crude received as royalty from the Barco Concession.

A round of investigations by the Colombian executive and congress confirmed the initial two charges and reported that installations had even been demolished. The revelation that oil output from the Barco Concession would soon start a rapid decline caused another shock, and no less sensational was the discovery that the government inspectors at the Barco Concession had been on company payrolls for decades.[7]

Each new finding increased the pressures to halt the probes, and soon the emphasis shifted to covering up the facts. Not all the evidence could be destroyed though, and enough of it survived to support the conclusion that no one dared to suggest at the time: From the start of oil exports in 1939 until 1964 when at last the Colombian government established fairly effective vigilance, the output of the Barco Concession had been at least 50 percent more than what the official figures reported, and probably even higher.

Only gradually starting to discover this startling information, the workers in the Barco oil fields went on strike; they also had specific labor grievances, in particular against the recent practice to hire contractors rather than permanent employees. The workers had been urging the government since 1961 to call for reversion of the concession before 1981, and they had become the most enthusiastic backers of the na-tionalization campaign. But the support of the workers was no match for the influences of the Colombian elite. The names of those individuals involved in the Barco Concession reads like a Who's Who of the Colombian elite: Besides the ever present Barco family, there were the Holguíns, Mario Laserna, and other scions of prominent Colombian dynasties, bonded together by their shared ownership of 4 out of the total 100 units of the Barco oil fields. The annual payments each of these elite Colombians received was very small by international standards but immense at the local level; it was not so much that the elite received only 4 units, but rather than the rest of the Colombians had been denied any share in the remaining 96 units. The results of this policy of depriving Colombians of the oil wealth could be seen most vividly among the peasants living near the Barco Concession (and also the Barrancabermeja concession) who for decades had remained trapped in the most abject poverty untouched by the petroleum wealth that flowed out for export.[8]

Not even the revelation that the two oil companies had speculated in foreign exchange during the 1962 devaluation could keep the campaign against the Barco Concession alive; by the end of 1963 most of the issues had been hushed up and the workers' strike brought to an end. Attention shifted temporarily to an oil discovery south of the Barco Concession proper.[9] So lavish had been the profits that Texaco and Mobil, like Exxon in Barrancabermeja, had neglected to search for oil outside the boundaries of the concession. To the west, mountains sharply reduced oil possibilities; to the north and east, the Venezuelan frontier blocked access. But what about to the south? Into this gap stepped Chevron, partly guided by geologic evidence, but mostly because of a different process. Chevron did not like government concessions because no matter how long they were granted for, they eventually ran out. Instead, Chevron embarked upon a vast project, apparently the largest in all of Latin America, to find and index every land transaction that had ever taken place in Colombia. The other oil companies repeatedly made fun of this vast undertaking, but it was solidly grounded in Colombian law, which upheld private rights to the subsoil in the land titles acquired before 1873. Somewhere along the way during this forty-year research project (which provoked incessant offers of land sales), Chevron came upon valid titles to the lands south of the Barco Concession; these were promptly purchased and a wildcat well was drilled (Zulia-1).

This Zulia field was extremely profitable, and Chevron officials could not help but boast to the other oil companies that a week's production had paid all the costs of their massive titles search. The exploitation of Zulia followed the general practice of the oil companies of draining the most accessible deposits, which later left Colombia without oil to face the 1973 energy crisis. Furthermore, the Chevron oil field behaved like the Barco Concession (not surprisingly, since it was a geologic continuation of the Barco field); that is, production rose dramatically for a few years then peaked, only to decline rapidly by the late 1960s. Thus, the decline in the newly discovered Zulia field paralleled the expected fall in output of the Barco Concession, which in 1970 reached 5 million barrels only with great difficulty,—quite a drop from the 9 million produced annually up to 1965.

Oil production was declining so fast that Texaco and Mobil reluctantly concluded that turning the fields over to Ecopetrol before the 1981 reversion was their best alternative. The two oil companies had not set aside pension funds for their employees (the Americans had to be paid in dollars), and since this new growing expense now coincided with shrinking oil output, they decided to shift the burden to the state. The administration of Misael Pastrana Borrero (1970–1974) agreed to the oil companies' plan, but first it wanted for electoral purposes to get some nationalistic mileage out of the deal. The goal was to have the government appear to be striking a blow against imperialism: The workers were easily convinced to stage a strike in 1971, and finally in 1972 Texaco and Mobil turned over their shares to Ecopetrol for "free," of course on the condition that Ecopetrol would assume the responsibility for pensions.

Production continued to decline under Ecopetrol in spite of renewed drilling. Secondary recovery, which had already begun under Texaco and Mobil, merely prolonged the agony of the fields into the 1980s. In conclusion, the rescue of the Barco Concession had come so late and against such powerful influences that it turned out to be nothing but a meaningless victory.

Battle for the Refineries

On 1 April 1961 Ecopetrol assumed control of the Barrancabermeja refinery, which had been operated up until then by Exxon under a ten-year contract. Exxon wanted a renewal, and many Colombians feared that the complex refinery functions were beyond the capabilities of the National Petroleum Company. These fears proved groundless.[10] Instead, upon taking over the refinery, Ecopetrol made certain important discoveries. The most startling was that for large imports of crude, foreign suppliers gave bulk discounts that could make prices up to 40 percent lower than the world market price. Ecopetrol now began to reap these profits, which it sorely needed to face a new pair of problems. Prior to 1961, Ecopetrol could sell excess crude abroad to earn foreign exchange credit, but afterwards, the crude did not cover the refining capacity and extra crude had to be purchased in dollars—although in fact most of it came from the other smaller Colombian fields still in the hands of the private companies. Second, the rapidly rising internal consumption, coupled with the fact that the previous expansion had been too small, made an enlargement of the refinery an urgent matter.

In August 1961, almost immediately upon taking over, Ecopetrol embarked on a "Partial Expansion," which consisted of creating the units to handle other by-products and in enlarging the capacity to refine lubricants. A major expansion of the capacity to produce gasoline and other fuels was such a vastly larger undertaking that considerable study went into finding the best alternative. Foreign currency was needed to finance equipment purchases abroad, but the oil companies blocked Ecopetrol's requests for a loan from foreign institutions in 1962, thus setting back the whole project.

The reason for the loan denials became clearer when Shell and Mobil presented a proposal in 1962 to set up a refinery in Bogotá. Shell wanted to refine the crude from its concession in front of Barrancabermeja and, like Mobil, wanted direct access to the profitable distribution market in Bogotá; in effect, these goals meant blocking Ecopetrol. In 1963 Shell and Mobil were joined by Exxon, which wanted to refine the crude it had found in a concession near Neiva as well as to safeguard its share in the profitable Bogotá retail market. With Ecopetrol tied down by Colombia's lack of foreign exchange credit, the proposal of the trio had every certainty of success—had not another proposal from a most unexpected quarter gained time for the National Petroleum Company. The oil companies could compete furiously against each other and could have bitter disagreements among themselves, but for the first and only time in the period covered in this book, they presented a divided front in public. Texaco offered to build a refinery in Bogotá to process its crude from Neiva and other fields, provided Ecopetrol had a 50 percent share, which Texaco would kindly finance. Obviously, Texaco held some secret grudge against the other three oil companies (probably because of their refusal to participate in Amazon oil) and was now trying to get even by seeking out Ecopetrol, normally the real enemy, to block the other companies.[11]

The Colombian government was thoroughly perplexed, since it had to choose between the National Petroleum Company expansion at Barrancabermeja, the Exxon-Shell-Mobil proposal, or the Texaco-Ecopetrol formula. To complicate matters further, Texaco said it would go ahead with its refinery at Bogotá even if the other three companies built their own. A bitter debate raged in the press over a supposed constitutional freedom to refine; in essence, the argument was over whether the state had authority to stop any company from establishing a refinery. Not wishing to get caught in a battle between giants, Ecopetrol trimmed its sails and reduced the size of the Barrancabermeja project, hoping that the proposed refinery in Bogotá would cover part of the expected demand. In April 1963 Ecopetrol agreed to participate with Texaco in the Bogotá refinery, and there matters rested when Enrique Pardo Parra became minister of mines and petroleum in May 1963.

Upon taking office, the new oil minister consulted extensively within the government and soon discovered that Ecopetrol had never wanted the refinery in Bogotá and had only acceded to the plan in order to retain a share in the refining business. He moved gradually during the rest of 1963 to the viewpoint that Ecopetrol should have first option to build the Bogotá refinery but could have other oil companies as partners. This decision in effect excluded Exxon, which was highly opposed to participating in any partnerships with the state, and thus the Exxon-Shell-Mobil proposal, in spite of bitter public outcries, finally disappeared.

Texaco still pushed ahead, but it had left itself vulnerable to attack on one side. Neiva, the region that held most of the oil that would be refined in Bogotá, and then Caldas and Boyacá each clamored for the refinery that, for such poverty-stricken provinces, became a life-or-death matter. It simply became political suicide to build any refinery at all in

Bogotá, and the Colombian government simply had no choice but to tell Texaco that the deal had to be canceled.[12]

Texaco felt deeply offended, not only at this last decision but even more at being outmaneuvered, and it took sweet revenge in the sacking of the westernmost Amazon deposits. But it could not forget the episode of the Bogotá refinery, and to pay back the Colombian government with its own medicine, Texaco orchestrated a huge campaign from 1964 until the mid-1970s to have Ecopetrol build a refinery in Tumaco (the port terminal for the Amazon oil), and at one point even had Buenaventura named as another possible site. These regional requests, in particular the intense pressure from Neiva and Tumaco, distracted the government from more important issues, and in the end none of those regional refineries was ever built. After so many delays, Ecopetrol at last returned to its plan of enlarging the Barrancabermeja refinery from a daily capacity of 46,000 barrels to 75,000 barrels. In spite of hostility by the oil companies, the Inter-American Development Bank granted a very favorable loan that provided the needed foreign currency for the project, which was finally completed in 1967.[13]

Pipelines Across Colombia

Nationalistic efforts were also directed toward gaining control of the pipeline network, which had fallen under the grip of the oil companies. Access to the capital city of Bogotá, the largest market in the country for gasoline and refinery products, was central to any nationalistic strategy. Ecopetrol, which owned the pipeline from Barrancabermeja to Puerto Salgar, sorely missed the Puerto Salgar–Bogotá segment, which belonged to the provincial government of Cundinamarca but was in fact under the control of Exxon because of a mortgage. Ecopetrol had offered repeatedly to buy the pipeline, but not until a financial crisis brought the provincial government to the brink of bankruptcy did Cundinamarca finally agree to sell it to the National Petroleum Company in September 1960.

As part of the sale agreement, Ecopetrol was saddled with repayment of the loan Exxon had made to the provincial government, but now the loan was no longer on generous terms, so that Exxon turned a nice profit. No less significantly, Ecopetrol had to immediately engage in a costly program to enlarge the capacity of the Puerto Salgar–Bogotá pipeline from 12,000 to 20,000 barrels per day. This enlargement in turn rendered the Barrancabermeja–Puerto Salgar segments too small, requiring corresponding increases in their capacity.[14]

These construction projects took years and swallowed up sizable sums of capital, so that Ecopetrol, on the doorstep of Bogotá, was kept away from the retail sale of gasoline and lubricants in the country's most profitable market. The oil companies were gradually learning from the Colombian elite that to block state expansion was not as profitable as taking advantage of it. Based on the generous clauses of the 1952 Petroleum Code, the oil companies assigned themselves low rates as well as a whole host of privileges and benefits—in effect making Ecopetrol subsidize them for using the state pipelines.

Nationalists had been irked since the 1950s with these spreading abuses, but the manager of Ecopetrol, Mario Galán Gómez, lacked recourse as long as legal jurisdiction lay with a Ministry of Mines and Petroleum overly sympathetic to the oil companies. When Enrique Pardo Parra became oil minister in 1963, he immediately approved Galán's requests. The oil companies then took advantage of the many delaying tactics built into Colombian administrative procedures to postpone a final ruling on the matter. Even without taking the matter to the sympathetic courts, they secured an arrangement from Ecopetrol whereby the extra fees for using the pipeline were not paid but merely charged to an account. Whenever Ecopetrol attempted collection, the oil companies threatened to pass the fees on to the consumers in the form of higher gasoline prices; the fear of protest demonstrations over gasoline hikes immediately evoked pressure from the Colombian elite for Ecopetrol to grant the oil companies more time. What the "more time" was needed for became clear in early 1966: The oil companies had been eagerly awaiting Enrique Pardo Parra's dismissal so that they could promptly seize upon the next oil minister not only to wipe away the huge sums the oil companies owed Ecopetrol for using the pipelines but also to institutionalize the "tradition" of having Ecopetrol subsidize their pipeline use.[15]

Outmaneuvered in Bogotá, Ecopetrol counted on outflanking Exxon in the Pacific coast provinces by means of an overland pipeline from Puerto Salgar to Cali. The refinery products from Barrancabermeja would then be cheaper than when brought by the long route from the Cartagena refinery via tanker across the Panama Canal and then from Buenaventura by the Pipeline to the Pacific. Exxon had long before foreseen this danger and had consequently maneuvered to delay construction for one reason or another. Moreover, Ecopetrol's repeated requests beginning in the late 1950s failed to convince the provincial government of Caldas, through whose territory the pipeline would pass. To make this segment of the overland line unnecessary, Ecopetrol extended a segment of the Pipeline to the Pacific north from Cali to Cartago, where trucks transported the refinery products to Caldas. For the supply of Medellín, the provincial government of Antioquia had constructed its own line to Cantimploras.

Ecopetrol still insisted on building the overland pipeline, but another complication arose when private stockholders sold Ecopetrol 40 percent of the shares in the Pipeline to the Pacific Company (leaving majority control in Exxon's hands). This transaction, which was very profitable for the private investors, consumed Ecopetrol's capital and assured five more years of life for the Pipeline to the Pacific; not until 1968 did the National Petroleum Company complete the overland pipeline from Puerto Salgar to Cartago. After it was finally completed, the Cartago-Cali segment carried the bulk of the refinery products, although, in an attempt to keep the Buenaventura-Cali line alive, the pipeline was remodeled to handle the excess fuel oil produced by the Cartagena refinery.

Once the Cartagena refinery was disposed of in 1974, as far as Exxon was concerned the Pipeline to the Pacific had outlived its usefulness and could be sold to Ecopetrol. Enough time had been gained for members of the Cali elite to enter the gasoline retailing business in close association with the oil companies, and henceforth, just as in Bogotá, Ecopetrol had to begin subsidizing private use of the pipelines won after such long battles.

Notes

1. *El Tiempo*, 20 Dec. 1958, 5, 7 July 1960; *Economía Grancolombiana* 1 (1959):289–326; *Vínculo Shell* 14 (1961):16–19.

. 2. *El Siglo*, 16, 30 April 1963. The warning was heeded by Belisario Betancur, who did not again intervene in petroleum policy (although later in Spain he brokered numerous oil deals) until he became president of Colombia (1982–1986) and duly turned over the Llanos oil for sale to the oil companies at rock-bottom world prices.

3. *El Siglo*, 31 May 1963; *El Tiempo*, 30 May 1963.

4. *El Siglo*, 29 May 1963; *Vínculo Shell* 16 (1963):7–9.

5. *El Siglo*, 7 March 1963; Ministerio de Minas y Petróleos, *Memoria de 1965* (Bogotá: Imprenta Nacional, 1966), pp. 67–71; *El Tiempo*, 6 April 1965.

6. Previous paragraphs depend on *Fortune*, Nov. 1965, pp. 105, 206–207; *New York Times*, 25 Oct. 1965, 3 April 1966; U.S. Senate, Committee on Foreign Relations, *Survey of the Alliance for Progress: Colombia—A Case History of U.S. Aid* (Washington, D.C.: GPO, 1969), pp. 27–40.

7. *El Siglo*, 19 April, 3 June 1963; Alvaro Concha, *La Concesión Barco* (Bogotá: El Ancora, 1981), pp. 110–113.

8. Philip W. Bonsal Report, 22 March 1956, 821.2553/3-2256, RG 59.

9. The rest of the section relies on David Bushnell, *Eduardo Santos and the Good Neighbor, 1938–1942* (Gainesville: University of Florida Press, 1967), p. 95; *El Tiempo*, 27 May 1971; Concha, *Concesión Barco*, pp. 121–138.

10. *El Tiempo*, 7 April 1959.

11. *Economía Grancolombiana* 3 (1961–1962):95–101; *El Siglo*, 18, 19 April, 4 May 1963; *El Tiempo*, 19, 21 April 1963.

12. The three previous paragraphs draw from *El Siglo,* 1 Aug. 1963, 1 Nov., 13, 16 Dec. 1963; *New York Times,* 3 Aug. 1963.

13. *El Tiempo,* 27 Aug., 24 Sept. 1966, 14 Oct. 1970; *Wall Street Journal,* 21 July 1971.

14. *Economía Grancolombiana* 3 (1961–1962):95–101.

15. The rest of this section is based on *El Tiempo,* 23 April, 30 July 1965; *New York Times,* 6 June 1965.

6

The Final Outcome

The nationalistic backlash spent itself in costly attacks that achieved few lasting results. The underlying structures assured that the flow of events moved against increased participation by the National Petroleum Company. The foreign oil companies, like expert marksmen with only a few shots left, still intervened, with telling effects in cases involving Amazon oil and foreign exchange, but so close had their alliance become with the Colombian elite that direct efforts were required less frequently. Thus, the foreign companies merely watched as Ecopetrol drifted into the white gasoline quagmire, and only a few shoves—with the blessings of the elite—were needed to push Colombia over the precipice of having to import massive amounts of oil just as the 1973 energy crisis was beginning.

Amazon Oil

The Amazon jungle, one of the world's natural wonders, stretches in an unbroken sweep from the foothills of the cold Andes mountains to the equatorial currents of the Atlantic Ocean. Dense vegetation with trees towering 120 feet high and an annual rainfall of 200 inches makes the Amazon one of the most inhospitable places for man on earth, but the lure of its vast untapped resources has proved irresistible over the centuries. In earlier times the main prizes were gold, diamonds, rubber, and tropical woods; in the twentieth century attention has focused on the discovery of other natural resources, in particular the vast pools of oil that flow under the tributaries of the Amazon river.[1]

Accounts by adventuresome explorers had convinced the oil companies to send teams of professional geologists into the vast Amazon jungle starting in the early 1920s. The absence of any effective government controls in those isolated regions allowed the oil companies freedom to search undisturbed for signs of the illusive black gold and even to drill in the headwaters of the Amazon river, a large area shared by Colombia,

Ecuador, and Peru. On the Peruvian side, Exxon culminated these explorations with the announcement of the discovery of the Ganso Azul fields in the late 1930s, but on the Colombian side, all that the national government received were reports about the existence of large oil reserves at undisclosed spots.

When an American engineer asked in the 1920s for an oil concession covering the entire Colombian Amazon, the central state was startled and asked a German geologist, Dr. H. Hubach, to make an examination of the area. Hubach reported back in 1932 with a formal recommendation that the Colombian state itself exploit the very abundant Amazon oil. Exxon, as the holder of the Barrancabermeja concession, had a monopoly on Colombian output at that time and wanted neither a rival field nor a state operation. At the suggestion of Exxon, president Olaya Herrera (1930–1934) dropped the Hubach proposal in exchange for much needed support in the conflict against Peru, a war partially sparked in the first place by rivalry between oil interests over frontier concessions.

The activities of the oil companies in the Colombian Amazon are not known for some time after 1932. In 1948, however, Texaco confessed to drilling four wells, obviously as part of an earlier ongoing process. Texaco provided an ingenious explanation, saying that all four wells had been abandoned because they had struck asphalt clays at a depth of 3,000 to 5,500 feet; yet those very same regions, when drilled to over 6,000 feet in 1963, had "surprisingly" yielded large amounts of oil! Clearly, the Texaco fields at Orito, the westernmost Amazonian deposits, had been found at least by 1948, probably in the late 1930s when Exxon discovered its own fields on both sides of the Colombian-Peruvian border. In 1948, with cheap Middle East oil flooding world markets, the urgency to exploit Amazonian oil vanished and the wells were plugged, thus leaving behind a reserve to be tapped when it become convenient for the oil companies as part of their worldwide long-term strategies.[2]

By the mid-1950s, events such as the 1956 Suez crisis indicated that excessive dependence on Middle East oil was becoming too risky and that alternative oil supplies, preferably in the Western Hemisphere, soon had to be exploited. Among the first to sense this shift was Johnnie Bower, the local manager of Texaco in Colombia, who wanted to have a major "new" field ready for production. As a first step Texaco obtained the concession for the Orito field in 1954, but Bower knew the company needed allies, not to provide funds but in order to stage a huge strategic movement. Two companies pooling their influence and contacts would have a higher likelihood of pulling off the coup than just one by itself. Bower's first choice was Shell because of its valuable influence in Colombia as well as its experience in bordering Ecuador, but Shell adamantly refused to get involved. Texaco finally cajoled Gulf into a 50 percent share of the deal, but Gulf's heart was never in the project; Texaco remained the real force and was legally in charge as the "operator."

Texaco, after accusing the other oil companies of lacking the guts to get into a real deal, proceeded to unroll the first part of the planned scenario. On 1 July 1963, the drilling rigs—which, in contrast to 1948, did not "stop" at 6,000 feet—found oil at the well called Orito No. 1. Other nearby discoveries soon followed, but the Orito field always remained the main one on the Colombian side. Right on schedule, two months later in September 1963, Texaco was pressing for a pipeline to transport the crude to a seaport, but an unforeseen event held up plans. When drilling had begun on 20 March 1963, a submissive minister of mines and petroleum was in charge, but on 1 July 1963 none other than Enrique Pardo Parra became the oil minister. Without his approval, the crude pipeline could not be built, but the more he learned about Amazon oil, the less he liked the whole project with Texaco. Pardo Parra instead began seeking formulas to have Ecopetrol exploit those fields, possibly in combination with Petrobras, the Brazilian National Petroleum Company, which had shown interest in having crude shipped downstream to Brazil. Before the oil minister's bold plans could take form, the foreign companies engineered the maneuver that brought him down in 1965.[3]

Texaco celebrated the fall of Pardo Parra with wild parties. The new oil minister—who could not wait for the opportunity to do everything the oil companies wanted—immediately approved the pipeline, but because of the real natural obstacles involved in crossing the Amazon jungle and then going over the Andes mountains, it was not completed until 1969. Meanwhile, it was time to unveil another part of the grand strategy. In 1964, following closely upon the Orito discovery of 1963, Texaco and Gulf obtained huge concessions in Ecuador across the border from the Colombian fields. Texaco and Gulf held 2.5 million acres on the Colombian side and 3.5 million on the Ecuadorian side. Just as in Colombia, oil had been discovered in Ecuador in the 1920s, and the honor of "rediscovery" fell to Texaco in 1967; the most spectacular wells in Ecuador were in the world famous Lago Agrio field, with gushers soaring high into the atmosphere. This oil in the middle of Ecuador's Amazon flowed out to Orito through a spur of the newly constructed pipeline, which then continued on to the seaport of Tumaco.[4]

For three years Texaco and Gulf exported huge quantities of Ecuador's most accessible (and thus cheapest to extract) oil via the pipeline in Colombia. The exact amounts are known only to the oil companies, which submitted doctored figures in order to reap huge sums of pure profit at a time when Ecuador's fields were supposedly not producing. Rumors finally reached the Ecuadorian government, which then demanded its own pipeline, but this request had long been expected and the oil companies too easily complied. When the pipeline across Ecuador was completed in 1972, the plundering in no way ended; rather, it may have increased because henceforth Texaco and Gulf had a choice. According to how susceptible to persuasion officials in either the Colombian or Ecuadorian line happened to be, unreported quantities of oil could be shipped in either pipeline (the two lines actually combined to form a single U-shaped one). In both Ecuador and Colombia, the same result had been achieved—that of exporting the cheapest oil before the 1973 price rise; after 1973 the deposits that remained were more expensive to extract but were still highly profitable because of the increased prices. In effect, Ecuador's Amazonian oil became the first line of defense to counter the price hike in Middle East oil, and continued production in Ecuador during the rest of the 1970s and the 1980s, along with taking other areas of the world out of reserve, eventually brought down oil prices by the mid-1980s.[5]

The oil companies, however, did not want to spend their cheap reserve deposits to bring down oil prices too fast after 1973, because precisely what they wanted was to dispose of the reserves that were more expensive to exploit while the prices were still high. Thus, although Ecuador was allowed to continue producing and even to nationalize its oil sector and create CEPE, the Ecuadorian National Petroleum Company, for the oil fields in the Colombian Amazon a different fate was in store. In 1970 Texaco and Gulf began to pursue a rapacious policy of pumping the wells as fast as possible; this practice meant not only draining the fields but actually ruining them permanently. In accordance with standard conservation practices, the life of a field and total output are increased by pumping smaller annual amounts over a larger number of years, thus preventing the rapid advance of underground water. Instead, Texaco and Gulf pumped the wells as fast as possible, shortening the life of the fields, yet the Colombian elite did not allow civil and criminal charges to be brought for this wanton destruction. A few officials at the Ministry of Mines and Petroleum (but not the minister himself) and Ecopetrol tried to use an inspection process to slow down this deliberate wrecking of the fields, but nothing could stop Texaco and Gulf, which left a legacy of irreparable ruin in the manner of the former buccaneers. The Colombian government, which, in order to justify the extraordinary privileges granted to Texaco, had proclaimed in the 1960s that oil was the salvation for the Amazon, now changed its tune; beginning in 1972 high officials played the new line that "the future of the region is not in oil."[6]

The sacking of the Colombian oil fields went unabated until 1973, when Gulf panicked at the growing risk of a popular outcry in either

Colombia or Ecuador and decided to concentrate on the latter country. Gulf put its 50 percent share in the deal up for sale, and the shares were then taken over by a consortium formed by Ecopetrol, but it was too late; Texaco had already ruined the fields permanently. Thus, on the eve of the 1973 energy crisis, Colombia was deprived of the known oil fields whose deposits, had they been saved for the post-1973 period, would have kept Colombia from having to spend its foreign exchange to import petroleum at high world prices. Something else bothered the executives of other oil companies: As they pored over the export figures of Texaco's Orito operation, even after doubling them and without counting Ecuadorian production that went through the Tumaco pipeline, the amounts were still too small. The feeling remained that Orito was only the tip of the iceberg and that other vast pools of oil lay elsewhere in the jungle that covers nearly half of Colombia, raising the question of what else lies under the vast Amazon basin.[7]

The Foreign Exchange Trap

One of the fundamental principles of oil company operations in Colombia was to avoid any exchange controls over crude exports. This rule had, among other effects, two main advantages for the foreign companies: (1) large quantities of oil could be exported without being reported in the doctored figures, and (2) the huge 90 percent profit margin in Colombian operations could be transferred abroad without having any effect (not even inflation) on Colombia's economy. This latter factor was always well appreciated by the Colombian elite; however, over the decades some questions occasionally came up, and although before the 1960s these questions were always silenced before they attracted widespread attention, in order to avoid future embarrassments the oil companies deliberately confused foreign exchange controls with related issues as a diversionary tactic.[8]

Exxon took the lead in this battle by continuously urging a lower exchange rate for the crude that was imported for its Cartagena refinery—imports that at first glance seemed absurd, since Colombia exported crude until 1974. In fact, since the 1920s Exxon had engaged in the well-entrenched and highly profitable system of exporting the oil from Colombia (but without earning any foreign exchange credit for the country) and then having Colombia import—at world prices and in dollars—most of the gasoline and refinery products consumed in the country. This arrangement did not end in 1961 when Ecopetrol at last took over the Barrancabermeja refinery because Exxon had cleverly maneuvered to gain control of the Cartagena refinery, which was inaugurated in 1957, thus giving the immensely harmful system a new lease on life under a slightly different variant.

Ecopetrol itself needed dollars to import some crude because production from the Barrancabermeja fields did not cover the capacity of the refinery. But the cost of this procedure was really a minor consideration, especially because the National Petroleum Company could obtain bulk discounts of 43 percent under the world posted price. Exxon, of course, demanded for its Cartagena refinery foreign exchange that the Central State Bank supplied until 1962 at a rate close to that of the free market. In addition, Exxon received a subsidy for selling gasoline in Colombia at a price higher than its import cost, a traditional measure that since the 1920s had forced the Colombian consumer to pay the highest gasoline prices in the world. To reduce internal consumption, Exxon had pursued a policy of keeping gasoline prices as high as possible, while Ecopetrol had asked for lower increases. During the 1960s this upward tendency slowed down somewhat because Ecopetrol, by then interested in capital accumulation, was more easily tempted to accept high gasoline prices in order to conserve large profit margins. Thus, an uneasy alliance on this point sprung up between Exxon and Ecopetrol from 1962 until 1974.[9]

Exxon began a more subtle maneuver when Colombia devalued its currency in 1962 from 6.70 pesos to the dollar to 9 pesos, the latter being the free exchange rate. The Cartagena refinery had been importing crude for some time at the 6.70 rate, which made for small profit margins but *not* huge losses, as Exxon claimed. But beginning in December 1962, Exxon too was entitled to buy the dollars for crude imports at a fixed official rate of 9 pesos per dollar. However, as an apparent "sacrifice" to the new monetary stabilization program, the oil companies did not press very hard for an increase in the number of pesos they received in exchange for the equipment imported for operations in Colombia, so that the exchange rate went up only 7.10 pesos per dollar.[10]

This second exchange rate was more a subsidy than a foreign exchange control mechanism because the oil companies secretly reexported their machinery out of Colombia once they had finished drilling. Economists fascinated themselves adding up the incredible capital sums that supposedly flowed into the country as a result of the "investment" that the oil companies brought into Colombia, which somehow managed to remain as poor as always. Oil minister Pardo Parra was not so easily fooled, and in July 1965 he took steps to begin reducing the immense benefits the oil companies received from the foreign exchange privileges (which also extended into excessive tax advantages); but, as has been explained in the previous chapter, these steps only hastened his fall from the cabinet post.[11]

Colombia devalued the peso again in 1965, but this move did not stop the open market exchange rate from floating upwards, so that Exxon's ability to buy dollars for importing crude at a rate of 9 pesos to the dollar became a very juicy additional subsidy for its refinery operations. Even though Pardo Parra's attempts to tamper with this arrangement had been beaten off in 1965, new forces were gaining momentum to raise the rate substantially. Exxon orchestrated a whole campaign among foreign financial institutions based on the false claims that Colombia faced another foreign exchange crisis because the country had failed to provide enough incentives for private oil explorations. The 1967 devaluation gave an air of credence to the claims, and in response to intense pressures from the oil companies and foreign institutions, Colombia issued a decree with the new "incentives" in November 1967. The government raised the rate for calculating the pesos given to oil companies in exchange for imported oil equipment from 7.10 pesos per dollar to 16.25. As far as the exchange rate for the purchase of crude for the refinery, the decree merely transferred authority to a newly created special Commission of Prices (within the Ministry of Mines and Petroleum), which actually did not tamper with the old rate of 9 pesos per dollar. As the owner of the Cartagena refinery, Exxon received the lion's share of the benefits, but the rest of the oil companies, less favored, threatened to publicly blast the new decree as unworkable. They in fact were only looking for a pretext to transfer their own operations to other parts of the world. After heated sessions and the granting of unnamed concessions, Exxon finally secured the acquiescence of the fellow companies and the oil minister proudly stated to the press that Colombia was on the eve of a new wave of exploratory activity. In reality, the oil companies could not pack fast enough to abandon the country before the 1973 energy crisis struck.[12]

Another decree of 1967 (no. 444) instituted a mechanism of "mini" devaluations: Each day the value of the peso would go down slower or faster, but always a few points, in relation to the dollar. No matter how slow the peso declined in value, every little drop made the rate that Exxon was paying for its imported crude a veritable fountain of wealth. Thanks to this subsidy, from 1967 to 1971 Exxon reaped immense profits from its refinery operations in Cartagena, which had already been booming in the early 1960s. Nevertheless, Exxon was careful not to raise the already high gasoline prices too fast because it did not want to overly antagonize the Colombian elite, who bought gasoline for their automobiles. By keeping the gasoline hikes to modest proportions, Exxon easily secured the backing of Ecopetrol, and Ecopetrol's own capital accumulation also increased. This last phenomenon, however, worried Exxon: As much as the U.S. company loved swimming in huge profits, if this meant enriching the National Petroleum Company, the price was too high.

Although the Colombian government was subsidizing Exxon to keep gasoline prices down for the Colombian elite, Exxon knew that one day some official would realize that the same effect could be achieved much more cheaply by subsidizing Ecopetrol. Exxon therefore had to take preventive action. The Misael Pastrana Borrero administration (1970–1974), one of the purest expressions of elite ideas, shared the same concern about a runaway Ecopetrol and was even willing to have the elite pay higher gasoline prices if this was the cost for retaining its preeminent position as the ruling class. The Pastrana administration carefully staged the necessary maneuver in June 1971. First of all, and for nationalistic propaganda, the government announced that henceforth Exxon would have to purchase the imported crude at the going market rate for dollars, which at that moment had already reached 19.80 pesos. The next step followed according to plan: Exxon promptly transferred the entire raise in the exchange rate to consumers in the form of higher gasoline prices. Such a drastic jump of nearly 100 percent in the price of gasoline would have produced mass violence and uprisings in the – streets had not the Pastrana administration been ready with the final and most deadly measure: Private bus lines (owned by elite members) received a special subsidy so that passenger fares did not go up even a cent. The funds came from Ecopetrol, which henceforth was permanently weighed down with the huge and growing payments needed to keep the private bus lines in Colombia running at subsidized fares, a situation that has not changed to the present.[13]

With this last masterful move, Exxon considered its refinery mission in Colombia completed. Even with buying crude at the free market exchange rate, the Cartagena refinery was turning over a nice profit of at least 15 percent annually after inflation and taxes. However, giving up the Cartagena refinery actually benefited Exxon: First, the foreign exchange situation of Ecopetrol was aggravated because it could not buy dollars as easily from the Central State Bank as Exxon, and short of dollars the National Petroleum Company could not carry out vast explorations for oil. Second, by saddling Ecopetrol with a huge debt in 1974 for the purchase of the Cartagena refinery at outrageous prices, still another burden was placed on the National Petroleum Company. The next year, Colombia began to import more oil than it exported, precisely when the energy crisis drove oil prices to their highest levels in world history, so that Colombia's dollar reserves were permanently drained to buy expensive oil abroad. The crude from Colombian fields under the control of the foreign companies continued to flow abroad without any exchange controls, and this fundamental principle remained intact.

From Bottled Gas to White Gasoline

The distribution of gas entered into a new stage when Ecopetrol, after long and complex maneuvers, gained a 50 percent share of the Colombian Gas Company by 1961. The National Petroleum Company hailed this acquisition as a crucial step to curtail the monopoly that private companies had over the distribution of bottled gas, but the celebration was premature. During the 1950s the Colombian Gas Company had grown into a big corporation that was no longer the best instrument for the purposes of the oil companies, in spite of the fact that from its foundation in 1946 it had been under the absolute control of Exxon. Since the mid-1950s the oil companies had helped to establish small firms to distribute bottled gas, sometimes by extending credits or other favors, at other times by channeling gas to the new outfits from their own fields.

Consequently, by 1961 when Ecopetrol took over, the other sources of gas were under the control of the foreign companies and the Colombian Gas Company was limited to the gas from the Barrancabermeja fields. Ecopetrol's fields were palpably insufficient, so that the Colombian Gas Company was left exposed as the perfect scapegoat to blame for the bottled gas shortages and held up as another example of the inherent inefficiency of state activity. The other 50 percent share of the Colombian Gas Company was still in the hands of institutions and individuals close to the foreign oil companies. A veritable army of fifth columnists undermined the work of this state company from the inside and at the same time fully reported the details of its inner workings (and some of Ecopetrol's). This inside information made it possible for the foreign companies to make tactical moves to keep the Colombian Gas Company permanently off balance. For example, a maneuver was engineered to make Ecopetrol sell 0.5 percent of its shares, thus reducing its control to 49.5 percent, but the National Petroleum Company managed to retain control by transferring the 0.5 percent to the National Federation of Coffee Growers, which always voted with the state. However, there was no denying that by one tactic after another, the state's efforts to enter the retailing of bottled gas had been decisively hamstrung.[14]

The field was thus left open for the private gas firms, which proliferated during the 1960s; by 1972 they numbered 184, broken down into 38 in the Atlantic coast provinces, 23 in the area served by the Barco Concession, and 123 in the rest of the country, concentrated mostly in Bogotá and Bucaramanga. In spite of the claims of those who praised the benefits of free competition, the operations of those firms were disastrous—and not only because the service was poor and expensive. Most of these distributors were fly-by-night outfits bent on making the quickest dollar. Not satisfied with a huge profit margin, they paid very low wages, exploited child labor, and tried to cut on expenses in every way possible, even changing their company names to avoid paying debts. Gas for them was a short-term opportunity to be exploited to the last drop without any attention to safety: Bottles exploded and the predilection for defective equipment scored an incredibly large number of accidents, with daily deaths occurring at a frightening frequency. Rather than vigorously prosecuting the private gas distributors, false charges were leveled at the Colombian Gas Company, which, as a state enterprise, had scrupulously observed safety precautions. The attempt to discredit the Colombian Gas Company had another motive, and in 1966 a docile oil minister could not resist reducing the amount of gas that Ecopetrol could sell to its subsidiary Colombian Gas Company—a maneuver aimed solely at favoring influential private distributors.[15]

The Colombian elite, so opposed to having Ecopetrol distribute bottled gas, insisted that state activity was inherently wasteful but watched unperturbed the annual burning of millions of cubic feet of natural gas by the private oil companies. This practice had become so entrenched in the Colombian oil fields that even when the gas that came up from the well was bottled, once the storage capacity was filled the rest was burned in the atmosphere. The companies simply refused to build any additional facilities for gas; at the same time, they would not plug the wells until the last drop of oil had come out, thus depleting underground pressure and reducing the potential gas recovery. The situation was only made worse in the early 1960s when three concessions in the Atlantic coast region, El Difícil, Cicuco, and Jobo, turned out to be gas rather than oil fields. Rather than turn over these fields to Ecopetrol for rational exploitation, the oil companies embarked upon questionable practices to make a quick profit.

The oil companies claimed that the market for bottled gas was too small to justify the operation of these fields and would be warranted only if large industrial consumption appeared. A number of factories in Barranquilla converted to natural gas for fuel, the government installed gas turbines in Barranquilla and Cúcuta to generate electricity, and as a last step, a group of private investors set up a factory to extract fertilizer and other chemicals out of the gas. A gas pipeline was even constructed from Cicuco to Barranquilla, and indeed, on paper, the projects sounded very promising. The oil companies, which reaped profits from selling the surplus gas, gained immense good will as the promoters of these projects, which were bringing progress and prosperity to the Atlantic coast provinces.[16]

These prospects soon were darkened by a number of complications, and as usual, the state and not the oil companies received the blame. Most of these industrial and electrical projects to consume natural gas did not come on stream until the late 1960s and a few not even until the 1970s, and by then the gas reserves had already been burned into the atmosphere. The oil companies drilled new wells as soon as a new plant or factory started to consume gas, but the results were counterproductive: The additional wells produced twice the gas needed and sometimes even more, and all of the excess production went up in flames. Such a rapid pace of extraction drastically shortened the life of the gas fields, which behave like oil fields in that the smaller the amount taken out each year, the larger the total output over many years. The proven reserves that should have provided twenty or thirty years of useful life for the gas-consuming projects turned out instead to run out in five and sometimes fewer years. By the late 1960s, Barranquilla and Cúcuta already faced electricity shortages because their turbines lacked gas, and the central state, the owner of the power authorities, was held responsible.

Gas was still cheaper than other energy sources for cooking. Demand rapidly rose during the 1960s, and the gas shortages of 1963 and 1966 failed to serve as warnings. Those shortages had been overcome because Ecopetrol, the only company that did not burn off the excess gas, had taken extraordinary measures—in particular, reducing gasoline output (which had to be compensated for by expensive imports)—to increase the production of bottled gas. By the late 1960s, unless it was put in charge of the other gas fields in the country, there was nothing Ecopetrol could do to solve the impending shortage in bottled gas. Already, many persons of the lower class could not find any gas to buy and powerful influences were needed to secure a share of the scarce gas. As the population of Bogotá swelled past the 3 million mark, more than half of the inhabitants lacked adequate energy sources to cook their meals, and in desperation turned first to kerosene and increasingly to white gasoline.[17]

Electric stoves (that occasionally ran out in the stores) were in any case not within reach: In 1970 the Bogotá Light and Power Company was in the same situation as in the 1940s. On both occasions the utility lacked the funds needed to double its capacity in order to meet consumer demand—a very clear indication that the electrical expansion of Colombia had fallen considerably behind the country's real needs. The distribution of coal had long since been discontinued in Bogotá, but since the supply of white gasoline did not expand rapidly enough, irate housewives from the poor neighborhoods stormed gasoline stations in November 1972. Whenever the lines of people holding cans and jars and waiting to buy white gasoline grew, politicians promised easy solutions. Ecopetrol finally was forced to channel its dwindling capital into the production and sale of white gasoline at subsidized prices, which put yet another unbearable burden on the National Petroleum Company. In response to intense political pressure, the government, rather than blaming the oil companies, put the responsibility squarely upon Ecopetrol, even though Ecopetrol had warned of the coming problem since the 1960s to no avail.[18]

Colombia found itself in a disastrous situation in the early 1970s. With the easily tapped gas fields converted into flames, the country was left without the reserves to weather the 1973 energy crisis. The large amount of capital sunk into gas-consuming factories and power plants became a worthless investment and proved a drain on both the country's scarce capital and the gas reserves. Lastly, Ecopetrol was forced to produce and subsidize white gasoline to supply the cooking needs of the urban lower class, particularly in Bogotá, at a huge loss. The votes of the lower class were easily manipulated, and politicians perpetuated themselves in office by keeping the price of white gasoline down and securing its distribution in favored neighborhoods. These practices effectively drained Ecopetrol's resources without, in the long run, doing anything to raise the abysmally low standard of living for the lower class, which forms the overwhelming mass of the Colombian population.

Toward Massive Oil Imports

So large were Colombia's oil deposits that even draining the westernmost Amazon fields did not have to turn the country into a major oil importer. Besides the black gold that lurked in other parts of the Amazon, various regions contained oil deposits waiting to be tapped. Sufficient oil to cover Colombia's oil needs was available, provided of course that Ecopetrol could exploit the fields rather than the foreign companies, which merely exported the crude without leaving foreign currency behind.

By 1966 it was clear that in order to meet the expected shortage of crude, the Colombian government needed to assign maximum priority to drilling and exploration by the National Petroleum Company. But the incoming Carlos Lleras administration (1966–1970) had a different priority. Upon taking office, the Lleras administration's first urgent order of business was to bury the "Report on the Participation of the State in the Exploitation of Petroleum."[19] This study had been commissioned by oil minister Pardo Parra and was handed in after his dismissal; the report had lived on beyond its progenitor's public life and had caused considerable public controversy when it was partially leaked to the press. In 1966, the oil companies published a "Summary," which in fact contained only evidence favorable to their cause. Widely distributed, this "Summary" of the "Participation" report was full of technical terms and jargon hard for the public to follow. Gradually the controversy over the "Participation" report waned and the Lleras administration succeeded in closing once and for all the nationalization campaign that had so bothered the oil companies.

Out with the "Participation" report went the government officials who had supported the nationalistic campaign, to be replaced by individuals who converted the Ministry of Mines and Petroleum into a dependency of the foreign oil companies. However, Ecopetrol was still on the loose, and the Colombian government, against a backdrop of public declarations of praise for the National Petroleum Company, slowly took steps to restrict or at least delay state petroleum production. The tactics were interlocking and complementary, each one building upon the other to produce a cumulative effect. An important move involved some smaller concessions renounced by the oil companies between 1956 and 1961: The government claimed that those lands had fallen into a legal limbo and refused Ecopetrol's requests to drill on them. Only in 1969, after years of lengthy and repeated efforts, could Ecopetrol at last start to drill those highly promising lands, but by then the state company had been sidetracked into channeling its exploratory work into less promising areas.

Another case concerned the Shell concession located in front of the Barrancabermeja refinery (across the Magdalena river), an ideal source for crude that until then had been largely exported. Ecopetrol secretly negotiated to buy back that concession twelve years before its expiration in 1979, but before the deal could be closed it was leaked to the press in 1967. Negotiations stalled, the sale price shot up, and Shell began to remove equipment. Ecopetrol was now deprived of this crude, which it should have received for free, and instead Shell was pumping the wells faster to export more crude. So much oil had been extracted that Ecopetrol at times considered withdrawing the purchase offer. Furthermore, the public had begun to associate the transaction with rumors of corruption and fraud among high government and Ecopetrol officials. Nevertheless, the National Petroleum Company preferred to trust the advice of the geologist Daniel Trompy, who prior to his death in 1971 performed his last service to Colombia. Secretly brought to Colombia under a disguised identity, Trompy confirmed to Ecopetrol that this field, which he had discovered in the 1930s, contained more oil than even Shell suspected and was worth many times the purchase price.[20]

Taken over by Ecopetrol in 1974, the Shell field was Colombia's only cushion to soften the blow of the post-1973 energy crisis. Other fields, known collectively as El Roble, Conchal, and Limón, had been spirited away by then. These fields were in the area surrounding the Barrancabermeja concession and right next to an Ecopetrol wildcat that had confirmed the existence of a pool of oil. The companies had been rebuffed in their attempts to keep Ecopetrol out of these surrounding areas, and to make up for their losses, Exxon, British Petroleum, and Sinclair presented petitions in 1952 asking for concession over El Roble, Conchal, and Limón, and to make the fight more worthwhile, at the same time moved the boundary lines right up to the Ecopetrol's wildcat well. The companies had no legal right to present the petitions, since these areas had been reserved for Ecopetrol, and moving the boundaries was a criminal offense. But rather than initiate criminal proceedings against the oil companies, the government allowed a civil case to drag out in the courts during the 1950s and 1960s. Not even a cease and desist order was possible, and so Exxon, British Petroleum, and Sinclair merrily pumped huge amounts of crude while the case was still pending. The field was so abundant that Ecopetrol counted on extracting substantial quantities of crude once the Colombian Supreme Court handed down the final verdict in 1972. To the stunned surprise of the country, the Supreme Court did not even consider the criminal violations but instead enriched Colombian jurisprudence with the really original concept that a petition presented to the government must be considered a petition accepted in good faith.[21]

The loss of El Roble, Conchal, and Limón was a staggering but not final blow. Ecopetrol in the late 1960s was already taking the first steps to expand beyond the Magdalena valley and begin exploratory activity in other parts of Colombia. Ecopetrol had never understood why the Ministry of Mines and Petroleum had lost all interest in the Llanos after the fall of Pardo Parra in 1965. Its curiosity aroused, Ecopetrol began to accumulate abandoned and apparently worthless concessions in the Llanos. It did not begin to drill immediately though because, starting in 1969, concessions in other regions of Colombia, such as the Caribbean coast, came into its hands. The National Petroleum Company was soon swamped with lands and was at a loss as to where to send its scarce drilling equipment. But at some point Ecopetrol wildcatting on its own could not help but stumble upon the pools of Llanos oil, especially because the first Llanos concessions of 1969 sat right upon the site of the "discoveries" in the 1980s.[22]

The oil companies foresaw a period of higher oil prices in the 1970s that gave them the opportunity to dispose of their more expensive crude deposits; their plans would be wrecked if Colombia flooded the world market with cheap oil. The oil companies elaborated a threefold strategy to delay the entry of Llanos oil until the late 1980s when low prices once again prevailed. First of all, the oil companies waged a long campaign to convince the Colombian government to keep Ecopetrol concentrated in the Magdalena valley. The deposits in the valley, although far from exhausted, could not match the pools of Llanos oil that had never entered production. Thus a turnabout took place: While in the 1950s the oil companies had denounced the National Petroleum Company's activities in the Magdalena valley, in the 1970s this area was considered Ecopetrol's proper sphere while proposals for the Llanos were bogged down in endless legal and bureaucratic objections.[23]

Second, influences were moved inside Ecopetrol to restrict its purchases of drilling equipment during the 1970s. The money always seemed to vanish from the budget whenever Ecopetrol wanted to buy or replace drilling equipment; at times; the state company had to rush out to rent rigs at exorbitant prices for short periods. This scarcity of rigs was artificial, but it gave various oil companies an excuse to "spontaneously" step forward with offers of becoming "associates" in Llanos exploration, thus completing the last element in their threefold strategy. The terms were generously sugarcoated: Ecopetrol did not have to invest a cent in these associated ventures until the wells actually started producing, and then would receive half of the crude produced. The real problem was that while for Ecopetrol this arrangement was a jump into an unknown region, for the oil companies it meant sailing in charted waters. The oil companies pointed Ecopetrol toward areas without any oil, while with their own equipment, they looked for just enough oil to cover their expenses, chalking up at the same time an impressive number of dry holes to further disillusion Ecopetrol about even the possibility of finding oil in the isolated vastness of the Colombian Llanos.[24]

Ecopetrol fell squarely into this well-laid trap and was left wandering in the Llanos for over a decade without making any significant finds. This lack of results fortified the arguments of the Colombian elite, who from the start had felt that the state, because of its inherent inefficiency, should not be involved in exploration activities that more properly should be left to the foreign companies. The ground was thus ripe for the oil companies to launch yet another public campaign seeking new "incentives" for oil exploration. There is no need to inflict upon the reader the details of that campaign, which flared intermittently under the administrations of Misael Pastrana Borrero (1970–1974), Alfonso López Michelsen (1974–1978), and Julio César Turbay Ayala (1978–1982).

Colombia had always imported crude and refinery products while the oil companies exported large amounts of Colombian crude, but the difference between imports and domestic consumption had shrunk thanks to Ecopetrol's efforts during the 1950s and 1960s. After 1973 the situation became critical because Ecopetrol no longer enjoyed bulk discounts for purchases but instead had to pay record high world prices for the massive oil imports. During the 1970s, when the Llanos oil should have enabled Colombia to save large sums of scarce foreign currency, Colombia was instead incurring huge expenses (wiping out the benefits of the boom in coffee prices during the 1970s) to cover the deficit in the domestic supply of petroleum. The country was deprived of the capital needed to embark upon the large-scale economic development needed to pull the masses of the population out of poverty. Colombia thus missed its last chance in the twentieth century to escape the stifling bond of underdevelopment; this failure also extended to electricity, the subject of the next part of this book.

Notes

1. The first three paragraphs of this section rely on the Ernest Kornel report, 28 July 1921, 821.6363/171, Record Group (RG) 59, National Archives, Washington, D.C.; René De La Pedraja, *Historia de la energía en Colombia, 1537–1930* (Bogotá: El Ancora Editores, 1985), pp. 192–193.

2. Warren report, 16 June 1948, 821.6363/6-1048, RG 59.

3. *El Siglo*, 16 March 1963; *New York Times*, 4 Oct. 1963.

4. John D. Martz, *Politics and Petroleum in Ecuador* (New Brunswick, N.J.: Transaction Books, 1987), pp. 46–47, 53–55; *Oil and Gas Journal*, 6 March 1967; *New York Times*, 6 Sept. 1966, 20 March, 18 April 1967.

5. *Oil and Gas Journal*, 24 July 1967, 20 Oct. 1969; *Wall Street Journal*, 9 July 1969; *New York Times*, 26 March, 10 July 1971; Martz, *Petroleum in Ecuador*, pp. 57–62, 105–110.

6. George Philip, *Oil and Politics in Latin America* (Cambridge: Cambridge University Press, 1982), pp. 274–277; *El Tiempo*, 9 Oct. 1971, 6 July 1972.

7. *Oil and Gas Journal*, 7 Aug., 4 Sept. 1972, 10 Sept. 1973; *El Tiempo*, 3 Dec. 1972.

8. The discussion in the first three paragraphs of this section draws on República de Colombia, *Memoria del Ministro de Minas y Petróleos de 1965* (Bogotá: Imprenta Nacional, 1966), passim, especially pp. 56–57; *El Espectador*, 30 April 1963.

9. *Vínculo Shell* 125 (1964):41–42; *El Siglo*, 22 Aug. 1963.

10. U.S. Senate, Committee on Foreign Relations, *Survey of the Alliance for Progress—A Case History of U.S. Aid* (Washington, D.C.: GPO, 1969), p. 158; Colombia, *Memoria de Minas y Petróleos de 1965*, pp. 52–63, 302–303; *El Tiempo*, 29 June, 3, 18 July 1965.

11. *New York Times*, 3 April 1966; *El Tiempo*, 3, 4 Nov. 1967; U.S. Senate, *Survey of Alliance in Colombia*, pp. 152, 157.

12. República de Colombia, *Un acto de gobierno: la variación en la tasa de cambio para la refinación de petróleo crudo* (Bogotá: Banco de la República, 1971), pp. 5–13; *El Tiempo*, 25, 26 June 1971.

13. *El Siglo*, 25 Jan., 15 May 1963; *El Tiempo*, 13, 23 Jan. 1963; 5 May 1966.

14. Colombia, *Memoria de Minas y Petróleos de 1965*, pp. 21–24; *El Tiempo*, 13 Jan., 5 April 1961.

15. *Economía Grancolombiana* 5(1961–1962):213–215; *El Tiempo*, 17 Dec. 1963; *El Siglo*, 21 Feb. 1963. The discovery of the Guajira off-shore gas deposits in the 1970s appeared to reverse the trend described in this and the following paragraph, but its effect was only temporary.

16. *El Tiempo*, 12 July, 16 Sept. 1967.

17. Ibid., 4 Jan., 14 Feb. 1970.

18. Ibid., 3, 8 Nov. 1971.

19. Centro de Información de la Industria Petrolera, *Informe de la Comisión de Estudio Sobre la Participación del Estado en la Explotación del Petróleo Resumen* (Bogotá: CIIP, 1966), pp. 1–18; *El Tiempo*, 29 Aug. 1966; Colombia, *Memoria del Ministro de Minas y Petróleos de 1966*, pp. 67, 72–75.

20. *El Tiempo*, 31 Jan. 1967; *Oil and Gas Journal*, 20 Feb. 1967.

21. *El Tiempo*, 22 Nov. 1972; Colombia, *Memoria del Ministro de Minas y Petróleos de 1965*, pp. 24–30, 375–384.

22. *Oil and Gas Journal*, 21 Oct. 1968, pp. 60–61; *El Tiempo*, 5 Oct. 1970.

23. *Oil and Gas Journal*, 16 June 1969; *El Tiempo*, 10 June 1971; *New York Times*, 25 Jan., 3 May 1971.

24. *El Tiempo*, 3 Dec. 1970; 13 Oct. 1972.

PART TWO

Electricity

7

The U.S. Utilities in Colombia

The entry of the American and Foreign Power Company into Colombia in 1927 marked the beginning of a new stage in the electrical development of the country. Among its many accomplishments, the American utility was responsible for bringing a modern, efficient service to areas that had been lagging behind even by Colombian standards. Furthermore, the American and Foreign Power Company began for the first time in Colombia's history to consider electricity within a national perspective, rather than from the purely local angle followed up to that time. Yet an increase in the pace of electrification was not welcomed by all the elite members in some Colombian cities, as the section in this chapter on Cali reveals.

Spread and Consolidation

Speculation in the United States during the 1920s had reached an all time high, and holding companies for utilities provided very lucrative opportunities. The biggest of the holding companies, Electric Bond and Share, decided in 1927 to go to Latin America to repeat takeover practices that had reaped large profits in the United States. Certainly, Electric Bond was not the last company to assume that what was valid at home should also work abroad. The company thus established a subsidiary, American and Foreign Power Company, with Floyd B. Odlum as president, who went on a world tour to buy utilities in Latin America and other continents both directly and through agents. In a first round of purchases for American and Foreign Power, Odlum acquired properties in Cuba, Ecuador, Guatemala, and Panama by April 1927; by October of that year holdings extended to Brazil, Colombia, and Mexico, and acquisitions in other countries soon followed.[1]

The American and Foreign Power Company entered Colombia from the two coasts: One drive through the Atlantic coast acquired the utilities at Barranquilla (the largest city in this area), Santa Marta, and other smaller towns; a second drive from the Pacific coast acquired the port town of Buenaventura and from there pushed inland to purchase utilities in Cali (the most important city), Palmira, and Buga (see Map 2). South of Cali lay the sleepy colonial town of Popayán: Its city council stubbornly resisted the tempting offers to sell, at one point even threatening the two local private utilities with expropriation if they dared to sell. By this action Popayán effectively kept the American and Foreign Power Company from linking the Cali utility with its other holdings to the south in bordering Ecuador.[2]

The local manager, Hiram S. Foley, temporarily dropped the push to the south and instead marshaled forces against a vastly more significant target: the Bogotá Light and Power Company. As will be explained in the next chapter, this Bogotá company was owned by private investors and the city government, and as the largest and most valuable utility in the country, its possession was crucial to achieving control over Colombia's electricity resources. In late 1927 Foley had rejected a bid to purchase the private utility at Bucaramanga because it was too far north to affect the impending clash with Bogotá, and instead he planned a two-pronged drive, buying first the utilities immediately to the north of the capital at Zipaquirá, Chía, Cajicá, Nemocón, and Cogua (with control over the Neusa river; see Map 3, p. 202), and then those to the south and west in Girardot, Tocaima, Agua de Dios, and finally Honda. To link the northern network with the southern utilities by transmission lines, all the American and Foreign Power Company needed was to purchase the Bogotá Light and Power Company. To accomplish this final goal Foley showed up in the capital city in June 1931, more as a triumphant conqueror than a peaceful businessman.

His fame had preceded him, and all of Bogotá was talking nervously about the many takeovers he had masterminded throughout the country and wondering how long Bogotá could escape falling. Foley's behavior, rather than removing these fears, only confirmed the worst of them, since "after long years in Mexico, he is imbued with the idea that American foreign investment should be protected by the armed forces of the United States."[3] The president of Colombia, Enrique Olaya Herrera, an unconditional ally of the United States, gave Foley full support, and the politicians in the city council, not daring to risk the president's wrath, meekly agreed to sell the city's shares in the Bogotá Light and Power Company.

A huge public debate raged for months, with Foley's old colonialist mentality effectively outraging those with nationalistic sensibilities in Bogotá. In the final analysis, the decision was in the hands of the private shareholders, primarily the Samper family, who had the controlling voting interest on the utility's Board of Directors. Nationalistic feeling

MAP 2

seized the private owners, and the manager, Francisco Samper Madrid, explained to the mayor of the city that giving up the utility meant nothing less than surrendering an important instrument that was desperately needed to save the Colombian nationality from external threats of absorption. These were the Colombians of the generation that had witnessed the rape of Panamá in 1903. Colonialist Foley, rather than trying to dispel these fears, built upon them in order to secure submission. Furthermore, Colombia in those same years was surrendering valuable petroleum deposits such as the Barco Concession to U.S. companies, and nationalistic elements decided to make a last stand in the case of the Bogotá Light and Power Company against U.S. penetration. The stand was successful, and Foley temporarily withdrew from the city, cursing the U.S. government for not having sent troops to teach the "natives" a lesson once and for all.[4]

Unfortunately, the efforts of the nationalists in this case were misdirected. The experience of later decades showed that if Colombia wanted economic prosperity, the petroleum deposits rather than the Bogotá Light and Power Company should have been saved. Foley was still undaunted, and he continued after 1931 to press for the acquisition of the Bogotá utility to complete a national network over the whole of Colombia. The takeover attempt slowed down considerably after 1936 because New York headquarters refused to release any more funds and insisted on making the Colombian subsidiary stand on its own resources. As a matter of fact, Electric Bond and Share came to have second thoughts about its entire Latin American investments because most of the utilities had trouble earning a 5 percent annual profit: Venezuela, with a 7 percent return was the highest, while Colombia, making a 1 percent return, was the worst of all. The abject poverty of the Colombian masses had caught the company by surprise: How could public relations campaigns convince people to stop eating so that they could buy electricity? Attempts to raise local capital by issuing stock attained only very modest results, and the Colombian subsidiary gradually settled into the long-term struggle of adjusting to a backwards country that would not escape underdevelopment during the twentieth century.[5]

For people in such depressingly poor conditions, any rate for electricity was too high, and this discontent was ably manipulated at times by local merchants and brokers who felt ignored by the American and Foreign Power Company. In effect, the Colombian subsidiary obtained its loans and purchased directly from the United States instead of going to the local intermediaries, who wanted to earn commissions. The merchant-brokers belonged to the influential families of each city, and they often manipulated public opinion to embarrass the U.S. company, such as in Barranquilla in 1932, in Honda, in Santa Marta, and in other places. Almost continuous agitation took place in Cali, but demands for expropriation at Barranquilla in 1939 precipitated the events that paradoxically allowed the American and Foreign Power Company to function in Colombia during the next two decades.

Foley, seeing that U.S. troops were not coming to bail him out, decided to imitate the tactics of the U.S. oil companies: He halted expansion work and announced in Barranquilla that the American and Foreign Power Company would make no more installations for service, not even for one-horsepower motors. This announcement in 1939 evoked a threat from the city council of Barranquilla to expropriate the utility. Curiously enough, nationalization with compensation was Foley's desired goal, and he admitted that "his company really would like to sell and get out of Colombia, even at a loss."[6] The American and Foreign Power Company expected similar nationalization proceedings to begin at Cali, and it could easily dispose of the smaller holdings in other parts of Colombia. The main reason why the operations of the American and Foreign Power Company had become unprofitable in Colombia was the refusal of the newly created state regulatory commission to approve raises in rates. The new commission had been established in accord with laws passed in 1936 and 1938, clearly after 1927 when Electric Bond and Share had bought its first Colombian holdings on the assumption that the liberal privileges originally accorded by the city councils, in particular with regard to rates, would remain indefinitely in force. The U.S. company had a strong case to seek redress through litigation, since a "good faith" argument could be made to uphold the existing rights. At least a dozen lawsuits were in progress, but not too surprisingly, the U.S. company wanted either to find an easier solution or to get out.

The U.S. government did not sent troops and instead just sent Spruille Braden as the new U.S. ambassador, apparently all that was needed. Braden recommended that C. E. Calder, the president of American and Foreign Power Company, come down from the United States to negotiate directly with the minister of development and Colombian President Eduardo Santos. Calder (even though invited by Undersecretary of State Sumner Welles) preferred to handle things from a distance and instead sent a delegation composed of one of his vice presidents and headed by Máximo Zepeda, a former minister of foreign affairs in Nicaragua. Conversations began in August 1939, and in January 1940 President Santos, under special authority from the Colombian congress, issued a decree empowering the central state to sign a contract with the U.S. utility recognizing its right to charge adequate rates. Even with the backing of Santos and Braden, the contract was delayed by nationalistic officials in the Ministry of Development who felt that the U.S. company was receiving unduly favorable treatment. Braden finally invoked diplomatic channels to press home the issue with the Colombian minister of foreign affairs on 13 November 1940, and the contract was signed the next day and soon entered into force.[7]

Thanks to Braden's intervention, a precipitate withdrawal by the U.S. company, which would have caused immense and irreparable damage to Colombia, had been averted. Even with the approval of favorable rates, the Colombian subsidiary did not make any profit remittances until 1948; clearly the American and Foreign Power Company was not draining the country like the oil companies. In spite of its valuable contributions—above all, that of relieving the central state of the burden of having to electrify many regions in Colombia, the U.S. utility became a permanent target for nationalistic attacks, generally manipulated by the merchant-brokers, which considerably weakened its resolve to stay in the country. Of the nationalistic attacks, the most bitter occurred in Cali, the topic of the following section.

Setback in Cali

The strongest agitation against the American and Foreign Power Company took place in the city of Cali. The purchase of the Cali utility from the Eder family in 1928 had gone smoothly, but in late October 1931 the U.S. company faced a strong protest movement, which was more a result of the Great Depression than anything else. As the world economic crisis slowly pushed Colombia into virtual bankruptcy, the consumption of electricity in Cali declined. The company reduced its rates on three occasions in the vain hope of trying to keep customers who were rapidly falling into total poverty. Hardest hit was the middle class, which had experienced some prosperity during the 1920s; the situation of the lower class had always been so bad that it could not conceivably be made worse.

This sudden fall in status was sorely felt by a group of blacks and mulattoes who during the prosperity of the 1920s had been able to climb into the middle class in race-conscious Cali, and who now were desperately struggling to conserve their recently gained position. They turned to politics in 1931 as a substitute livelihood and soon had a well-organized political action group that called itself the Hindustanis, although the white elite more derisively called them the "black boys" (*negritos*), a nickname that made them even angrier. To win in electoral politics, they needed an issue that would mobilize votes for their slate, and this issue they found in the American and Foreign Power Company. The Hindustanis accused the utility, which was losing money at this point, of every conceivable misdeed and held it responsible for all of Cali's problems. Since the company was disconnecting service to those who did not pay, it inadvertently gave credence to the accusations of exploitation.[8]

The Hindustani group (typical of other popular movements that occasionally have swept through Cali) demanded lower rates and, for the very poor, free service. The elections gave the Hindustani slate all the positions in the city council, a dubious victory since the municipal government was bankrupt; soon the Hindustanis realized that other channels were needed to bring more pressure upon the U.S. company if they were to at least partially fulfill their campaign promises. On 8 November 1931 the Hindustanis organized a boycott against the company and urged customers not to pay. The campaign soon extended to other parts of the city, and a blockade around the company offices kept clients from paying their bills; when the newspaper *El Relator* denounced the boycott, its offices were stoned. The governor of the province was a weak figure who avoided taking strong action against the Hindustani-led city council or against the demonstrators, who by now were even blocking the movement of the company's trucks and employees.[9]

The American and Foreign Power Company decided to appeal to President Enrique Olaya Herrera, who promptly issued strong orders to support the utility company. Since the municipal police were becoming increasingly reluctant to take sides, the Colombian government sent troops to Cali in early December 1931 as well as to garrisons in nearby towns just in case the violence assumed more dangerous proportions. Order returned with these strong measures, and although the company proposed a fourth rate reduction of 20 percent, the Hindustanis still clamored for a 70 percent reduction. Protests, after dying down over the holiday season, revived again in late January 1932. The Colombian government decided that a strong governor in the province along with more reinforcements was in order. With the full backing of president Olaya Herrera, the new governor, Valentín Ossa, negotiated secretly with the U.S. company, the Cali elite, and the Hindustanis and managed to close the whole episode without recourse to force.[10]

The Hindustani movement had by 1932 largely spent itself, only to be replaced by another force that was much more powerful and long lasting—the merchants and brokers of Cali. This group, left out of the utility's equipment purchases, wanted to participate in all the lucrative opportunities that the position of intermediary could offer. The merchants and brokers thus pushed for the city to purchase the U.S. company, supposedly on nationalistic grounds but actually to gain a share in the allocation of juicy contracts. The merchant-brokers waged an intense campaign in favor of expropriation beginning in 1933, but without success, since the city government simply lacked the funds for the compensation. They tried another tactic in 1941 when the provincial government and the city of Cali established a rival company to construct a hydroelectric dam near the city: The new company was promptly bled to death by the merchant-brokers, and the wartime shortages of equipment provided the excuse to quietly dissolve the company.[11]

The idea of a separate company did not disappear, however, it was revived again in February 1944 when the national, provincial, and city governments created the Anchicayá Power Authority. The primary obligation of this new power authority was to construct a dam at Anchicayá (Map 2), but from the beginning it was swamped with administrative problems and, above all, the problem of swallowing up funds faster than they were received. The merchant-brokers concluded that Anchicayá would never get off the ground until the U.S. utility in Cali was expropriated, and they organized another protest movement in March 1944 to take advantage of a 10 percent increase in rates. A general strike soon paralyzed Cali, and to end the strike the city council authorized the expropriation of the utility. Everything had happened so fast that even the Colombian government questioned how "spontaneous" all the demonstrations had really been, and it began to look for another alternative.[12]

The Colombian government presented a formula in late March 1944 to incorporate the Cali holdings of the American and Foreign Power Company into the existing Anchicayá Power Authority. The U.S. company, which at that time was investing in a dam at the Nima river, would continue to handle most operations, including the retail and distribution of electricity, while the Colombian government would contribute its authority as well as funding to carry out the larger hydroelectric projects. The U.S. company was genuinely interested in this arrangement, and a very promising partnership between the government and the American and Foreign Power Company was in the offing. Many details had to be worked out for this totally novel proposal to become reality; in 1945 the proposal was partially transformed into a plan to set up a partnership between the U.S. company, the city, and private Colombian investors. The final shape of the arrangement, which would have permitted foreign capital investment, provided a way to escape the shortage of funds, a problem soon to become endemic throughout Colombian utilities.

As a matter of fact, the city and provincial governments could not accept the proposal for the simple reason that they lacked the sums to cover their required shares. The merchants and brokers, who were totally opposed to the plan, created a committee to lobby for the total and complete expropriation of the utility, whose properties would pass into the hands of the city government. The reason for this insistence was very clear: While the American and Foreign Power Company was in charge, the merchants and brokers would be deprived of the juicy contracts. The U.S. company had announced its willingness to sell in 1944, provided proper compensation was paid, and as a matter of fact company officials were getting tired of the entangling protests to the point of gradually going sour on Cali.[13]

Negotiations dragged out during the rest of 1945 and 1946, and finally in 1947 an agreement was reached for the city to buy the Cali utility. The threat of a new popular protest in July 1947 had hastened the negotiations, and the nearly bankrupt city government bound itself to purchase the U.S. company's holdings. This long struggle had delayed electrification, since neither the state nor the utility company had begun the construction of new electrical projects.[14] The Anchicayá Power Authority was likewise bogged down, and many years had been wasted. The city government of Cali was saddled with a debt that became a nightmare for future mayors to the point that in 1954 the city government opened secret overtures to the American and Foreign Power Company hoping that it would again agree to run the power system.[15] Clearly a precipitate expropriation for the benefit of the small minority of merchants and brokers had ruined Cali's electrical development, but at least in many other parts of Colombia the American and Foreign Power Company continued to operate successfully.

Notes

1. Mira Wilkins, *The Maturing of Multinational Enterprise: American Business Abroad from 1914 to 1970* (Cambridge: Harvard University Press, 1974), pp. 133–134; Spruille Braden, *Diplomats and Demagogues* (New Rochelle, N.Y.: Arlington House, 1971), p. 195; *New York Times*, 15 April, 19 Oct. 1927.

2. René De La Pedraja, *Historia de la energía en Colombia, 1537–1930* (Bogotá: El Ancora, 1985), pp. 138–139; *New York Times*, 15 March 1929; *El Siglo*, 24 April 1939.

3. 8 July 1939, 821.6463 Electric Bond and Share Co/27, Record Group (RG) 59, National Archives, Washington, D.C.; *La Opinión*, 28 Feb. 1931; *El Tiempo*, 23 April 1931; *Mundo al Día*, 21 April 1931.

4. *El Nuevo Tiempo*, 7, 14 June 1931; *El Tiempo*, 3, 6 May 1931; *Mundo al Día*, 7 May, 19 June 1931; *El Espectador*, 5 May 1931; *Gil Blas*, 19 June 1931; *Fantoches*, 27 June 1931; *El Diario Nacional*, 17 July 1931.

5. 14 April 1937, 821.6463 Electric Bond and Share Co/15, RG 59.

6. 8 July 1939, 821.6463 Electric Bond/27, RG 59; *El Tiempo*, 8, 13 April 1932; Braden, *Diplomats and Demagogues*, p. 212.

7. Spruille to William Braden, 15 July 1940, Box 7, Rare Book and Manuscript Library, Columbia University; 14 Aug. 1939, 27 Nov. 1940, 821.6463 Electric Bond, RG 59; Braden, *Diplomats and Demagogues*, pp. 194–196, 212–214.

8. Memorandums, 14 Jan. 1932, 14 Dec. 1931, 821.6463 Electric Bond, RG 59; *El Sapo*, 21 March 1931; *El Nuevo Tiempo*, 25 Oct. 1931.

9. *El Relator,* 10 Nov. 1931; *El Tiempo,* 10, 19 Nov. 1931.

10. Memorandums, 14 Dec. 1931, 14 Jan. 1932, 18 Feb. 1932, 821.6463 Electric Bond, RG 59; *El Tiempo,* 7, 13 Dec. 1931; *El Espectador,* 19 Jan., 9 Feb. 1932; *El País,* 24 Feb. 1932.

11. *Heraldo Industrial,* 11, 12 Aug. 1933, 7 April 1934; *Nueva Era,* 14 April 1934; "Summary of Developments," 14 Sept. 1944, Records of the Office of American Republics Affairs, Box 34, RG 59.

12. *Liberal,* 27 March 1944; "Summary of Developments," 14 Sept. 1944, Records of the Office of American Republics Affairs, Box 34, RG 59; *New York Times,* 31 March 1944.

13. Commander Gerald C. Gross to Ambassador Wiley, 17 July 1945, John Wiley Papers, Box 5, Franklin D. Roosevelt Library; 19 Jan. 1945, 821.6463/1-1945, RG 59.

14. 7 March 1945, 22 Sept. 1947, 821.6463/9, RG 59; *El Tiempo,* 27 July 1946, 6 Aug. 1947; *New York Times,* 29 May 1946.

15. Memorandum, 10 June 1954, 821.2614/6-1054, RG 59.

8

The Private Colombian
Utilities at Bay

Ownership by private Colombian investors characterized a second type of utility. In the capital functioned the largest and most prominent of these, the Bogotá Light and Power Company, which, because of its excellent management by the Samper family, was the richest and most profitable utility in Colombia until the mid-1930s when the national and municipal governments allowed its immense potential to be wasted. In the provinces, the most successful private utility was the Bucaramanga Electric Company under careful administration by the Paillié family, but here again mistaken policies of the provincial and national governments threatened its great promise. In the countryside electricity was virtually unknown except for small, isolated factories; of these, the Industrial Corporation of Garzón was a good example, but it too later set precedents for perverting the nature and purposes of state involvement.

The Bogotá Light and Power Company

The fusion of two rival utilities was the immediate origin of the Bogotá Light and Power Company in 1927. As part of this arrangement, the city council used the proceeds from a loan by the New York firm of Baker, Kellogg & Co. to purchase the majority of the shares; however, municipal control was avoided by a voting arrangement in the Board of Directors weighted in favor of the private stockholders. The shares subscribed by the city council brought much needed capital into the Bogotá Light and Power Company, which now embarked upon the expansion plans long delayed by the ruinous competition between the two previous utilities. Work began immediately, and the Bogotá Light and Power increased its capacity to 14 megawatts by 1930 and to 22 megawatts by 1936.[1]

The expansion covered Bogotá's electricity needs until the mid-1930s, provided that rainfall was sufficient to keep the volume of the Bogotá river (the source of water for the hydroelectric plants) at adequate levels. The company had learned that prolonged drought during the summer months was inevitable at least once every five years; even more predictable was a massive public outcry whenever there was a failure to provide ample current throughout the year. To prevent public criticism from erupting, the company needed to enlarge its reserve capacity so that coal-fired plants would take up the slack whenever drought reduced the hydroelectric generation. The utility needed new financing to build the reserve steam plants, and after extended negotiations secured a loan in 1930 from the Swiss concern of Motor-Columbus. The U.S. firm Pan-American Utilities Company offered better terms, but the Bogotá company considered the offer nothing but another subterfuge in the power play by the American and Foreign Power Company; as will be recalled, in 1930 the nationalistic feelings of the Colombian owners had prevented the sale of the Bogotá Light and Power Company to the U.S. firm.[2]

In 1930 the Bogotá utility was again in a very solid position and had resumed its traditional high rate of internal savings, which made possible large expansions without recourse to more foreign loans. The company continued to enlarge the stations along the Bogotá river, but it soon saw the limits of this piecemeal approach and instead began to concentrate its efforts on two bigger projects. To tap the maximum potential of the Bogotá river and to regulate its flow, construction began on a reservoir dam at one of its tributaries, the Muña. This Muña reservoir was supposed to be in service by 1936 to cover expected demand until a larger and more dramatic expansion could take place. Seeing the demand for electricity in Bogotá accelerating so rapidly, the Bogotá Light and Power Company bought lands in 1931 to build a dam in the Guavio river that could have a potential as high as 500 megawatts—thirty times the existing capacity in Bogotá. Such an immense potential would guarantee Bogotá's electricity supply not only during the 1940s but even for the 1950s.

Incalculable benefits would accrue to Colombia, but before any substantial work could begin on Muña and Guavio, these projects were rudely interrupted by the Great Depression. Beginning in 1930, the wave of bankruptcies, crashes, and defaults swept almost all of Colombia into virtual ruin, yet towering above this panorama of economic desolation stood the Bogotá Light and Power Company. Not only had the utility company escaped unscathed from any ill effects of the Great Depression, thanks to its efficient management and its high rate of internal savings, but the company had reaped record high profits even after paying interest, dividends, and income taxes. And the estimates for the coming years promised even higher profits. The spectacle of the utility company wallowing in riches while the country sank deeper into ruin powerfully impressed the public, and indeed the Colombian government had been handed a unique opportunity to take decisive action that would have momentous long-term effects.[3]

Two opposite positions emerged as to what should be done with the accumulating capital and growing profits of the Bogotá utility. A first position, inspired by the ideas that would later be put into practice in the United States under the New Deal and that were already in force in the Soviet Union, argued that work should begin at once on the two hydroelectric projects at Muña and Guavio; they could be built simultaneously and completed much earlier than originally planned. The Colombian government could force the utility company to reinvest all of its profits into the expansion so that the demand created by these ongoing construction projects would create a powerful .stimulus to reactivate the economy, while the gigantic project of Guavio would shock the country not only out of the Great Depression but also out of underdevelopment. Consequently, rates should be kept as high as possible and even increased to assure the rapid accumulation of capital needed to finance these large projects without undue recourse to the foreign loans.

This plan meant transforming Colombia from a backwards agrarian society into a modern urban community, and needless to say, such prospects were not to the liking of most members of the Colombian elite, who shared the second opinion with the majority. The second position favored the government's extending a helping hand to those caught in the temporary jam of the Great Depression. Citing "humanitarian" arguments on behalf of the poor working class, most of whom lacked electrical service, the city council repeatedly lowered rates from 1931 to 1933, but the reductions favored upper class residences, shopkeepers, industrialists, and in particular, the merchants. Thus, rather than channeling the company's reserves into vastly enlarging Colombia's installed generating capacity, the funds went into subsidizing members of the Colombian elite, in effect bailing them out at the price of condemning the country to underdevelopment.[4]

The problem was not just that the profits accumulated before 1931 were distributed in the form of lower rates among the elite members; more serious was the decline in income, which substantially curtailed the company's ability to generate a high rate of internal savings. The company continued to be a profitable undertaking—taxes, interests, and dividends were paid punctually—but nothing could replace the loss of income caused by the lower rates. Consequently, the company had to postpone the Muña reservoir owing to lack of funds and push the Guavio project further into the remote future. Thus, in 1939 when the Muña dam should have been in operation, the Bogotá Light and Power Company instead was forced to float a loan to finance its construction. This was the company's first bond issue, and it was a total success. Local Colombian banks sounded out beforehand had agreed to subscribe the loan. On the eve of World War II the security offered by the utility company was a powerful incentive to investors, who actually over-subscribed, and this success emboldened the company in 1941 to launch another bond issue, which was also a success. The utility had to divert some of these sums to steam plants and to the stations along the Bogotá river in order to avoid excessive shortages of electricity, and installed capacity reached 40 megawatts in 1943. Work on the Muña dam was pursued but its completion required more sums to compensate for the diverted funds.[5]

Bond issues appeared to have become the saving formula for the utility. Indeed, this was the only alternative because the city council, in response to electoral pressures, had decreed rate reductions in 1941 and again in 1942 even in the face of rationing because of drought. But before the financial situation could reach a crisis, it was overtaken by a parallel development. A major reason why the city government had bought shares in 1927 was to keep the utility under Colombian control. This attitude was reversed in 1930 when the city council, under pressure from President Enrique Olaya Herrera, wanted to sell to the American and Foreign Power Company. It was the private investors who had blocked the sale. Temporarily rebuffed, the U.S. utility had embarked upon an acquisition campaign, buying up as many of the private shares as could be enticed away from private Colombian investors, so that the next purchase attempt would not be halted so easily. However, New York headquarters gradually became skeptical of these moves and concluded that the operations of its Colombian subsidiary, besides being unprofitable, were already overextended and thus refused to release more funds to complete the acquisition of a majority control. Nevertheless, a substantial number of shares had been bought by 1934. By then, however, the Colombian government was no longer as enthusiastic about having the American and Foreign Power Company operate the Bogotá utility.

A partial alternative to the U.S. menace came from the Swiss. The Swiss concern of Motor-Columbus had extended foreign credit to the Bogotá utility in 1930, but this loan could not be repaid in foreign currency after 1933, when Colombia became the last Latin American country to stop payments on its foreign debt.[6] The Bogotá Light and Power Company had the funds to pay, but only in Colombian currency. After complex negotiations, which dragged out from 1933 until 1938, Motor-Columbus agreed to exchange the pending loan for shares—

issued expressly for that purpose—in the Bogotá Light and Power Company. The city government still held the majority of the shares, with the remaining shares divided almost equally between Motor-Columbus, the American and Foreign Power Company, and private Colombian investors, predominantly the members of the Samper family. A careful balancing act ensued, with the Samper family playing off the city against either or both of the foreign companies in order to retain control over the Bogotá utility.

By 1939 the company was really a "mixed" operation, although in the practice of its daily operations, distribution of dividends, and payment of taxes it continued to function as a private firm. The replacement of most private Colombian investors by the foreign companies meant that the Samper family, in order to retain control, had to accede to many unsound petitions from the city council, in particular to rate reductions, as in 1941 and 1942. These measures could not but undermine confidence in the solidity of the company. To meet the ongoing expenses of constructing the Muña reservoir, the company had to make a third bond issue in 1943, but unlike the first two, this 1943 issue was a failure: Investors did not think a company that charged such low rates would be able to repay the loans and meet the interest payments. This conclusion was unfortunate, since the loan was sound and the electricity business was profitable. Although the company could not raise enough capital out of income because of the low electricity rates, it could guarantee a return on the investment. In order to avoid halting work on the Muña reservoir, the utility agreed to issue shares. Subscription to these shares was assured because Motor-Columbus and the American and Foreign Power Company had saved all their accrued dividends from their stocks in local banks and were willing to reinvest. These stock purchases doubled the respective number of shares of the two foreign companies, each of which now held almost one-fourth of the total shares, reducing at the same time the city government to the position of single largest stockholder.[7]

The Samper family had to continue its balancing act, playing shifting combinations against each other, and the whole situation was a time bomb that could explode at any moment. By the end of World War II, the company admitted in 1945 that it was facing a crisis because the rapidly rising demand for electricity had outstripped the influx of capital, so that the effects of the 1943 share subscription had long since worn off. As the Bogotá Light and Power Company entered the postwar period, the utility desperately looked for new sources to finance the long overdue expansion projects needed to meet the growing demand for electricity in Colombia's capital city.

The Bucaramanga Electric Company

The largest city between Bogotá and the Venezuelan frontier 400 miles to the north, Bucaramanga, was the site of the second most important private utility in Colombia during the 1930s and 1940s. The Bucaramanga Electric Company had undergone several reorganizations since the pioneering years in the 1890s when it first introduced hydroelectricity into Colombia. The Paillié family, descendants of nineteenth-century French immigrants, had been the owners since 1927. There were other minority stockholders, such as the Ogliastri and Clausen families, but in principle the company was kept in the hands of the Paillié family by a contractual clause that required the permission of all the stockholders to sell shares to outsiders and by the practice of offering new share issues only to the present holders. The Bucaramanga Electric Company was never able to shake the image of a closed group that exploited its monopoly position. In fact, the opposite was the case: The Paillié family members had extensive dealings in real estate and retailing—activities which generated the bulk of their income—and they entered electricity more from a desire to acquire prestige and to endow their native city with a utility company comparable to Bogotá's.[8]

During the 1930s the company had made small additions to its generating capacity, but the recurrence of droughts strongly suggested that an exclusive dependence on hydroelectricity should be avoided. Because Bogotá was surrounded with abundant coal deposits, steam generating plants had been the obvious solution, but no mines were within easy distance of Bucaramanga, which until 1960 remained one of the most isolated cities in Colombia, without even paved roads for access. Fortunately, a solution was found nearby in the Barrancabermeja oil fields: Exxon agreed to supply fuel for diesel engines to move the new electric generators in Bucaramanga. The utility ordered two diesel engines from England in 1940, but World War II paralyzed both their shipment and manufacture.

During the war the existing plants worked smoothly in spite of the lack of imported spare parts, but without foreign generating equipment, the utility could not expand its capacity. The inevitable electricity shortage was cited by other members of the Bucaramanga elite as justification for a different solution. Some elite members felt threatened by the ascendancy that the Paillié family was acquiring in the city because of its multiple economic activities; moreover, the merchants and brokers in the city resented being left out of the commissions on equipment purchases, as the Bucaramanga Electric Company did its own procurement without involving other intermediaries. Local politicians were easily tempted by the prospects of bringing the utility under their control to reward political debts, and they eagerly provoked a series of clashes between the company and the city council over the latter's nonpayment of its light bills.[9]

Rebuffed by the Bucaramanga Electric Company, the politicians joined with the merchants and brokers in hopes of establishing a rival, more pliant public utility, yet they totally underestimated the magnitude of the challenge: One study commissioned by the provincial government and the Bucaramanga city council claimed that a 2-megawatt plant would suffice to cover the needs of the city for the next fifty years! More careful studies soon revised both this estimate and the expected costs upwards to a degree that convinced the provincial and city governments that they could not afford to create a rival public utility to harness the waters of the Lebrija river. Only the central government possessed enough resources to carry out such a large undertaking in Bucaramanga. After intense lobbying and political pressures, the Colombian government finally agreed to provide 51 percent of the capital for the new Lebrija Power Authority, which was formally created in 1943. The state provided annual installment payments between 1943 and 1946, but capital did not accumulate because the money was spent faster than it came in. No complaints arose, however, because the recipient of the procurement contracts issued by the new public authority was the Bucaramanga elite, who only wished an indefinite continuation of this lucrative relationship. Work on the Lebrija dam scarcely started, and the initiative for generating electricity remained with the Bucaramanga Electric Company.[10]

Once World War II was over, the first item of business for the private utility was to put the equipment ordered in 1940 into service. The two diesel engines finally arrived in 1947 and after a speedy installation were on line to compensate for the drop in generation caused by the droughts of the late 1940s. The company also had ordered another water turbine in 1946, but it did not reach Colombia until 1948, when it was finally installed. The Bucaramanaga Electric Company did not want to have only diesel engines, which required higher fuel expenses, and instead banked on the drought years coming to an end. Although rationing was temporarily imposed in 1949, the drought ended in 1950 and 1951 with abundant rainfall that made possible a more profitable operation thanks to a greater reliance on the cheaper hydroelectricity.[11]

The company was aware that further expansion—both in diesel and hydroelectric power—was in order, but it trusted on its tried and proven way of raising capital. From 1945 and continuing on an almost annual basis until 1950, the Bucaramanga Electric Company financed its expansion out of dividends. The close family links, and the fact that all the relatives had other sources of income, allowed them to save the dividends and reinvest them into the next year's issue of shares. In this way, the Paillié family retained control over the company and at the same time, owing to its own high rate of internal savings (which, besides the dividends, included setting aside capital reserves), the company paid for expansion in capacity easily and without recourse to outside financing. This success was largely due to the extremely able management of the last two presidents of the company, Enrique Paillié and Victor Paillié, both of whom kept very tight reins on the company and did not allow the slightest waste but at the same time encouraged moderate growth in consumption by a reasonable rate policy.[12]

The method by which the Paillié family financed expansions during the 1940s strikingly resembled what the Samper family had practiced in Bogotá during the first decade of the twentieth century—practices that had led to a form of state participation in the case of the Bogotá Light and Power Company. At least as far as the 1950s were concerned, the central government could safely leave electricity in the hands of this company—one of the most successful utilities in Colombia wholly under private ownership—and instead channel its significant but limited resources into the immense task of meeting the crying needs of many other regions of the country. The failure of the Lebrija Power Authority, which so far had accomplished nothing, did not, however, prove to be sufficient warning for the central government, which, unwisely, and in response to local pressures, began to harass the Bucaramanga Electric Company. The merchants and brokers mobilized protests that convinced the government to delay a 1947 request for a rise in electricity rates for three years, so that the company, receiving less income, necessarily slowed down its expansion (although still another water turbine was ordered). The private utility did some intense lobbying of its own in Bogotá and at last convinced the Colombian government in 1949 to authorize the overdue hikes in rates. Beginning in 1950, a period of abundant rainfall guaranteed higher profits because a greater reliance on hydroelectricity reduced operating expenses.[13] The Bucaramanga Electric Company prepared to embark upon a period of large-scale expansion to meet the growing demand in the city, but the Paillié family had overlooked some powerful political forces that would soon give their opponents an opportunity to strike a deadly blow (see Chapter 10).

The Industrial Corporation of Garzón

An example of a third type of private utility was the Industrial Corporation of Garzón, which was founded in 1915 to grind imported U.S. wheat. The company converted the original water mill to hydroelectric power in 1921 and began to sell electricity to nearby homes from a very small 25-kilowatt plant. An enlargement to 65 kilowatts in 1932 allowed the company to also sell current for the electric motors in the town's small workshops. The flour mill was typical of the kinds of industries that had branched out into the utility business, like the Obregón enterprises in Barranquilla, but in the case of Garzón the utility was located in the isolated and normally backwards Colombian countryside, in effect providing this one spot with a headstart on rural electrification.[14]

The Industrial Corporation reaped high profits every year during the 1920s and the 1930s. The many applications for electric service in homes and shops convinced the company to construct a hydroelectric plant at La Pita, which would increase the capacity tenfold to 850 kilowatts. Local short-term credits financed the purchase of the General Electric equipment and covered installation expenses, but when work began in 1947, the initial optimism faded. Trusting the assurances of the consulting firm of Vicente Pizano Hernández, the corporation had underestimated the costs, but later, rather than overrule him, it instead acceded to complete the purchases with cheaper equipment from local distributors of European manufacturers. Adding the European parts to the General Electric equipment produced a hodgepodge of brands that did not fit together, and in any case the funds ran out before the hydroelectric plant could be finished. The creditors, in particular the Bank of Bogotá, prepared to pounce on the assets of the corporation.

Word of this imminent bankruptcy spread rapidly, and the stunned owners of the company could not understand how decades of large annual profits had given way in less than a year to financial collapse. The Industrial Corporation of Garzón frantically searched for help in 1948, but with very little success. An issue of shares failed to attract new stockholders, and the owners either could not or would not buy more shares. Neither local private banks nor those in Neiva or Bogotá showed any interest in extending any more short-term credits. State banks were approached, but their charters prohibited making loans to private utilities.

With nowhere else left to go, the corporation approached the newly created Electraguas, an agency of the Colombian government charged with developing the country's water and power resources. At the prodding of a high Electraguas official from Neiva, the state agreed to extend the loan. The company appeared to have been saved, but when the director of Electraguas, Julián Cock, traveled to Garzón in August 1948 to personally inform the Board of Directors that by law the only way the state could provide funds was by buying shares, the board immediately ignored the offer, since it was an article of faith with private business to refuse government partnership in any enterprise. However, barely three months later in October, the Industrial Corporation could no longer avoid the hard facts—it was either bankruptcy or the state. Reluctantly, the board consented to the latter.

Electraguas conditioned the purchase on changing the voting rights at stockholders' meetings so that the one-fifth of the total shares purchased by the state would have equal representation, since the existing voting system penalized large stockholders. But when the corporation complied with the required reform, another state agency that regulated private companies knocked down the change. The old voting system, which in effect meant leaving the company under complete private control, remained in force. Both the private owners and Electraguas considered the entry of the state into the Industrial Corporation of Garzón as a temporary emergency measure that would end once the company was back on its feet. Nowhere was there a realization that bigger projects, vast by local standards, were simply out of the reach of private enterprise, not only because of the lack of capital but also because of the strain placed upon the scarce technical and managerial talents. As elsewhere in Colombia, in Garzón the central government gradually stumbled into playing a role in electric power, but rather than directly facing up to the challenge in a coherent and planned way, found itself trying to keep private enterprise alive.[15]

Electraguas continued subscribing to more shares to meet mounting expenses until by 1950 it became the majority shareholder, but always with a minority voice in the Board of Directors. The only real solution was to fuse the corporation with the recently created Huila Power Authority, which served the province around Neiva. Precisely to avoid that fusion, Electraguas agreed to purchase from the company the excess current to electrify small rural towns near Garzón; the Huila Power Authority installed the transmission and distribution system at its own cost. But the success of the project depended upon the completion of the hydroelectric plant at La Pita—no easy task because the plant required extensive repairs to compensate for the previous deficiencies in construction. Both directly and through the Huila Power Authority, Electraguas poured money into the company, but with no visible results. The Industrial Corporation of Garzón, which had been so loath to accept government participation, was now discovering the benefits of state money: The company spent funds as rapidly as they were provided, even buying a brick factory that eventually failed. The Board of Directors refused to heed any advice from Electraguas, and the state agency had no choice but to begin judicial proceedings against its own company in 1953.

The creditors moved even faster in their attempts to seize the assets of the corporation, and to head off this danger, Electraguas reluctantly accepted a proposal in 1954 to separate the company into two—one for the flour mill, the other for the utility. The separation meant favoring those speculators who had accumulated shares at giveaway prices, but unfortunately this was the only way the state could keep the electric plants—at the price of having to pay all the outstanding debts of the Industrial Corporation of Garzón. To run up as many debts as possible, the corporation—with the guidance of the former high official of Electraguas who was now one of the stockholders—procrastinated putting the agreement into effect until 1955. The value of the assets the state received was dwarfed by the sum of money it had poured into the corporation over an eight-year period without any apparent results.

In spite of this outcome, the private sector did not consider Garzón a failure, and as a matter of fact, of the three utility companies discussed in this chapter, the Industrial Corporation of Garzón looked most to the future. The highly profitable eight-year relationship with the state had come to an end only because private individuals had overreached themselves, but the pattern of milking the state had been established.[16] The search was on in Huila and elsewhere in Colombia to find ways to permanently transfer funds from the rich state utilities to private individuals, and Garzón had shown it could be done.

Notes

1. Empresas Unidas de Energía Eléctrica, *Informe del gerente, 1930* (Bogotá: Cromos, 1930), pp. 9, 11; René De La Pedraja, *Historia de la energía en Colombia, 1537–1930* (Bogotá: El Ancora, 1985), pp. 87–88.

2. Empresas Unidas de Energía Eléctrica, *Informe del gerente, 1929* (Bogotá: Cromos, 1929), pp. 6, 20–21; De La Pedraja, *Energía*, p. 89.

3. *El Espectador,* 23 Dec. 1931; *Nuevo Tiempo,* 16 March 1932; Empresas Unidas de Energía Eléctrica, *Informe del gerente, 1931* (Bogotá: Imprenta de la Luz, 1931), pp. 13–14; *Fantoches,* Oct. 1931.

4. *Nuevo Tiempo,* 16 March 1932; *El País,* 4 April 1932; *El Tiempo,* 14 Nov. 1933; *El Espectador,* 15 March 1932.

5. Empresas Unidas de Energía Eléctrica, *Informe del gerente, 1939* (Bogotá: Prag, 1939), pp. 8–9; Ibid., 1943, pp. 6–9; *El Tiempo,* 3 April 1932, 21 Jan. 1942; *El Espectador,* 6 March 1942.

6. David Bushnell, *Eduardo Santos and the Good Neighbor Policy, 1938–1942* (Gainesville: University of Florida Press, 1967), pp. 67–68; Stephen J. Randall, *The Diplomacy of Modernization: Colombian-American Relations, 1920–1940* (Toronto: University of Toronto Press, 1977), pp. 70–72.

7. 14 April 1937, 821.6463 Electric Co./15, Record Group (RG) 59, National Archives, Washington, D.C.; Empresas Unidas de Energía Eléctrica, *Informe, 1942* (Bogotá: Prag, 1943), pp. 6–7; *El Espectador,* 31 July 1942.

8. De La Pedraja, *Energía,* pp. 106, 111.

9. Compañía Eléctrica de Bucaramanga, *Informes y balances, 1946* (Bucaramanga: Editorial Selecta, 1947).

10. *Liberal*, 30 Aug. 1945, 2 Feb. 1946, 28 Feb. 1947; *El Tiempo*, 1 March 1946.

11. Compañía Eléctrica de Bucaramanga, *Informes y balances, 1947* (Bucaramanga: Editorial Selecta, 1948); Ibid., 1950 and 1951.

12. Printed handbills of Compañía Eléctrica de Bucaramanga announcing share issues, 1946, 1947; Compañía Eléctrica de Bucaramanga, *Informes y balances, 1948* (Bucaramanga, Editorial Selecta, 1949); 24 July 1951, 821.2614/7-2451, RG 59.

13. De La Pedraja, *Energía*, pp. 72–75; *El Liberal*, 12 Jan. 1947; *El Tiempo*, 16 Jan. 1947.

14. De La Pedraja, *Energía*, pp. 104, 134–35.

15. Instituto Nacional de Aprovechamiento de Aguas y Fomento Eléctrico, *Informe del gerente, 1954* (Bogotá: Aedita Ltd., 1954), pp. 9–11, 34.

16. In 1956 one of the private speculators who had most benefited from the previous transactions sued Electraguas for damages, hoping to milk even more funds out of the state.

9

From Municipal
to Central State Action

A third type of utility were those owned by the city governments. This type existed throughout Colombia but was most pronounced in the provinces of Antioquia and Caldas. In Medellín, the capital of Antioquia, functioned the Medellín Municipal Power Company, the second largest utility company in the country and the best example of city government ownership. The difficulties Medellín faced were also experienced by other municipal utilities; thus, by the 1930s, municipal ownership ceased to spread, and by the 1940s the city utilities were gradually being absorbed into state organizations, with two exceptions. No takeover goals had motivated the central government when it first entered the electricity business in the 1930s. But diverse political pressures soon dragged the state into regulating the larger companies and providing subsidies for struggling utilities.

The Medellín Municipal Power Company

A pioneer of municipal electrical service, Medellín had the largest city-owned utility in Colombia. A great sense of public duty had characterized the operation in its early years, but by the late 1920s the members of the city elite could no longer resist the immense opportunities for personal profit. Merchant-brokers negotiated a loan in the United States after having obtained secret authorization from the city council and also signed contracts for equipment purchases. The U.S. Senate investigated these transactions, and although much of the evidence had disappeared, no doubt remained that this wave of speculation had greatly benefited the merchant-brokers of Medellín. The resulting loan financed the installation in 1932 of the first 10-megawatt unit of the hydroelectric plant Guadalupe I, thus tripling the previous capacity of 5 megawatts.[1]

The desire of commissions on the part of the local merchant-brokers had endowed Medellín with a supply of electricity supposedly too big for a modest city like Medellín, yet when the city council set rates very low in an effort to dispose of the huge surplus capacity, this had the unforeseen result of initiating a period of lively economic activity. As a result, demand grew so rapidly that the first unit of Guadalupe I installed in 1932 became too small by 1936 and the Medellín Municipal Power Company had to install in quick succession the three remaining 10-megawatt units in 1938, 1939, and 1942. These expansions were never made in time to avoid repeated power shortages, and the capacity of each unit was loaded as soon as it came on line. These enlargements required investments that were huge by Medellín's standards, and only by a combination of manufacturers' credits and a 1938 bond issue were funds gathered with great difficulty; the city government subscribed a majority of the bond issue, while industrialists and local banks assumed the remainder.[2]

Finding the funds for each additional unit became more and more difficult since the Colombian banking system had never developed the ability to extend long-term loans and instead remained in the profitable stage of extending only high-interest short-term commercial loans. By 1942 the Medellín Municipal Power Company concluded that foreign financing was the only alternative left for the pressing expansions needed to meet the rapidly rising demand for electricity. World War II, which had already delayed the completion of Guadalupe I until 1942 because of the shortage of shipping space, had likewise dried up foreign credits, so power shortages and poor service continued to plague Medellín. In 1943 negotiations with the Export-Import Bank began so that Medellín would be first in line when the credits were again opened at the end of the war. The Export-Import Bank duly granted a loan of $3.5 million in 1946 for the Río Grande hydroelectric project, while the National Association of Industrialists collected sums for another loan to cover local expenses in pesos. The factory owners were extremely concerned over power shortages that crippled their factories, and they were making huge sacrifices, in effect decapitalizing their industries in order to finance the Medellín Municipal Power Company. It was clear that the industrialists could not sustain this high rate of saving, and as a matter of fact in later decades these earlier efforts returned to haunt many factories that, by neglecting to renew their equipment, became less competitive by the 1970s.[3]

Some work had begun on Río Grande even before the end of the war, but the approval of the Export-Import Bank loan in 1946 did not immediately intensify the pace because by then the Medellín Municipal Power Company was reconsidering the whole project. Guadalupe II, with a potential of 250 megawatts, had from the earliest studies appeared as the logical continuation of Guadalupe I, but this large figure of 250 megawatts had scared local officials. Instead, they opted for a smaller expansion of only 50 megawatts in Río Grande, but this project would take longer to bring on line because expensive tunnels had to be dug underground to carry water to the turbines. It was the first time that these underground construction techniques were to be used in Colombian power projects, and their mastery took considerable time.

Not unexpectedly, construction moved forward slowly on the Río Grande project until the shortages and severe rationing of electricity in 1946 convinced the Medellín Municipal Power Company to divert funds into the first 10-megawatt unit of Guadalupe II. When completed in 1949, this first unit brought temporary relief to the city's supply of electricity, yet something was clearly wrong when simple arithmetic revealed that for the same price, Medellín had received only 10 megawatts of Guadalupe II instead of the originally planned 50 megawatts of the Río Grande project. Furthermore, the municipal utility fell months behind in its payroll and laid off most of its personnel, and work on the Río Grande project was paralyzed. To bail out the municipal utility, the Medellín city council turned to the Colombian government and received several large loans from national government institutions, in particular from the Central State Bank. Bogotá was willing to extend additional loans to ensure the completion of the Río Grande project, but only on the condition that the central government be allowed more control. This price was too high, and in order to conserve its cozy relationship with the city utility, the Medellín elite once again sought financing from the Export-Import Bank so that the foreign loan could counterbalance the growing influence of the Colombian government.[4]

U.S. manufacturers eagerly backed the loan application, but the Export-Import Bank was very unhappy at the way the earlier loan had been spent and did not want to lend any more money until the Medellín Municipal Power Company adopted better operational methods. As a first step, the Export-Import Bank urged the utility to hire a reputable firm of U.S. engineers to point out what the problems were. This was a tough request for the Medellín elite, but between having Bogotá or the Americans look over the company's records, the elite preferred the latter; consequently, Gilbert Associates Inc. was hired early in 1950 and by October of that year had completed its report.[5]

The findings were extremely revealing about the operations of government institutions in Colombia, be they municipal or national organs. The problem, according to Gilbert Associates, was with the Board of Directors: Only three were businessmen, while of the other four, three were city council members and one was the mayor of the city, thus giving the politicians a majority. The highly politicized control had brought about unfortunate consequences—for example, a high turnover rate among utility executives and a diffusion of authority that made carrying out orders a slow and doubtful process. The company had made profits, but these had been transferred into the common revenues of the city so that, in effect, the city government was using utility funds to balance its budget rather than to finance enlargements of hydroelectric capacity. Needless to say, there was no reserve capacity for emergencies and demand had repeatedly outstripped the supply of current. The rate structure subsidized residential consumption and penalized factories— thus slowing down industrialization—because the politicians found it more acceptable to push through rates that, while appearing to favor the lower classes, in fact favored upper class residences. The interest payments on the outstanding loans placed such a huge burden upon the company that it desperately needed relief. The report recommended that the temporary moratorium which the Central State Bank and the National Association of Industrialists had granted should be extended.

No less serious were the problems with the Río Grande project, which were at least as bad as those faced in the construction of Guadalupe I and II. Gilbert Associates revealed the reason for all these project complications: Infuential brokers had negotiated contracts for local construction companies that lacked experience and skills. Continuous cost overruns and malfunctions in the equipment were the result, so that from the late 1930s frequent interruptions in service were the rule. In the case of the Río Grande project, the money had simply vanished with very limited construction work done. The Río Grande engineering study had been sloppily finished in a rush in 1946, and serious errors existed in the original design. To correct these defects the utility had incurred additional expenses. So badly had the planning been done that the transmission network lacked the capacity to carry the current from the new plants to the city, and the urban distribution network was in such a bad state that it could not handle the additional loads.

Gilbert Associates recommended, besides a whole host of technical changes, that the Board of Directors be changed to give businessmen a majority so that the Medellín utility could be run on sound principles. The Export-Import Bank conditioned the second loan on the acceptance of this recommendation. Unfortunately, this diagnosis by Gilbert Associates partially missed the cause: it was not the politicians who were responsible for the sorry state; rather, it was the existence of a class of businessmen, the merchant-brokers, who continually jockeyed for contracts from the Medellín Municipal Power Company. The politicians served a useful role by harmonizing the conflicting demands of rival merchant-brokers; if businessmen predominated on the Board of Directors, they would exploit the municipal company for their individual benefit rather than that of a larger class.

The Medellín elite did not want a few of its members to receive such extraordinary privileges, but at the same time it needed the Export-Import Bank loan to escape control from the central government in Bogotá. Trapped between the two alternatives, the members of the Medellín elite bitterly fought each other until they reached a deadlock; the most that the Medellín elite could promise the Americans was that the mayor would be a "businessman"—under a very loose definition. Assistant Secretary of State Edward Miller, who was very familiar with these intra-elite fights in Latin America, concluded that this was about all that could be achieved and that the United States, as a good faith gesture, should grant the second Export-Import Bank loan. The funds went to purchase the two 25-megawatt generators, all that was needed to complete the Río Grande project formally inaugurated in 1952. Good luck had accompanied the Medellín elite this time, but it had received the message that the municipal utility had to be handled better in the future, or at least more discreetly.[6]

The new hydroelectric plant at Río Grande still did not allow Medellín to catch up: Although installed capacity had doubled from 25 megawatts in 1938 to 51 in 1949, Gilbert Associates had calculated that capacity should have quadrupled. In effect, with each new project, the delays in carrying it to a conclusion and the cost overruns meant that the lag increased even faster. Occasionally, a big project appeared to temporarily put supply ahead of demand, but the latter quickly overtook the former. Having the utility company owned by the municipal government was very convenient for the local elite, but it was an arrangement that could be generalized to other cities only if they possessed at least some capital and managerial talent.[7] In practice, the only city outside of Medellín that had been able to sustain a municipal utility company was Bogotá, starting in 1951. For the rest of Colombia, areas in which neither private nor foreign utility companies operated had no choice but to direct their desperate pleas for help to the government in Bogotá.

The Origins of Central State Intervention: Electraguas -

From the introduction of electric service into Colombia in 1890, the central government had almost never intervened and had left the task of supervising the private utility companies to the city and provincial governments. The state had all the constitutional powers to intervene, but government leaders had no awareness of the need to provide a coherent blueprint for electrification across the country. As a result, costly and irreparable mistakes multiplied and Colombia lagged behind in electrification.

Curiously enough, concern for this lag was not what led the government to begin more active participation in electricity. As Colombia's population mushroomed during the first half of the twentieth century, the agricultural frontier expanded as well, bringing not only greater pressure upon the land but also upon the supply of water. Quarrels over water rights, very rarely provoked by electric plants and usually the result of conflicting claims between landowners, had broken out throughout Colombia. The clashes escalated to the point where the city and provincial governments found themselves unable to cope. To meet the situation, the Colombian congress approved Law 113 in 1928, which for the first time vested in the national government the authority to grant all future concessions over water rights. However, this law did not have an immediate national impact, since the concessions previously granted to the utilities by municipal and provincial governments remained valid; only as landowners and utilities needed more water to meet rising demand would the authority to grant future concessions gradually come into full play.[8]

A few cases did come up from the very beginning; for example, the Medellín Municipal Power Company made several applications of the law in the late 1920s that raised the question of whether the power to grant a water concession gave the government the authority to set rates for utilities that used the water. A bitter legal debate raged over the extent of the state's jurisdiction, and to decide the issue, the congress passed Law 109 in 1936. This law directly stated that the Colombian government had the authority to set rates for those utilities enjoying concessions granted after 1928 (but without usurping the right of city councils to set *lower* rates). Furthermore, the law created an office in the Ministry of Development to supervise and regulate the rates. As far as companies enjoying earlier municipal or provincial concessions went, the government could do nothing to alter the situation. However, the American and Foreign Power Company did not like the drift things were taking and initiated a lawsuit to declare the law unconstitutional. The judicial system upheld the validity of the legislation.[9]

Foiled in this approach, the American and Foreign Power Company expressed its total dissatisfaction and began a campaign that—thanks to the help of U.S. Ambassador Spruille Braden—resulted in a separate law that promised fair rates for the U.S. utility company. The Medellín Municipal Power Company fared better than others because the central government did not want to ruffle the feelings of that most sensitive region. The Bogotá Light and Power Company, however, faced a difficult task. As the holder of a national water concession, the utility was caught in a cross fire between both city council and state regulation. Representatives of the Bogotá utility talked with the minister of development and the president of Colombia to impress upon them the need for a rate increase to keep expansion work from coming to a halt; the arguments were persuasive, and the central state authorized a hike in 1939, but this was not the end of the problem. Two years later, the Bogotá Light and Power Company saw the earlier efforts undone when the city council decreed rate reductions. Only by appealing to the central government did the company halt further reductions; in any case, the Bogotá utility had fallen into a position of undue dependence on the will of Colombian government officials—a dangerous dependence that would bring harmful consequences ten years later.

Important as the authority to fix the rates was, officials at the Ministry of Development felt that this approach was too narrow and pressed for more decisive state intervention in electrification. Congress agreed, and it passed Law 126 in 1938 to authorize the central government to contribute funds for municipal and provincial electrification projects. Congress also gave the authority to regulate rates a new stature by transforming the former office into a state regulatory commission; it did not, however, set up this commission as an independent agency, so that over the next thirty years it wandered back and forth among different ministries. The 1938 law furthermore declared the municipal ownership of the private utilities to be in the public interest and to that effect authorized the national government to extend loans so that poor city governments could buy out private investors. Congress had inserted this last measure into the bill to placate public protests against high rates in Bogotá, the goal being to threaten the Bogotá Light and Power Company with expropriation as a means to push rates down.[10]

Congress appropriated funds in the national budget to the state regulatory commission, which then distributed money for the construction of small municipal plants. This first taste of central state money whetted the appetite of the city governments for more funding to face their myriad problems. In response to powerful local pressures, the central government created in late 1940 a special Municipal Development Fund to finance the construction of water and sewage systems, primary schools, hospitals, and electric plants. Originally administered by the state regulatory commission, by the late 1940s the fund had become an independent agency in its own right and in the early 1950s became known as the Institute for Municipal Development. Its most important contribution to electricity was the installation of small generating plants needed to power the pumps of municipal water systems.

On closer analysis, however, the results of central government participation in electricity were disappointing. The rate-fixing authority became meaningless because it was constantly overruled by intense local political pressures, and the sums appropriated by the congress were small and highly irregular. The state regulatory commission and the Ministry of Development found themselves distributing pittances to many towns and small cities and then teaching local officials how to read manufacturers' catalogs so that the city governments could order the proper equipment from foreign factories. The equipment ordered usually only provided power in the 100-kilowatt range and were frequently fueled by diesel or gasoline, so that besides being expensive to operate, they did not solve a town's electricity needs and had no noticeable effect upon the country's total electrification. The officials at the state regulatory commission were the first to realize that this poorhouse method was not working, and to buttress their arguments for a bolder approach, they first began to gather information on Colombia's electrical plants.[11]

The state regulatory commission concluded that in the congress's haste to approve the 1938 law authorizing the expropriation of private utilities (none had so far been purchased), two fundamental issues had been neglected. First and foremost was the lack of adequate funds; to depend on the national budget for these purchases brought them into competition with many conflicting pressures that scarcely left anything for electricity. Second, in the rush to help local utilities, the government had fallen into the piecemeal allocation of minuscule plants; this wasteful approach had to be replaced by large hydroelectric projects to cover the needs of two or even three provinces at once. Such vast undertakings could not be carried out without a coherent national plan; government officials talked about hiring some U.S. experts at the end of 1943 to elaborate the plan, since nobody in Colombia knew what planning was all about, but the proposal floundered with the change of ministers. The idea remained in the background and was finally carried out ten years later in 1954 when the first national electrification plan was developed. But by then, as the next chapter will show, political and economic realities had imposed a schedule for electrification independent of any nationwide planning considerations.[12]

In 1944 the state regulatory commission launched the trial balloon of creating a bank for electrification, with the capital to come from a special "electric tax" levied on consumers—in effect a disguised rate hike. The logic behind the bank was irrefutable—namely, that consumption had to be sacrificed in order to finance capital investment—but no politician would survive such a proposal, and it died quickly. In 1945 a modified formula called for the establishment of an Institute for Electric Development, which could be financed by several possible alternatives. Initially the proposal fared badly because members of the Colombian elite were not interested in long-term electrical development; all they wanted was to ensure very low rates for themselves. The proposal did not die this time, however, because it was joined and eventually overtaken by a parallel movement. The owners of large landed states had always clamored for flood protection and some irrigation, and to meet these demands the Colombian government had created local commissions in different parts of the country to study and solve the water problems. In response to this proposal to establish an institute to handle electrical development, the landowners quickly asked themselves a question: If electricity could have its own institute, why not one for water also? But the national government could not afford two institutes, in spite of the fact that water and energy, as two of the most fundamental essentials for human society, would seem to amply qualify for the undivided attention of separate institutes. Gradually the consensus formed to fuse the functions of water and electricity into a single institute. The proposed institute would be for both electrical development and water, but before the bill was approved, a highly indicative change in priority occurred: The order was reversed and in the final draft the title became the Institute for Water Usage and Electrical Development (although in the common abbreviation, Electraguas, electricity at least remained first).[13]

With the support of the major landowners, congress at the end of 1946 easily passed Law 80, which created Electraguas to carry out flood control, irrigation, and electrical projects throughout the country. Congress introduced one major innovation of far-reaching significance into the law: Besides any additional appropriations in the national budget, Electraguas would regularly receive all royalty income from the petroleum concessions. Here at last the crucial link was made between petroleum and electricity, and the nonrenewable natural resource was reinvested into developing permanent sources of energy in the form of hydroelectricity. The royalties paid by the oil companies were so small that the full potential of this measure was never realized, but at least congress had set electricity financing in the right direction. When Electraguas began to function early in 1947, the newly created institute discovered that the national government had no major electrification projects in mind and that the real purpose of Law 80 had been to channel the oil royalties into the pockets of major landowners. Thus, in the first few years of operations, Electraguas literally found itself mired in the mud as it attempted to provide the pet irrigation works demanded by the landlords for their estates.[14]

The city of Medellín soon dumped the huge expense of canalizing the Medellín river on Electraguas, and the institute, whose first manager, Julián Cock, was from Antioquia, quickly acceded. Not willing to fall behind, the Bogotá city council joined with landlords of surrounding estates to urge flood control for the Bogotá river. Yet even Electraguas realized that not enough funds were available for such a vast undertaking.

To appease the recurrent political pressures, Electraguas proposed instead to stop the annual floods of La Picota (one tributary of the Bogotá river) to the south of the capital. But since the surrounding lands belonged to the Colombian government, the city council and the major landowners soon lost interest. By the time Electraguas had elaborated a construction project for La Picota in the 1950s, unscrupulous real estate speculators had "invaded" the state lands with squatters, thus occupying the area reserved for the proposed reservoir. With no dams to stop the water at La Picota, the families who lived in abject poverty continued to be flooded out of their slum dwellings each year. But anywhere else, their situation would have been even worse.[15]

As if Electraguas did not have enough problems, the rate-fixing authority of the state regulatory commission had not been transferred to the new institute, leaving a huge gap in its limited range of powers. This lack has been sorely felt down to the present, but so intense have been the political pressures upon rate fixing that not until a major transformation occurs in Colombian society will the state be able to join all aspects of electrification into a single powerful agency. In the late 1940s Electraguas was the best Colombia could do, and the new officials, full of enthusiasm and great hopes, prepared to tackle head on the immense problems of electrification that soon fell upon the institute, as the next chapter shows.

Notes

1. U.S. Senate Finance Committee, *Sale of Foreign Bonds or Securities in the U.S.*, 3 Parts (Washington, D.C.: GPO, 1932), Part 3; René De La Pedraja, *Historia de la energía en Colombia, 1537–1930* (Bogotá: El Ancora, 1985), pp. 96, 98; *Revista Empresas Públicas de Medellín* 2 (1980):11.

2. E. Livardo Ospina, *Una vida, una lucha, una victoria* (Medellín: Empresas Públicas de Medellín, 1966), pp. 456–457; *El Diario*, 7 Oct. 1938; *Liberal*, 10, 24 Oct. 1941.

3. 13 Feb. 1943, 821.6463/39, Record Group (RG) 59, National Archives, Washington, D.C.; *El Colombiano*, 16 March 1946; *El Tiempo*, 12 Feb., 7 April 1942; *El Liberal*, 8 Nov. 1945.

4. 19 April 1950, 821.2614/4-1950, RG 59; *El Liberal*, 15 June 1943, 1 Sept. 1948; *El Tiempo*, 7 March, 21 June, 14 Aug. 1947, 22 Oct. 1948.

5. The discussion in this and the following three paragraphs is based on 25 July 1950 and Gilbert Associates Reports, 821.2614/7-750, 11-1351, RG 59.

6. 30 Oct. 1951, 821.2614/10-3051, RG 59; Memorandum of Conversation, 31 Oct. 1951, Office Files of Assistant Secretary of State Edward G. Miller, Box 4, RG 59; *New York Times*, 18 May 1952.

7. Ospina, *Una vida*, pp. 458–464; *Revista Empresas Públicas de Medellín* 2 (1980):21–34.

8. De La Pedraja, *Energía*, Chaps, 3, 4.

9. *El Siglo*, 30 March 1939; *El Tiempo*, 18 Aug. 1937.

10. *La Razón*, 7 Sept. 1938, *El Tiempo*, 23 Oct. 1937; *El Espectador*, 7 Oct. 1938.

11. Instituto Nacional de Aprovechamiento de Aguas y Fomento Eléctrico, *Informe del gerente, 1954* (Bogotá: Aedita Ltd., 1955) pp. 37–42; *El Tiempo*, 6 Feb. 1940; *Colombia Económica* 3 (1944):95–97.

12. Gibbs & Hill, Inc., and Electricité de France, *National Electrification Plan*, 3 vols. (Bogotá: Multilith, 1954); *El Tiempo*, 19 Dec. 1943.

13. *Colombia Económica* 3 (1944):278–280; *El Tiempo*, 24 May 1945, 12 April 1946, 28 Aug. 1946; *El Siglo*, 29 May 1946. As of this writing, water still does not have a separate national institute, with most (but far from all) of the responsibilities for flood control and irrigation located in the Colombian Institute for Agrarian Reform in a strange aberration of its main function.

14. *El Tiempo*, 26 April, 18 Oct. 1947; *El Siglo*, 5 March 1947; Electraguas, *Informe, 1954*, pp. 62–64.

15. *Liberal*, 12 Dec. 1947, 13 Jan. 1948; *El Siglo*, 18 Jan. 1948; *El Tiempo*, 7, 9 Dec. 1947.

10

The Decisive Clashes

The fate of twentieth-century Colombian electrification was decided during the 1950s. In a first round of clashes, the Colombian government was able to turn failures at Caldas, Anchicayá, and Lebrija into victories, thanks to timely support from the Harry S. Truman administration. From there on everything was downhill, whether in Bogotá, the site of the largest utility in the country, or in Cali, one of the largest cities in Colombia.

The Initial Successes

Electraguas continued to be overwhelmingly concerned with water works until confronted in the late 1940s with three hydroelectric projects that permanently changed the focus of the agency's activities. Before explaining how that transformation came about, some background on the origins of the three projects in Caldas, Anchicayá, and Lebrija is in order.

Caldas

Inhabitants of the province of Antioquia had moved south in the nineteenth century to colonize the new province of Caldas, now famous because on its mountain slopes grows the finest Colombian coffee. Although coffee was the main source of foreign exchange for Colombia, once the vast dollar earnings of the Caldas coffee crop were distributed across the whole country, not much was left to meet that province's needs for imported equipment. Caldas faced other problems as well: It had tried to imitate Medellín's example of developing municipal utilities, but the cities in Caldas were too small to raise local capital. In 1944 the municipal electric company in Manizales, the capital city of Caldas, gave up the struggle for hopeless and in February 1944 fused itself into a newly 'created Caldas Power Authority whose ostensible purpose was to tap funds of the central state.[1]

As the example of Manizales was followed in cities throughout the country, each municipal electric company (except for Medellín and Bogotá) fused during the 1940s and 1950s into a regional power authority belonging to the central state. With the promise of state funds, the local expenses of the Caldas Power Authority were covered but the foreign exchange problem was still left unsolved. A quick solution came from an unexpected quarter. In May 1944 two technicians from the Soviet embassy in Bogotá, who had been sent to inspect the hydroelectric site, offered all necessary technical assistance with the goal of eventually working out a barter agreement whereby Caldas' unsold coffee could be exchanged for Soviet generators and other electrical equipment. The possibilities of this proposal were immense, not only for Caldas but also for other projects, and at the very least provided an alternative to the handful of multinational corporations that monopolized the manufacture of heavy electrical equipment. None of this impressed the elite of Caldas, which abruptly rejected the proposal without even letting the central state consider it. The Soviets were understandably upset by the behavior of an ally against Nazi Germany, yet not until the 1970s did the attitude of the Colombian elite mellow to the point of considering the barter of coffee for Soviet equipment.[2]

Colombia's rejection of the Soviet offer in 1944 was approvingly noted by U.S. officials, and the Caldas elite confidently counted on being rewarded by preferential treatment from the United States as soon as World War II ended. Very careful technical studies were completed, and in May 1946 the Caldas Power Authority presented a loan application for $1 million to the Export-Import Bank to cover the foreign exchange costs of installing a 10-megawatt hydroelectric station at Manizales. The Export-Import Bank had approved a larger loan for the Medellín Municipal Power Company, and a favorable decision was eagerly awaited. As the months rolled by, Colombian officials in the United States began to worry and rumors circulated that powerful U.S. groups were blocking the loan application. The Caldas Power Authority asked the Colombian government to find out what was causing the delay; soon Assistant Secretary of State Spruille Braden explained that until the city government of Manizales worked out an agreement to repay its foreign debt, the hostility both of the Republican-controlled Congress and the Foreign Bondholders' Protective Council made it impossible to grant a loan to the Caldas Power Authority.

During the friendlier New Deal years, the Colombian government had settled its foreign debt in a satisfactory manner, but of the city governments, only Medellín and Bogotá had reached workable agreements. Most municipal utilities, cut off from foreign loans because of the default by their city governments in the 1930s, now had an added incentive to turn electric service over to the national government, whose foreign credit was good. In the case of Caldas, the strategy did not work because the Women's Benefit Association of Port Huron, Michigan, which had bought heavily into Manizales city bonds during the 1920s, stubbornly refused to recognize the Caldas Power Authority as a central state institution distinct from the Manizales city government. This situation created an embarrassment for the U.S. government, which could not in good faith reject an application from an institution belonging to a national government whose foreign debt had been settled years before, so as a good bureaucratic solution, the Export-Import Bank just sat on the application. The province of Caldas was left to pay the price of a permanent power shortage, which sharply restricted its economic growth. Yet it had only itself to blame for rejecting the Soviet offer so quickly. By 1948 the Caldas Power Authority had concluded that the 10-megawatt plant was insufficient and that a 20-megawatt plant was needed. The national government continued to provide the funds for local construction costs, but for the imported machinery, the problem only became worse.[3]

Anchicayá

Opposition to the American and Foreign Power Company's holdings in Cali had led to the creation in February 1944 of the Anchicayá Power Authority with ownership distributed among the national, provincial, and city governments. The main proponents were the merchants and brokers of Cali, who had resented being excluded from the profitable procurement contracts for the U.S. utility. They had been joined by the local engineer Espíritu Santo Potess, who was fascinated with the possibility of building a large hydroelectric project of 41 megawatts at Anchicayá gorge (the U.S. utility considered other sites more attractive, rightfully as later it turned out). As Potess carried out the water and engineering surveys with unusual dedication, the money allocated for the study of this and other nearby sites was well spent—something not usually the case in Colombia. The Colombian congress since 1938 had passed several pieces of pork barrel legislation calling for the construction of a dam near Cali, and now that a specific proposal existed, thanks to Potess's diligence, the regional politicians pressed the national government to release the promised funds. The Central State Bank still had $600,000 from an Export-Import Bank loan earmarked for electrification, and now, in response to regional political pressures, the government parceled sums out to the power authorities of Anchicayá, Caldas, and Lebrija.[4]

This money soon ran out, and Cali clamored for more funds; some merchant-brokers used the tactic of threatening to proceed on the project without the central state's participation—an empty bluff since already by the end of 1945 the central state's share in the Anchicayá Power Authority had risen to more than half and had continued to rise. Upward revisions of the budget needed to construct the Anchicayá project had led the national government to seek a partnership with the American and Foreign Power Company, but this proposal was rejected by the merchant-brokers of Cali, who wanted undisputed control over the new power authority. If there was not enough money to build the Anchicayá plant, it was hard to see how funds could be found to purchase the U.S. utility in Cali, yet incredible as it might seem, not even bankruptcy stopped the city government from buying the properties in 1947 after a long and drawn-out struggle.

The U.S. government did not receive the news well in 1944 when it learned that part of the proceeds from the Export-Import Bank loan had been diverted into the Anchicayá Power Authority, a competitor against the U.S. utility. Thus, when the Colombian government later sought a separate Export-Import Bank loan just for Anchicayá in 1946, the application was held up—first to try to prevent the purchase of the U.S. utility and then to assure the payment of the compensation. In effect, the merchant-brokers of Cali had maneuvered to deprive the city both of the U.S. utility and the Export-Import Bank loans. The very narrow class interests of the Cali elite, hiding behind regional aspirations, had blocked both the larger national interests as well as the local ones, and consequently, from 1947 on the city suffered poor and insufficient electric service.[5]

This adverse situation did not evoke complaints because the construction work that had begun on Anchicayá in 1945 satisfied the real objectives of the merchant-brokers. Huge sums were poured into the project, and by 1949 twice the original budget had been spent but not even one-third of the work was completed. The project called for an arched dam, but since it was the first of this type in Colombia, its final costs could not be accurately predicted. A one-mile long tunnel—the second in Colombia after Río Grande near Medellín—would carry the water from the dam to the turbines through very hard crystalline rock in one part and slate in the other. Less than one-third of the mile had been dug, and to save money, no sealing was planned for the inside of the tunnel; so to prevent cave-ins, water could not flow under pressure, thus considerably reducing the electrical output. The site had many other problems as well, not the least of which was its inhospitable nature, which led the engineers to conclude that the only place work could be carried out comfortably was underground in the tunnel. But with money running out quickly in the late 1940s, work gradually ground to a halt in Anchicayá.[6]

Lebrija

In both Cali and Bucaramanga, state intervention paralyzed electrical development. The only difference was that while in Cali a U.S. utility was driven out, in Bucaramanga the victim was a private Colombian company. As explained in Chapter 8, the establishment of the Lebrija Power Authority in 1943 signaled the beginning of the end for the Bucaramanga Electric Company. This private company had achieved the unique feat in Colombia of accumulating enough capital to finance its own enlargement. Once the provincial government decided to press on with the construction of the Lebrija dam after 1946, the private utility slowed down the tempo of its expansion plan because, as a tax-paying company, it was in no condition to compete against a subsidized tax-exempt state company. In spite of the many privileges state ownership accorded to the Lebrija Power Authority, the merchant-brokers sank it into near bankruptcy and construction work only advanced slowly in occasional bursts. From 1949 on the city of Bucaramanga experienced power shortages for which neither the private utility nor the Lebrija Power Authority claimed responsibility. As a stopgap measure, the power authority negotiated an agreement to install two diesel engines for the private utility to distribute the electricity, but when these new units came on line, the output was still too small. The Lebrija dam—with construction at a standstill—was the only possible solution.[7]

The Central State Fills the Breach

The administration of Mariano Ospina Pérez (1946–1950) could no longer ignore the clamor for better electrical service and between 1948 and 1949 proceeded to dump the problems of Caldas, Anchicayá, and Lebrija into the lap of Electraguas. The transition was a bit too sudden for an institution which up to that moment had dealt mainly with complaints by large landowners about their cows drowning during flooding; but in all justice to the new state institution, it bounced back quickly to try to assume a commanding role in the electrification of Colombia.

Monumental as the technical and engineering problems were, Electraguas immediately concluded that the real insurmountable obstacle was lack of money, and more specifically, lack of foreign currency. Since the Export-Import Bank would not lend, other sources had to be found. Encouraging news came in early 1948 with reports that the World Bank had made a loan for electrical expansion to Brazil—the first such case in South America. This and other leads were worth exploring, and so a Colombian delegation (the first of many) traveled to the United States. This group consulted the Export-Import Bank to no avail, and although some financing by New York banks was possible, without a doubt the most advantageous terms came from the World Bank.

The Colombian government presented loan applications for Caldas, Anchicayá, and Lebrija, but the weight of the past hung heavily over these negotiations. In the case of Caldas, the Colombians worried excessively that the Manizales debt default would block the loan. The fears proved groundless, for as far as the World Bank was concerned, the slate had been wiped clean, and it clearly understood that the Caldas Power Authority was a national and not a municipal institution. In the case of Anchicayá, the expropriation proceedings against the American and Foreign Power Company in Cali had given the region a bad name in New York financial circles. Moreover, Cali's failure to settle the last outstanding payments for the purchase of the U.S. utility had kept this resentment alive. The World Bank never did raise the issue, but just to be on the safe side, the Colombian government expedited the final settlement of the Cali expropriation.[8]

The World Bank did express concern over the fate of the Bucaramanga Electric Company and wanted to ensure that private capital would suffer no harm as a result of the proposed loan. In fact, the expropriation was motivated by political hostility in the Conservative Party against the Bucaramanga Electric Company. Merchant-brokers eagerly backed the Conservative administration of Laureano Gómez (1950–1951) as a way to deprive the Paillié family of their control over the private utility. The World Bank's warning forced the Lebrija Power Authority to offer a high price for the Bucaramanga Electric Company in order to avoid having any criticism from the private owners reach the World Bank. The private owners still refused to sell, and by 1950 the World Bank had concluded that the ideal solution was to make the loan to the solid and well-run Bucaramanga Electric Company so that it could purchase the bankrupt Lebrija Power Authority. Knowledge of the World Bank's changed attitude put provincial officials into a panic. They were under strong pressure from the Conservative Party to buy out the Paillié family as a political reprisal. The Lebrija Power Authority pressed hard by legal as well as heavy-handed methods to close the deal before the private owners could find out that they enjoyed World Bank support. The Paillié family finally capitulated and sold the private utility in December 1951.[9]

Colombia had sent other loan applications to the World Bank during the late 1940s besides the ones for the hydroelectric projects at Caldas, Anchicayá, and Lebrija. The World Bank, which was just beginning operations in Latin America, decided for the first time in its history to send a study mission to survey the whole country's needs. Each of the projects was justified on its intrinsic merits and was backed by technical and feasibility studies, yet it was not clear how they all fit together into a coherent plan for the country's whole economy, nor whether more significant projects should be pursued. To answer these questions, the World Bank sent a mission headed by the American economist Lauchlin Currie, who arrived with his team early in 1949 and finished work by the middle of 1950. The report ratified the hydroelectric projects but dealt Colombia a cruel and unexpected blow when it argued against the Paz del Río steel mills, which had become a symbol of widespread enthusiasm among the Colombian public. The World Bank stood behind the study mission and refused to consider Paz del Río for financing. Undaunted by this setback, the administration of Laureano Gómez proceeded to find more expensive private financing for Paz del Río, and French credits were eventually forthcoming to erect the first modern steel mill in Colombia.[10]

This should have been the end of the matter, but instead the World Bank was furious to see the advice of its study mission not only ignored but openly defied. The World Bank decided that the time had come to teach a lesson to a future borrower: If Colombia did not immediately drop the steel mill, then all its requests—the most important of which were the hydroelectric loans—would be rejected. As news of the ultimatum reached the Colombian government, utter hopelessness set in: Colombia had to choose either the trio of Caldas, Anchicayá, and Lebrija, or Paz del Río, but it could not have both. Borrowing from French banks had been on prohibitive terms for the steel mill and could not be repeated for the trio of hydroelectric projects, yet abandoning either project was political suicide. Electraguas had exhausted its budget and its future income had been spent months in advance; government revenues were already overcommitted. Clearly, huge mistakes had been made in driving the American and Foreign Power Company out of Cali and the private utility out of Bucaramanga, but couldn't Colombia be given another chance to wipe the slate clean and start all over?

Colombia now found itself trapped in a dead end; the national government, frozen into paralysis, could only plead for a solution from any of its officials. With this blanket authorization, the Colombian ambassador to the United States Eduardo Zuleta Angel, decided to sound out the assistant secretary of state, no longer the probusiness Spruille Braden but rather Edward Miller, who had consistently shown himself in private to be extremely sympathetic to the plight of Latin America. At a meeting with Miller, the Colombian ambassador mentioned that Colombia was having difficulties with Paz del Río; Miller confessed that he had not had the time to follow the difficulties in detail but understood that for Colombia at least this was a beginning. Encouraged by the tone of the reply, Zuleta pressed on and said he really had come to raise a related question to see what advice Miller might give. Gingerly, Zuleta explained that the World Bank, in order to impose some sort of ideal plan, was depriving Colombia of its hydroelectric projects as the price for Paz del Río. A totally surprised Assistant Secretary of State immediately volunteered to make some phone calls; Miller obviously called the right people, and the objections vanished. Although to save appearances the World Bank delayed the final loan signatures, the logjam had been broken.[11]

The Colombian government now rejoiced at the news and with the sums that flowed into Electraguas was now able to initiate full-scale construction on Caldas, Anchicayá, and Lebrija. Not only would the new plants greatly increase the generating capacity in their respective regions, but the power authorities could actually become profit-making enterprises. With the proceeds, Electraguas could pay for other projects and eventually reach the point of becoming a self-financing institution. Present revenues could be used to cover future projects without recourse to foreign loans, which, even when on favorable terms, were still a serious drain for a capital poor country like Colombia. But before Electraguas could take steps to convert these idyllic prospects into reality, the plans were rudely interrupted by the outbreak of a ferocious struggle over the purchase of the Bogotá Light and Power Company.

The Loss of Bogotá

The critical situation of the Bogotá Light and Power Company did not change with the end of World War II even though spare parts and new equipment, as well as the possibility of foreign borrowing, gradually became available again. Also, two changes had taken place in the circumstances of the Bogotá utility. First of all, the American and Foreign Power Company, in response to the protests against its subsidiary in Cali, had decided to sell its shares in the Bogotá utility as part of a policy of retrenchment in the unprofitable Colombian operations. The departure of the U.S. company left the Swiss firm of Motor-Columbus as the single largest private stockholder, thus permanently weakening the Samper family's ability to control matters by playing the Americans off against the Swiss. Second, in an effort to save some measure of influence, the Samper family, close friends of Alfonso López Pumarejo, an ex-president of Colombia, now convinced him to participate actively in the affairs of the Bogotá utility as president of its Board of Directors— a position he had ceremoniously held since 1938. Beginning in 1945, he began to make his influence felt.[12]

López Pumarejo had the bonus attraction of having the Motor-Columbus representative to the Board of Directors under his thumb, thus checking the pressures from the Swiss company to manageable proportions. Furthermore, as an ex-president, López Pumarejo enjoyed considerable influence in the national and city governments. The fifty-year concession the city council had granted the company was about to expire in 1946, and thanks to López's efforts, the city renewed the concession. Yet the price of this "favor" seemed too high: In exchange for the renewal, the company had to sign an option giving the city government the right to buy the company at any moment if it had the cash to do so. López explained away this inconvenience, arguing correctly that the city was always short of funds, but the danger of expropriation remained hanging in the background.[13]

The precarious position of the Bogotá Light and Power Company was due to a lack of capital. The 1943 bond issue was still unsold in 1948, and to try to build up investor confidence, the company since 1946 had regularly played the market to keep the price of the bonds from collapsing. The Muña dam still needed work, while the really important projects, like Guavio, remained a dream. Construction did not stop, however, and could proceed both in Muña and in the plants along the Bogotá river because the company still retained a high rate of internal savings and foreign exchange was supplied by short-term accounts with the Chemical Bank and later also with the National City Bank. There was no doubt, however, that even these enlargements were not enough to meet the growing demand. Matters became even worse after 1946 when the national government printed large amounts of paper money only to see inflation accelerate.

Electricity rates remained frozen, which in real terms was equivalent to a price reduction because of the inflation, thus slowing down the expansion of the Bogotá Light and Power Company. This problem of low rates, endemic to both private and state utilities, only made more urgent the need to seek long-term foreign loans to finance the overdue expansion. Since 1943 Medellín had eagerly looked to the Export-Import Bank, which approved its application in 1946, but the Bogotá utility had been very slow to seek similar financing. Both Bogotá and Medellín had settled their municipal debts, unlike most Colombian cities, like Manizales, which remained in default. However, in the case of Bogotá, a group of American speculators had cornered a large number of the 1927 Baker, Kellogg & Co. municipal bonds, and not satisfied with the debt arrangement worked out between the Bogotá city government and New York bankers (which had been approved by the Department of State), clamored for even better terms. Capitalizing on the fact that the U.S. government considered the episode closed, the Bogotá utility needed to quickly and forcefully present its loan application to the Export-Import Bank. Instead, and at the suggestion of López Pumarejo, whose motives are open to question, the company delayed presenting the loan application until it was too late.[14]

Trusting once again to the judgment and international links of López Pumarejo, the Bogotá utility placed the initial contacts with the World Bank in his hands, thus bypassing Emilio Toro, the Colombian representative to the World Bank and other foreign lending institutions. López Pumarejo bungled the contacts with the World Bank; among other complications, he missed the crucial requirement that any application to the World Bank had to be presented by the national government as part of a larger package. When the company finally contacted Emilio Toro, he pointed out this and other requirements, but by then it was too late to include Bogotá with the initial batch of loan requests for the projects at Caldas, Anchicayá, and Lebrija. In 1948, the national government refused to include the Bogotá utility in the second batch of loan requests to the World Bank for reasons that will shortly be explained.

Cut off from even the possibility of Export-Import Bank or World Bank loans, the situation of the Bogotá Light and Power Company became really critical in 1947 when a severe drought struck the country. With minor interruptions, this drought continued into early 1948. It was one thing to deny requests for electric service due to insufficient capacity, but it was another to ration current because the low water volume reduced hydroelectric generation. The effects of the drought preceded its arrival, since in anticipation the manager of the company diverted scarce funds into stockpiling coal for the steam plants, thus slowing down construction on the hydroelectric projects even more. During the dry months, the company's income dropped because less electricity was sold. The rationing produced a public outcry, and as usual in these crisis situations, politicians rushed into the spotlight with all sorts of crackpot proposals—the most notable a suggestion to construct a huge steam plant at the Magdalena river.

While company officials listened to this and other half-baked proposals in silence so as not to antagonize the politicians, the utility quickly moved to obtain financing. The city government authorized a new issue of shares, but without funds to subscribe them, it worked out a curious arrangement whereby the company "loaned" the money at a low interest rate to the city. Motor-Columbus did bring foreign currency to subscribe its additional shares, but except for that amount and the interest payments from the city, the share issue was really just a stopgap measure. More decisive support came from the national government, which at last after so many decades was starting to realize the immense importance of electricity.[15]

The Central State Bank subscribed the outstanding bonds of the 1943 issue and quickly provided most of the funds for the 1947 issue. The

1947 bonds still did not cover all the capital needs, and the Central State Bank urged another bond issue in 1948, which it promised to subscribe in its entirety. By tapping the resources of the central state, the Bogotá Light and Power Company was at last gathering enough capital to finance the expansion plans; but no matter how generous the loans by the Central State Bank, their repayment was dependent upon increasing rates. In late 1947 the Bogotá utility presented its requests for a rate increase to the state regulatory commission and the city council, both of whom had to grant approval.[16]

With state funds now flowing into the company, the Bogotá utility confidently expected a favorable ruling in the requested rate hike, but the application was overtaken by an uprising in Bogotá on 9 April 1948. On that day the popular leader of the Liberal Party, Jorge Eliécer Gaitán, was assassinated because of high-level pressures from the Colombian elite; not surprisingly, cover-up efforts have prevented full disclosures, but the flow of events was quite clear. Outraged inhabitants of the lower class, whose tempers were on edge after having suffered months of drastic water and electricity rationing that had only ended in the first days of April 1948, now could no longer control their pent-up feelings and exploded, sending the capital city into a sea of panic and destruction. The uprising lasted for several days, causing untold thousands of deaths with burnings and the sacking of many buildings. Throughout the dangerous revolt, the officials and employees of the Bogotá Light and Power Company had stayed at their posts to try to keep service going; but whenever trucks tried to reach fallen lines for repair, shots broke out and with the police melted into the crowds, the company decided not to dispatch any more employees to get killed. After a few days, the first army units arrived to restore order and the utility could begin to assess the damages.

At first the company appeared to have escaped unscathed: The generating plants (all located away from the city), the transmission lines, and the substations were in perfect condition, leaving the damage localized to the distribution system within the city. In two weeks of furious work, all cables and transformers had been repaired and service was back to normal. This should have been the end of the matter, but gradually the bad news came out. During the uprising rebels had seized the national radio station to broadcast incendiary appeals, and it was not until troops recaptured the station that the broadcasts could be stopped. The utility had not sent workers to disconnect electricity to the radio station out of a concern for the employees' lives and in order to avoid blacking out a whole neighborhood, which would only create more panic. After the event, the Ospina Pérez administration cited this example of providing electric service to the subversive radio as proof that the utility had sympathized with the uprising. Furthermore, the administration, whose wanton negligence had allowed armed crowds to surround the Executive Palace (also the president's residence) now held the company responsible for not having come to repair the fallen cables which had left the president's home without electricity. Once peace had returned, the company urged that an underground cable be installed to supply electricity to the Executive Palace, but this suggestion did not stop the lingering resentment that spread among Conservative Party members. Fuel for the resentment came from the traditional Liberal sympathies of the Samper family and from the obvious fact that the head of the Board of Directors of the utility was Alfonso López Pumarejo, the most famous Liberal ex-president alive.[17]

The first reprisal of the Conservative government came quickly: The Central State Bank reneged on its commitment to subscribe the 1948 bond issue, which had been sent into a saturated bond market only because of the earlier urgings by Central State Bank officials. In spite of the company's most earnest entreaties, this loan was never fully subscribed, even though in 1949, to avoid lawsuits, the Central State Bank agreed to acquire one-third of the bonds. A second reprisal was no less deadly: The Conservative government continued to block access to the World Bank. It always found some excuse not to include the Bogotá loan application among Colombia's batch of requests to the international financial institution. Not unexpectedly, shortages of electricity became inevitable, and the type of rationing introduced during the 1947 drought returned with increasing frequency in subsequent years.[18]

The Central State Bank's refusal to subscribe the 1948 bond issue accelerated a process begun in 1944: As talk of a municipal takeover increased (and was reinforced in the 1946 option-to-buy contract), private investors—at first slowly, and then with growing momentum—proceeded to reduce the functions of the company. The Bogotá Light and Power Company, as the largest in the country, was not merely a profitable business for generating and selling electricity but had branched out into many other activities and was on the way to becoming a conglomerate. First of all, the utility built its own projects with almost no recourse to outside contracts (except for foreign technical advice). Thus, all the work of construction, maintenance, and repair for the dams and the steam stations, as well as for all the buildings, was carried out by the company itself. These practices saved the company from having to pay contractors' profits, not to mention the commissions of the brokers. Second, as the company embarked upon the prospect of building larger reservoirs, it purchased huge stretches of land, and to handle these transactions the utility founded a subsidiary. From here it was only a small step to engage in the real estate business with very profitable returns. Third, the company from the very start in 1900 had retailed electrical equipment and light bulbs, originally on a monopoly basis and later in competition with small merchants to restrain abuses. This Commercial Bureau of the utility always earned nice profits for the company, and not surprisingly, angry merchants who resented the competition had the retail store burned down during the 9 April 1948 uprising. Fourth, the company had acquired a varied portfolio of stocks in different companies, and although usually only a minority interest, the dividends plus rental income from leasing other properties rounded out the company's receipts. In the case of the Samper Cement Factory in Bogotá, although the utility was only a minority stockholder, Samper family members held a direct controlling interest, thus assuring a mutually profitable relationship between the Cement Factory and the Bogotá utility. The only thing the utility needed to function as a full-fledged conglomerate was a bank: In spite of several attempts, the Bogotá Light and Power Company could not find a formula to establish a bank, and this gap remained the crucial weak link that eventually brought down the whole edifice.[19]

With a municipal takeover impending since 1946, the company gradually divested itself of most of its other holdings so that whenever the government should decide to take over the installations, only a hollow shell would be left. The electricity business just by itself can be extremely profitable, but only when adequate rates can be charged, especially if a utility no longer has other sources of income to fall back on. The national government refused to allow a rate hike in 1947, and its harassment of the Bogotá utility became more blatant as the state regulatory commission gradually granted rate increases to the other cities in Colombia. Inflation continued, and with rates frozen at their World War II level and the cushion of complementary activities now dissolved, the company faced ruin. At last in 1949 the Colombian government was willing to grant the 30 percent raise requested in 1947, but by then the company claimed that although 60 percent was needed, maybe it could survive with a 40 percent raise. The rate increase took on a new meaning in late 1949 when a merchant-broker, Santiago Trujillo Gómez, became the mayor of Bogotá, since he was determined to have the city buy the company. The city government lacked funds, so the decision was placed squarely in the hands of the national government: If the rate increase was too small, the private stockholders would sell, but if adequate, they would continue to operate the company. There matters stood when Laureano Gómez became president of Colombia in August 1950.[20]

Gómez, as a Conservative president, allowed some continuity from the outgoing Conservative administration of Mariano Ospina Pérez. In the case of Bogotá, Trujillo Gómez remained as mayor but different ideas soon began to appear. The Laureano Gómez administration, responsible for unleashing a wave of violence of unheard proportions in Colombia, has not been given enough credit for its important initiatives to strengthen the central state, such as the creation of Ecopetrol and of the Paz del Río steel mill. Lingering in the minds of the principal members of this administration was the idea that a very strong central state apparatus was absolutely indispensable to Colombia's economic development and even to its survival. Unless the state controlled the main economic activities, narrow private interests would block any meaningful economic expansion. Upon examining the bulky dossiers on the Bogotá Light and Power Company, Laureano Gómez concluded that a municipal takeover would only hand over the utility to parochial interests and that the only way to assure meaningful central state action was to put Electraguas in charge of the Bogotá utility.

In October 1950 the government opened a line of credit for Electraguas in the Central State Bank to enable it to purchase the private shares of the Bogotá Light and Power Company. Taking everyone by surprise, Electraguas bought shares in small lots over a period of five months without sparking a speculative surge; finally, it had acquired almost all the private shares. Success was possible because the largest private stockholder, the Swiss firm of Motor-Columbus, fulfilled its promise of selling its shares to either the city or national government on the sole condition of receiving a cash payment. Electraguas saw itself so near to having the Bogotá utility in its grasp that it prepared to name its own candidate for the position of manager of the company and was planning a coordinate development for electrical resources in the Bogotá area and the surrounding province of Cundinamarca. Even with all the private shares, the central government still held only a minority interest in the Bogotá Light and Power Company, with the city government the majority stockholder. But just as had happened before in Caldas, Anchicayá, and Lebrija, new infusions of capital would after some years inevitably give overwhelming majority control to the central state, as indeed happened throughout the rest of the country.

Local parochial interests were no less intense in Bogotá than in other parts of Colombia, but in Bogotá the complaint was that the national institutions were bled to favor the provinces. The Bogotá Light and Power Company was a very profitable enterprise, and the Bogotá elite wanted to see it under local control. The merchants and brokers had already established close relations with the city council, which would repay votes and campaign contributions with juicy contracts, but even more motivated were the local banks, which did not want to lose the opportunity of placing high-interest, short-term commercial loans with the new municipal power company. The city government had been unable to raise a cent to purchase the company during the 1940s, but now that the threat of nationalization appeared, it managed to quickly gather from unusually friendly Bogotá banks all the sums necessary to purchase the private shares. As this move had come too late because the shares were already in the hands of Electraguas, an indirect maneuver was required. Citing a clause in the 1946 option agreement, which authorized the city to deposit in an account in the Central State Bank an amount equal to the value of the outstanding private shares whose owners could not be found or refused to sell, the municipal government now deposited an amount equal to the value of the shares Electraguas held. Such a move was a perversion of the original intent, since the clause had obviously been directed against private stockholders and not against the national government, and besides was blatantly unconstitutional as well as illegal. The private banks, which were determined to keep Electraguas out of the Bogotá utility at all costs, had openly defied the central state. Nevertheless, as the holder of sweeping constitutional powers, the state had the authority and the obligation to overrule any city or provincial government that flaunted independence, and the local governments were, in legal theory, nothing more than creatures of the central state. Electraguas confidently expected the national government to stop this defiant rebellion by the Bogotá city council. Although the Laureano Gómez administration was implacable about sending troops and police to crush the slightest sign of rebellion among peasants and workers, when confronted by the private banks it faltered in its resolve to defend central state prerogatives.[21]

The private banks had neutralized the central state, leaving the field wide open to the merchant-brokers, who pressed the attack until the city council claimed the Bogotá Light and Power Company as its property in 1951. Electraguas refused to accept the outcome and was only quieted by the consolation prize of keeping the money from the sale of the private shares to the Bogotá city council. These funds promptly flowed out to meet the crying needs for electricity in other provinces of Colombia. This temporary relief for Electraguas's finances could not hide the fact that without control over the Bogotá Light and Power Company, the national institute's ability to electrify Colombia had been permanently crippled. The interest groups that composed the constituency of the Bogotá Light and Power Company, busily enjoying their privileges, opposed all cooperation with Electraguas, and a silent rivalry developed between the two institutions that sometimes erupted into bitter clashes, as in the case of Zipaquirá.

Yet in 1951 the full implications of the loss of Bogotá were still not realized, since Electraguas hoped to make another try to capture Bogotá in the future using the commanding position attained by its many investments throughout Colombia, in particular the Anchicayá dam, the subject of the next section.

Disaster in Cali

Opening Rounds over Anchicayá

The World Bank loan of November 1950 saved Anchicayá. Work on the project had stopped in 1948, but not before devouring almost all the capital of the Anchicayá Power Authority. Construction resumed in 1951, but since the World Bank loan covered only the foreign exchange expenses, continuous appropriations from the national government remained indispensable. The Cali elite lobbied aggressively for additional central state funds but was totally adamant in rejecting any form of control or even supervision.

In November 1950 the first stage of construction began on the arched dam, according to the original plans of Espíritu Santo Potess. To proceed in such a way was highly debatable, since both the experience gained in construction during 1946–1948 as well as later surveys had confirmed the need to modify the pioneering studies in light of new information. Rather than change the blueprints, however, the Anchicayá Board of Directors covered up the many flaws by keeping the information hermetically sealed. They even refused to inform Electraguas what had been done with central state funds. The Anchicayá Power Authority promptly refuted any of the Electraguas engineers' suggestions by citing information that was known to have been false from the start, and some meetings degenerated into rowdy shouting matches. Electraguas, swamped with problems throughout the country and hoping for a change of attitude in Cali, allowed more than a year to slip by without coming to grips with the insubordination at Anchicayá. Letters to the Board of Directors usually went unanswered and at most inspired only vague replies. Finally in 1952 the national government decided to send the director of Electraguas himself, Julián Cock, to find out what was happening.[22]

Cock, as a representative of the central state, which held 51 percent of the shares, ordered the power authority's books opened and made a careful on-site inspection, only to find Electraguas's worst fears confirmed. In seventeen months of work, the main contractors had only done 10 percent of the project, which was supposed to be completed in a total of thirty-six months. Clearly the main contractors were not going to finish on time. Yet worse still was the fact that in an effort to compensate, the Anchicayá Power Authority had granted supplementary contracts to other builders, so that double the amount originally budgeted was now required to complete just a fraction of the project. Out of a desire to favor brokers with more commissions, the power authority had at last ordered sealing the walls of the mile-long tunnel to prevent cave-ins. No easy solution existed for the reservoir: Under one scenario sediment would gradually fill up the dam in six years; under a more favorable one the silting would take thirty years. But even the second estimate included the warning that at any moment landslides from the steep cliffs could overfill the entire reservoir. A much safer alternative was to build only the tunnel, but this approach would deprive the generators of a reservoir with reserve capacity for the dry summer months, the original justification for the project. Engineering and cost considerations demanded dropping Anchicayá and finding a different site.

The Anchicayá Board of Directors reacted violently to any idea of scrapping, much less even cutting back the project. Publicity and electoral purposes required building a dam, which could be showed off and photographed, not just a tunnel, and the Anchicayá board members, after heated sessions with cabinet ministers in Bogotá, finally convinced the national government to push ahead with the original design with one modification—that of replacing the concrete arched dam with a simpler curved gravity type. The power authority had no choice but to cancel the contracts of the original builders in 1953, and with this small confession of its past mistakes, once again was replenished by more funds from the central state. The national government, which had underestimated the power and ambitions of the Cali elite, dismissed the whole crisis too hastily as just another example of wild spending by provincial power authorities. In any case, an unrepentant Anchicayá Power Authority merrily continued along on its spending spree begun in the 1940s, favoring the local merchant-brokers with countless contracts for equipment, services, and supplies. Anchicayá was turning out to be one of the most important sources of income for Cali, and there certainly was no rush to finish the project; the longer construction work continued, the larger the sums of central state money that would pour into the pockets of the local elite.[23]

The dictatorship of General Gustavo Rojas Pinilla, coming to power in 1953, did not disturb this lucrative relationship; in fact, the national government routinely authorized more funds for Anchicayá in order to secure the wavering political support of the Cali elite. By 1955 when Electraguas had committed one-fourth of its entire budget to the project, only the first unit of 24 megawatts had been installed even though the funds for the first two 24-megawatt units had already been spent. The Cali elite prepared additional requests so extravagant that even General Rojas Pinilla had to reject them out of hand. Undaunted, the Cali elite embarked upon a twofold strategy to secure total compliance with its demands. The first part of this strategy called for bringing a foreign expert with an international reputation to Colombia.

Lilienthal and the CVC

The Cali elite had been very impressed with the World Bank mission headed by Lauchlin Currie, since at the very least the 1950 plan had made the idea of economic development fashionable. Currie himself had stayed behind to study individual Colombian provinces and cities. But for what the Cali elite had in mind, Currie would not do because his plan had a *national* perspective, which was precisely what the Cali elite was trying to avoid at all costs. Europe was just emerging out of wartime destruction, so the foreign expert Cali needed had to be an American with close ties to the World Bank and U.S. financial circles. Above all, the foreign adviser had to have an uncompromising commitment to regional over national development. The Cali elite sounded out its American friends like Milo Perkins for likely candidates, and a list gradually emerged. Very soon it became apparent that of the persons who met the qualifications, David Lilienthal, former head of the Tennessee Valley Authority, was the ideal candidate. Lilienthal did not know Spanish, but as far as the Cali elite was concerned, this was a positive asset: Since almost all the information was in Spanish, he could thus be kept from uncovering facts that they did not wish him to know.[24]

Lilienthal accepted the offer and came to Colombia in late February 1954, but before beginning his inspection work, he met with Colombian President Rojas Pinilla on 2 March 1954. The president admitted there was nothing wrong with the regional development approach, provided other provinces could participate, and he urged Lilienthal to visit other regions and even put a plane at his disposal for that purpose. A comparison made the American expert wonder: Whereas the Tennessee Valley Authority had been established by the federal government in a poverty-stricken area, the Cali corporation would be founded by the central state in one of the wealthier regions in Colombia. Lilienthal did travel in the president's plane to other provinces, but permanently surrounded by Cali elite members, he was constantly fed one-sided information on the merits of the Cali regional corporation, and his only other source of information were his talks with Rojas Pinilla. In justice to Lilienthal, he had not been the first nor would he be the last foreign expert to be bamboozled by narrow economic interest groups in Colombia.[25]

Lilienthal made no attempt to contact the national ministries or Electraguas to see what views and information they might provide, and after exhausting the data the Cali elite had wanted him to see, he returned to New York City to write the report he presented on 25 June

1954. He enthusiastically urged the creation of an autonomous regional corporation, the Corporación Autónoma Regional del Valle del Cauca (CVC), free of central state control and able to negotiate foreign loans directly with the World Bank and other overseas lending institutions. Lilienthal deferred to Rojas Pinilla's wishes only insofar as to state that the CVC could be the first of a series of similar regional corporations. The 25 June 1954 report was long on broad arguments on behalf of the CVC and purposely left the specifics for a later study, in effect bestowing carte blanche for the proponents of CVC. Rojas Pinilla could see no harm in the proposal, and naively thinking that this measure would satisfy the insatiable demands of the Cali elite, which was already draining Electraguas to keep Anchicayá going, on 22 October 1954 he issued the executive decree creating the CVC.[26]

The Cali elite still needed two follow-up studies to prove the technical soundness and the economic justification for the CVC idea. The CVC commissioned the first study directly with a local Colombian engineering firm, and perhaps not surprisingly, the lengthy tome that was forthcoming categorically used a variety of facts to prove the need for the CVC. The second study was more tricky: At Lilienthal's insistence, the World Bank had sent a mission to study the CVC as a first step to secure favorable consideration of loan applications. The mission, headed by Harold Larsen, did not limit itself to talking to the Cali elite or CVC officials but made an attempt to sound out the central state. The Larsen report accepted the existence of CVC but without any enthusiasm, and indeed this group was particularly worried by the lack of funds to finance the ambitious projects contemplated for water, electricity, and agriculture. To complement World Bank loans, at the very least the national government had to participate as a major stockholder in the new corporation. The Larsen mission did come out for the Calima dam as the most important project the CVC should next undertake, thus tacitly leaving open the door for World Bank financing.[27]

The critical report of the Larsen mission was not exactly what the Cali elite had wanted, yet they could live with it. On the pretext that it was a confidential World Bank document, the bulky Larsen report was kept out of circulation, and instead the highly favorable report by the local Colombian engineers was given wide publicity. There remained yet another hurdle: to contract the Calima dam with the World Bank, the national government had to place the application among Colombia's package of requests. Electraguas, starting to sense danger, bitterly opposed this arrangement on the grounds that it would only open the door to even more extravagant demands for aid, and most of Electraguas's efforts in 1955 were spent on this struggle.

To break the deadlock, the CVC brought Lilienthal back in 1956 to see if he could pry approval from President Rojas Pinilla not only to negotiate with the World Bank over the Calima loan, but even more boldly, to transfer Electraguas's shares in Anchicayá to CVC. At a meeting on 11 July 1956, Lilienthal pressed Rojas Pinilla, who agreed to the Calima loan negotiations with the World Bank; but the next day the defenders of a strong central state convinced the president to reverse this decision. Lilienthal, in protest, turned in his resignation as adviser.[28]

Anchicayá: The Last Battle

The end of the Lilienthal mission and the ensuing halt of all World Bank lending to Colombia found the Cali elite ready to spring the second stage of its strategy. Careful lobbying had convinced the National Planning Commission (forerunner of the National Planning Department) to recommend on 1 December 1956 that the CVC receive a huge appropriation of funds as well as the shares held by Electraguas in Anchicayá. Such a pork-barrel measure that sacrificed the interests of the whole country for the benefit of a privileged class in one region was only authorized by the tottering Rojas Pinilla regime because it was holding on for dear life; significantly enough, the proposal failed only because the Cali elite rejected the condition of changing the name of the CVC to the Rojas Pinilla Corporation.[29]

By April 1957 the entire Colombian elite had turned against General Rojas Pinilla; he was overthrown in May 1957 and replaced by a caretaker military junta until presidential elections could be held. The Cali elite decided to use this period of turmoil and transition to obtain its demands. In June 1957 new Minister of Development Joaquín Vallejo tried to convince the military junta to authorize the transfer of shares to CVC, and he carefully worded his arguments. Vallejo claimed that for the sake of effective action, electricity, flood control, and agricultural extension needed to be integrated into a single entity, and that since dams were needed for flood control at Timba and Salvajina, it was best to put electricity under the CVC for coordination as well. The obsolete provincial bureaucracies at Cali and Popayán (Caldas province had already refused to participate) would gradually be replaced by modern and dynamic public administration of the CVC. Minister Vallejo finished in a flurry claiming that CVC was a revolutionary experiment.

Normally such a combination of erroneous ideas would have been promptly refuted by Electraguas, but in the months of May–June 1957 this national institute was disorganized and under a cloud of public suspicion. In effect, between 1955 and May 1957, Electraguas had been fused along with the Institute for Municipal Development and a national housing agency into the mammoth National Corporation of Public Services, which had become so riddled with corruption during the last years of the Rojas Pinilla dictatorship that it had been promptly abolished and its individual agencies reconstituted. At last the military junta got around to appointing a new director of Electraguas, Carlos Sanclemente, who immediately sensed the dangers in the Vallejo proposals.

First of all, Sanclemente pointed out that Electraguas would lose its capital, since Anchicayá was its single largest investment and was rivaled in size only by Bogotá and Medellín. Second, the loss of Anchicayá rendered useless all previous efforts to coordinate a national program for electrification. The new director argued that the national government should be free to assign any profits Anchicayá might earn (and none were expected before four years) to benefit other regions, since it was elemental justice that national funds be spent for national purposes. Third, the transmission of electricity and flood control were more than enough to keep CVC busy, and saddling it with the huge cost of also generating the electricity would overburden its resources. As for Electraguas, Sanclemente was even more emphatic: The proposed measure meant nothing less than a "death blow" to its mission as the institute that coordinated national electrification.[30]

These irrefutable and prophetic arguments had no effect on Minister Vallejo, who on 4 July 1957 announced the national government's decision to turn Electraguas's shares in Anchicayá over to CVC, but they did have an impact on the manager of Anchicayá, Luis E. Palacios. Up to now a docile instrument of the Cali elite, Palacios panicked upon realizing that henceforth the power authority, which was already facing a monumental financial crisis, would have to survive without regular transfusions of central state funds. Palacios now joined with Electraguas to try to stop the transfer. But rather than fight him, the Cali elite decided to make the most of his concern by converting it into the basis for still another demand: CVC would receive the shares but not the debt of Anchicayá; the debt would remain the responsibility of Electraguas. This proposal amounted to nothing less than gutting the national government to subsidize the Cali elite, and the military junta did not even try to restore the sums Electraguas had lost.

Even this victory did not bring about an end to the matter. CVC kept digging up all sorts of old debts and unpaid bills that supposedly belonged to Electraguas, when in fact most had been backdated. When phony bills could no longer be plausibly presented, CVC officials began to seek "loans"—which they rarely repaid—and other forms of financial assistance from the national government. A $2.8 million World Bank loan in December 1958 eased the situation for the regional corporation somewhat, but in the case of foreign credits, CVC acquired the bad habit of having the national government guarantee a loan and then having it charged off to the account of a national institution like the Central State Bank or Electraguas. As had been repeatedly predicted, the Anchicayá reservoir duly silted up; to keep the plants operating, costly dredging became a permanent expense, wiping out the expected profit margin. After all the publicity the Cali elite had made about the CVC running Anchicayá, the province faced recurrent power shortages beginning in 1960.[31]

The claims for a revolutionary transformation can be summarily dismissed as pure rhetoric; in fact the CVC more than anything else reinforced the control of an exclusive elite over that region. The CVC served as a channel to finance the members of the Cali elite in one instance after another. The merchant-brokers obviously benefited from numerous lucrative contracts, but no less significant were the subsidies for wealthy industrialists by means of low electricity rates on the pretense that this would stimulate a period of rapid industrialization. The cement factory and the sugar mills, swimming in profits, could easily finance their own electrical power needs but were not about to reject an additional subsidy in the form of low industrial electricity rates. The industrialization of Cali was already an ongoing process prior to the creation of CVC, and although the cheap rates helped some small entrepreneurs, the main beneficiaries were the established wealthy industrialists.[32]

For the national government to continue subsidization of the CVC without having any control over it was certainly a striking phenomenon, yet explanations existed. A first reason reflected political rankings: Cali had become the third largest city in Colombia, displacing Barranquilla, and if the elites of Bogotá and Medellín were both allowed to have their own municipal power companies, why not Cali? Unfortunately, the Cali city government had grown too late and too little to absorb electrical generation. Furthermore, it tended to fall under the influence of popular groups, an inconvenience to the local elite who had to work out the substitute formula of forming a regional corporation under its close control. A second reason involved a certain perception shared by the Cali and Colombian elite: Both were gradually coming to the conclusion that rapid electrification was not in their best interests; thus, any formulas that interrupted or torpedoed electrification had to be given a fair hearing and even a trial period. The CVC guaranteed that the electrical supply in the province of Cali always lagged behind its real needs. But Electraguas, which even with reduced responsibilities could still channel its remaining resources to achieve decisive breakthroughs, was on the loose and had to be brought into line with the prevailing elite views, as the next chapter shows.

Notes

1. James J. Parson, *Antioqueño Colonization in Western Colombia*, 2d rev. ed. (Berkeley: University of California Press, 1968), chaps. 1, 2; Robert H. Davis, *Historical Dictionary of Colombia* (Metuchen, N.J.: The Scarecrow Press, 1977), pp. 68–69, 142; *Liberal*, 4 June 1945; *El Tiempo*, 20 Oct. 1945.

2. Howard Bowman report, 18 May 1944, 821.6461/2 Record Group (RG) 59, National Archives, Washington, D.C.

3. Eugene R. Black letter, 19 Jan. 1951, OF 313, Harry S. Truman Presidential Library; *El Siglo*, 11 Oct. 1946; *El Tiempo*, 21 Sept. 1947; *Liberal*, 2 July 1948; David Bushnell, *Eduardo Santos and the Good Neighbor Policy, 1938–1942* (Gainesville: University of Florida Press, 1967), pp. 70–79.

4. W. E. Dunn report, 21 Feb. 1944, 821.6463/47, RG 59; *Liberal*, 21 June 1943; *El Tiempo*, 17 March 1947.

5. Memorandums, 10 Oct. 1946, 4 Nov. 1946, Office of American Republics Affairs, Box 34, RG 59; *El Tiempo*, 29 Sept. 1947.

6. *Colombia económica*, no. 103 (Nov. 1950), pp. 1269–1270; *El Tiempo*, 17 March 1947, 3 July 1948; *El Espectador*, 12, 19 Nov. 1947.

7. Central Hidroeléctrica del Río Lebrija, *Breve reseña del origen desarrollo y proyecciones* (Bucaramanga: Editorial Oriente, 1950), pp. 7–12; 24 July 1951, 821.2614/7-2451, RG 59; Compañía Eléctrica de Bucaramanga, *Informes y balance, primer semestre de 1951* (Bucaramanga: Editorial As, 1951), p. 4.

8. Edward S. Mason and Robert E. Asher, *The World Bank Since Bretton Woods* (Washington, D.C.: The Brookings Institution, 1973), pp. 159–160; *Colombia económica*, no. 103 (Nov. 1951), pp. 1269–1270; *El Tiempo*, 20 July 1955.

9. Compañía Eléctrica de Bucaramanga, *Informes y balance, primer semestre de 1951* (Bucaramanga: Editorial As, 1951), pp. 4–5; Ibid., *Segundo Semestre*, pp. 3–4.

10. World Bank, *The Basis of a Development Program for Colombia* (Baltimore: Johns Hopkins University Press, 1950), pp. 419–423, 514–521; René De La Pedraja, *FEDEMETAL y la industrialización de Colombia* (Bogotá: Op Graficas, 1986), pp. 36–37; Mason and Asher, *The World Bank Since Bretton Woods*, pp. 300–302, 652.

11. Eugene R. Black letter, 19 Jan. 1951, OF 313, Truman Library; *Colombia económica*, no. 103 (Nov. 1950), pp. 1269–1270, no. 108 (Nov.–Dec. 1950), pp. 16–18.

12. Empresas Unidas de Energía Eléctrica, *Informes y balances, 30 diciembre 1938* (Bogotá: Prag, 1939), p. 1; Ibid., 1945; *El Tiempo*, 11 July 1945; *El Espectador*, 23 Feb. 1946.

13. *Liberal*, 3 April 1946; *El Espectador*, 23 June, 6 July 1945; Empresas Unidas de Energía Eléctrica, *Informes y balance, 1946* (Bogotá: Prag, 1947), pp. 4–5.

14. Ibid., pp. 5–6; *El Tiempo*, 5 June 1946; *El Espectador*, 9 May, 9 June 1947; *Liberal*, 24 May, 10 June 1947.

15. *New York Times*, 19 April 1947; Empresas Unidas de Energía Eléctrica, *Informes y balance, 1947* (Bogotá: Prag, 1948), pp. 5–6; *Jornada*, 18 April 1947; *Liberal*, 18, 22 April, 21 May 1947; *El Tiempo*, 14, 24 May 1947; *El Siglo*, 14 Jan. 1948.

16. Empresas Unidas, *Informes, 1946*, pp. 8–9, 10; *El Espectador*, 17 Sept. 1947; *Liberal*, 21 June, 17 Oct. 1947.

17. Herbert Braun, *The Assassination of Gaitán: Public Life and Urban Violence in Colombia* (Madison: University of Wisconsin Press, 1986); *La Razón*, 6 April 1948; *El Espectador*, 3 April 1948; *New York Times*, 18 Feb., 22 March 1948.

18. Empresas Unidas de Energía Eléctrica, *Informes y balance, 1948* (Bogotá: Prag, 1949), pp. 9, 11; *Liberal*, 1 July 1948; *El Tiempo*, 3 June 1948; *El Espectador*, 7 June 1948.

19. Empresas Unidas de Energía Eléctrica, *Informes y balances, 1940 to 1948*, passim; René De La Pedraja, *Historia de la energía en Colombia, 1537–1930* (Bogotá: El Ancora, 1985), chap. 3.

20. *Liberal*, 7 Oct. 1948; *El Espectador*, 26 Feb. 1948.

21. *New York Times*, 1 Dec. 1950, 30 March 1951; Empresas Unidas de Energía Eléctrica, *Informes y balance, 1950* (Bogotá: Prag, 1951), pp. 5, 7–8; *El Siglo*, 24 April 1950.

22. *Colombia económica*, no. 103 (1950), pp. 1269–1271; Instituto Nacional de Aprovechamiento de Aguas y Fomento Eléctrico, *Informe del gerente, 1954* (Bogotá: Aedita Ltd., 1955), pp. 12–13.

23. Manuel Carvajal, *Realidades de la electrificación en el Valle del Cauca* (Cali, 1969), pp. 4–5, 25–26; Antonio J. Posada and Jeanne de Posada, *CVC: Un reto al subdesarrollo y al tradicionalismo* (Bogotá: Tercer Mundo, 1966), p. 50; *El Tiempo*, 27 July 1955.

24. José Castro Borrero to Milo Perkins, 27 June 1953, David E. Lilienthal Papers, Box 294, Princeton University Library; World Bank, *Basis for Colombia*, pp. xi–xviii; David E. Lilienthal, *Venturesome Years* (New York: Harper & Row Publishers, 1966), p. 476. The published entries from the Lilienthal diaries used in this book have been checked against the originals in Princeton.

25. Lilienthal, *Venturesome Years*, pp. 487–490.

26. "Recommendations on the Establishment of Regional Development Authorities by the Republic of Colombia," New York City, 25 June 1954, Lilienthal Papers, Box 294, Princeton University; Posada and de Posada, *CVC*, p. 67.

27. World Bank, "The Autonomous Regional Corporation of the Cauca," Nov. 1955; CVC, "The Unified Development of Power and Water Sources in the Cauca Valley," Jan. 1956; Lilienthal to Robert Garner, 27 Aug. 1954, Lilienthal Papers, Box 294.

28. Diary entry, 13 July 1956, Lilienthal Papers, Box 202; David E. Lilienthal, *The Road to Change, 1955–1959* (New York: Harper & Row, 1969), pp. 99–103; Posada and de Posada, *CVC*, pp. 166–168.

29. J. Phillip Rourk report, 25 July 1957, 821.2614, RG 59; Posada and de Posada, *CVC*, pp. 167–168.

30. J. Phillip Rourk reports, 12 July and 25 July 1957, 821.2614, RG 59; Posada and de Posada, *CVC*, pp. 167–169, 178–179; *Relator*, 19 July 1957.

31. *Foreign Commerce Weekly*, 29 Dec. 1958; Manuel Carvajal, *Realidades de la electrificación*, pp. 6–8.

32. José Antonio Ocampo and Santiago Montenegro, *Crisis mundial, protección e industrialización: Ensayos de historia económica colombiana* (Bogotá: CEREC, 1984), chap. 7; Hugh Collier, *Developing Electric Power: Thirty Years of World Bank Experience* (Baltimore: Johns Hopkins University Press, 1984), pp. 94–95; *El Tiempo*, 25 Jan. 1966; Posada and de Posada, *CVC*, pp. 112–116, and see chaps. 7, 8 for an opposite interpretation about the impact of CVC.

11

Slowing Down the State

The loss of the Bogotá utility and the creation of the CVC sharply reduced the central state's sphere of activity. Colombia already was lagging in meeting electricity needs, and just how costly was the lack of a centralized power authority became apparent in the long and time-consuming struggle over the steam plants at Paipa and Zipaquirá. Electraguas had still not recovered from this effort when another event, The nationalization of the American and Foreign Power Company utilities, permanently crippled the central state's ability to effectively electrify the country.

Steam Plants at Paipa and Zipaquirá

Fifty miles north of Bogotá begins the densely populated region of Boyacá characterized by crushing poverty. To try to industrialize this very traditional agrarian society that had scarcely changed in three centuries, the national government resolved to establish the Paz del Río steel mill as a state-owned enterprise and the first modern steel mill in Colombia. According to the initial plan, a dam at Cusiana would provide cheap electricity to transform the local iron ore into steel as well as to supply the neighboring region. The ample hydroelectric potential of Boyacá easily guaranteed expansion for future needs.[1]

On closer analysis, however, cost considerations ruled out the Cusiana dam. Capital was very scarce because the World Bank, the Export-Import Bank, and other foreign institutions were opposed to the steel mill. Thus, the national government had to construct the Paz del Río project quickly and with the minimum expense. The Colombian government faced a difficult choice: to build either the Paz del Río steel mill or the Cusiana dam. Regrettably, the state abandoned the dam, and this move forced Paz del Río to set up a traditional blast furnace consuming coke produced from the nearby coal mines. To meet future demand for electricity in the mill, Paz del Río installed steam-generating plants that were expensive to run. Excess capacity from these plants would be sold during the initial years to the surrounding regions in Boyacá.[2]

The national government, in anticipation of the 1955 transfer of the steel mill proper to private investors, decided in 1953 to assume the distribution of the excess current (10 megawatts annually during 1954–1956). Simple calculations sufficed to convince Electraguas that another steam plant (of 25 megawatts) would be needed in Paipa after 1956 to meet growing demand from both the steel mill and Boyacá. Electraguas made a call for bids, but not fully confident of its technical expertise to judge a steam plant larger than any then in Colombia, it took the precaution of hiring a Belgian consulting firm to give an independent opinion. By the end of 1954, constant and meticulous studies had confirmed the best offer for the plant; all that remained was to award the contracts.

At this point the military regime of Rojas Pinilla intervened. Arguing that the project was too small, the government called for new bids for three units of 33 megawatts each; not only was each unit bigger than anything else in Colombia, but their combined capacity was also larger than Bogotá's, then the largest in the country. The only valid reason for such a monumental project was to attempt to break the gripping bond of poverty by a huge shocking blow, but actually its real purposes were less lofty; first to provide lucrative commissions and kickbacks to those involved in the negotiations, thus bolstering support from the private sector, and second, to gain political backing for the Rojas Pinilla regime in Boyacá.[3]

The speculation had been sparked by a French concern (Comptoir Industriel et Agricole de Vente à L'Etranger) that had offered financing for the Paipa project on the basis of no questions asked. The catch was in the equipment: Electraguas could choose only from a French manufacturer. But the lowest French bid was outrageously high compared to the prices of U.S. and other European suppliers. President Rojas Pinilla was at first seriously worried about such a huge difference in price. But when the director of Electraguas tried to return to the original bids made by the other manufacturers, he found himself without a job, and nothing more was ever heard about the president's intial worry.

The bids were duly awarded, and the factories in France put their idle capacity to work meeting these new orders; but before the French could celebrate their commercial coup, a snag held up the project. The foreign financing did not cover the substantial local expenses, for which Colombian currency was needed. Since the many projects of Rojas Pinilla to enrich the Colombian elite had drained the national treasury, a scheme emerged to tap the funds of the Bogotá Light and Power Company. As explained in Chapter 10, this company, as property of the city government, was independent of the central state. Hydroelectric power formed the bulk of the expansion plans for the capital city; in addition, to cover water shortages during the dry summer months, the Bogotá Light and Power Company had selected the coal mines at Zipaquirá (twenty miles north of the capital) as a site for a backup steam plant. Capitalizing upon this state of affairs, the Rojas Pinilla dictatorship now advanced a scheme to transfer the planned Zipaquirá plant to Paipa. The only additional expense the new plan entailed was the cost of installing the Paipa-Zipaquirá transmission lines needed to carry the large loads.[4]

Forced to join the scheme, the Bogotá Light and Power Company was nevertheless able to delay providing funds until the overthrow of Rojas Pinilla in May 1957. For more than two years starting from the middle of 1957, a ferocious battle raged between the interested groups. Electraguas was left in the worst possible situation with its mounting debt and dearth of construction. To avoid paying the costs incurred by contractors who benefited from commissions and the like, the Bogotá Light and Power Company wanted to get out of Paipa. As a matter of fact, the bitter struggle that had erupted did not reflect real institutional or technical differences but rather a clash between two rival factions of merchant-brokers that controlled both Electraguas and the Bogotá Light and Power Company. It was impossible to wipe the slate clean and start all over: French diplomats repeatedly protested and exerted pressure whenever they saw the contract threatened. But so unusual were the circumstances that by mutual accord the terms of payment had to be renegotiated.[5]

Meanwhile, the Bogotá Light and Power Company took the offensive with its counterproposal to set up the three 33-megawatt units in Zipaquirá rather than Paipa. Quite naturally a long round of bitter debate ensued over the location of the steam plant. Very technical reasons were marshaled by both sides to disguise the essentially political struggle for control.[6] Electraguas had no final authority in the matter and was not even vested with the power to approve electricity rates for the country. But to bring some pressure to bear upon the Bogotá Light and Power Company, which had requested a long overdue increase in rates, the minister of development finally agreed to intervene with the state regulatory commission: The company was forced to participate in Paipa in exchange for approval of the rate increase. Cornered only temporarily, the Bogotá Light and Power Company continued to drag its feet until May 1959, when it cleverly regained the offensive by maneuvering to secure a formal written agreement that made the World Bank the final arbiter of the steam plant's location. The company did not waste a minute in contacting two junior World Bank employees before Electraguas could reach them. The company's one-sided evidence convinced the World

Bank officials, who then criticized the whole Paipa project in the strongest terms.

Its hand strengthened by this opinion from the World Bank, in June 1959 the Bogotá utility denounced the agreement of the previous month as null and void. But in shelving the whole Paipa project, it had gone too far. Emilio Toro, a very dynamic member of the Electraguas Board of Directors, urged the Colombian government to go directly to the World Bank, However, after Carlos Sanclemente, the director of Electraguas, refused the order to go himself by turning in his resignation (which was not acepted), Toro proceeded personally on behalf of Electraguas to the Washington, D.C., World Bank headquarters in an effort to salvage what was possible out of the whole mess. Sanclemente considered it degrading in the extreme to have a foreign institution witness all this infighting. As a matter of fact, since 1957 he had repeatedly asked the national government to end the struggle with a decision that would enable Electraguas to get on with the rest of its overwhelming work. President Alberto Lleras Camargo, however, only kept himself minutely informed of everything that transpired.

Emilio Toro enjoyed direct access to senior World Bank officials and by July 1959 had already secured their approval for any workable agreement that would end this drawn-out struggle. The task was not as easy as it sounded, however. After considerable racking of brains at many meetings, a World Bank official came up with the suggestion of selling half of the Paipa equipment to CVC, which had received World Bank funds to purchase a steam plant for Yumbo next to the city of Cali. The proceeds from this sale would cover the costs of setting up the remaining half of the equipment in Paipa. Toro returned to Bogotá to seek support for the formula, but before Electraguas had time to consult with CVC, the Bogotá Light and Power company offered to buy one of the 33-megawatt units for its own steam plant at Zipaquirá. The CVC gladly agreed to purchase the Paipa-Zipaquirá transmission lines (which had not yet been put in place) for its network. Electraguas was charged with erecting the second 33-megawatt unit in Paipa, and as for the third unit (which, unlike the first two, was still in France), other arrangements would be made to placate the French. President Lleras Camargo finally told all concerned that this arrangement enjoyed his presidential blessing, and at long last 1960 saw work begin in both Paipa and Zipaquirá.

Why had the Bogotá Light and Power Company waited so long to make the saving proposal? Basically the utility had trusted too much in its hydroelectric expansion plans, which had underestimated demand. When the capital city faced the prospect of having power shortages for at least three years starting in 1960, the company realized that the only way it could increase electric generation quickly enough was by placing the Paipa 33-megawatt unit in Zipaquirá and getting it on line before the hydroelectric projects could be completed.[7] Although the World Bank had repeatedly urged that rates be increased even more—not for the purpose of accumulating capital but as a rationing device to reduce consumption—that was a solution that could not be sustained for long without incurring political costs. In any case, the five-year struggle had distracted and so weakened Electraguas that it was in no position to face new challenges—such as the nationalization of the U.S. utilities.

The Nationalization of the U.S. Utilities

The latest expansion plan of the American and Foreign Power Company called for installing more than 80 megawatts in new capacity throughout the plants of the Colombian subsidiary. This expansion, which was gigantic for Colombia, had been prompted both by rapidly rising demand for electricity and by the fact that by 1948 the Colombian subsidiary had begun to make annual profit remittances to the United States for the first time in its twenty-year history. Headquarters in New York now agreed to release funds, but capital continued to come mainly from two sources: the high rate of internal saving achieved by the utilities' very efficient operations, and the Export-Import Bank loans obtained only after intensive lobbying by the New York office. From January 1956 to February 1957, the American and Foreign Power Company installed a total of 19 megawatts in the cities of Barranquilla (with a 15-megawatt unit), Buenaventura, Girardot, and Honda—an operation that required no effort or sacrifice from the Colombian government and also brought scarce foreign currency into the country.[8]

With the first part of the expansion program in place, the company asked the Colombian government, as an incentive to complete the plan, for the right to remit any future profits abroad. The use of the word "profits" was unfortunate because it conveyed the idea that huge sums of money were being drained out of Colombia by the U.S. company. In reality, the first claim on remittances went to the susidized interest payments on the Export-Import Bank loans as well as to cover the manufacturers' short-term credits for equipment purchases. No problem arose while dealing with institutions like Electraguas, which understood that the collaboration of foreign capital, in particular the American and Foreign Power Company, was absolutely indispensable to reducing the lag in electrification. State funds could cover at most 40 percent of the power requirements. In early 1958 when Colombia once again was facing one of its recurrent foreign exchange crises, Electraguas renewed its support for the U.S. utility because its expansion could bring millions of dollars into the stagnant economy.

In the late 1950s, Electraguas was reforming its whole policy toward national electrification. The bitter battles over Bogotá and CVC that had ended in disaster had weakened Electraguas, and the struggle for Paipa had devoured time and money at an alarming rate. Spreading state funds thinly across the country clearly did not have any appreciable effect on the problems at hand, while the private Colombian utilities that still remained subsisted only to milk the state out of funds. In this bleak panorama, the only bright lights were the solid accomplishments of the American and Foreign Power Company. Quite realistically, Electraguas now decided to shape a policy that would build upon the company's often remarkable achievements. Henceforth, state funds would go to fewer government utilities, and those chosen few would also receive a greater amount of scarce managerial and technical talent.

As a corollary to this new policy, a number of state projects, such as the Cartagena utility and the Coello river dam at Tolima, would be sold to the American and Foreign Power Company. Speculators had wrestled the Cartagena utility out of the U.S. company and into the hands of the city government in the 1940s. Central state funds were then tapped to construct a steam plant at nearby Cospique, but the only visible result was a permanent flow of expenses due to constant rackets over contracts, supplies, and salaries. Electraguas soon realized that to stop the permanent drain on funds, the only alternative was to sell the Cartagena utility back to the American and Foreign Power Company.[9] Neither had speculation been absent in the case of the Coello river dam, but here the main problem was of a different nature. The Tolima Power Authority, short of managerial talent and funds, saw its attention monopolized by the task of trying to provide adequate electric service to the capital city of Ibagué; as a result, the Coello project was badly bungled. This failure contrasted sharply with the transmission network between Honda and Girardot that the American and Foreign Power Company had patiently built and later extended to neighboring towns like Mariquita. Although other transfers were under study, with the initiative always springing from the central state, the U.S. company was usually reluctant to accept the additional responsiblities.

By the 1950s the American and Foreign Power Company had some small hydroelectric projects on line and was planning a number of larger dams (such as in the Sierra Nevada de Santa Marta) that, when joined together by transmission lines stretching across the Atlantic coast, would considerably reduce generating costs. However, steam plants fired by oil (and some diesel engines) still comprised the majority of its installations, making the U.S. utilities very vulnerable to fluctuations in fuel prices.

World prices were in fact holding steady, but the company could only use Colombian currency because of foreign exchange controls. The 1958 devaluation of the peso meant that more pesos had to be spent for the same number of dollars which, in effect, raised the price of fuel. With this development, operating expenses shot up past the sale price of electricity. Inflation, the inevitable sequel to devaluation, meant that the rates, which had been frozen since 1949, did not really stay the same but actually declined. The profits of the American and Foreign Power Company disappeared, no more dividends left the country, and the company faced great difficulty meeting the interest payments on the outstanding foreign loans. By October 1959 patience had run out. Company officials formally told the minister of development that unless a rate increase was approved, the company would have to sell its properties to the Colombian government. The minister of development made the serious mistake of dismissing the company's offer as a bluff, and he did not bother to relay the warning to other government agencies, such as Electraguas, which would have immediately recognized the extreme gravity of the situation.[10]

A virulently anti-American official at the state regulatory commission continued to delay the rate increase, and quite naturally, consumption of electricity at the low rates climbed rapidly. The American and Foreign Power Company predicted that by 1961—much sooner than originally expected—the generating capacity in Barranquilla would be insufficient, and it placed full responsibility on the government for the inevitable shortages. The prospects of riots over power rationing gradually overcame the opposition in the state regulatory commission, which finally, on 1 August 1960, decreed a 40 percent raise in rates. In real dollars the increase was still less than the devaluation, but since the larger volume of sales made possible a greater total income, the company decided to proceed with its original expansion plans. The New York headquarters authorized the shipment of a 16-megawatt steam plant that previously had been detained in a U.S. factory, and the Colombian subsidiary rushed to complete the whole expansion program to stave off the impending shortages. The timing of the decree could not have been worse: In that very same month, Cuba nationalized the properties of the American and Foreign Power Company on the island as part of a series of moves that, years later, even Cuban government leaders admitted were premature.[11]

Two groups in Barranquila saw the precious opportunity to strike a blow. The first group was the merchant-brokers, who had for many years bitterly resented being left out of the bidding for the big contracts. Although the U.S. company procured whatever Colombian goods were available, purchases of imported equipment with their juicy commissions were negotiated directly by the American and Foreign Power Company without recourse to local intermediaries. In many cases, Export-Import Bank loans forced the U.S. company to buy products from the United States even though they were available in Colombia. The merchant-brokers cited these cases as a pretext to criticize the company when in reality the merchant-brokers themselves were just as quick to favor foreign goods because of their normally larger commissions. The second group, and no less important, included the local bankers and financiers. Their complaints against the American and Foreign Power Company were simple: Because of the company's high rate of internal savings and its ability to borrow at lower rates abroad, local financial institutions had been deprived of the opportunity to earn interest by means of the short-term loans so characteristic of Colombia's commercial lending.

The obsession with making quick commercial profits, even at the cost of sacrificing the whole country's electrical growth, drove the merchant-brokers, backed by the local financiers, to mobilize the consumers and the labor unions. This task was easy because the population of Barranquilla had grown accustomed to compensating for their very low incomes with cheap electricity. Placards covered the city and demonstrators took to the streets. To symbolize their dislike, the protestors burned effigies of "Reddy Kilowatt," the cute figure that the American and Foreign Power Company had used in publicity campaigns to ease acceptance of electricity in the homes. The misguided crowds soon turned to violence. They pelted the offices with rocks and bullets and almost burned them down. Even more serious, demonstrators attempted to destroy the power plants. Luckily, timely intervention stopped the damage. The purpose of these attacks was very clear: The greater the destruction, the larger would be the commissions to replace damaged equipment. The labor unions, enthusiastic over the example of Cuba, totally misunderstood the real objectives of the revolutionary struggle. Although in Cuba the utilities had been left for last, the Colombian laborers hastily concluded that their revolution would begin with the nationalization of the American and Foreign Power company.[12]

At first the national government postponed the new rates for 120 days. Since this measure did not quiet the protests, the government went even further and in an incredible reversal told the company to refund the additional receipts that had already been collected. This sorry spectacle of caving in to the demands of the merchant-brokers and the financiers in Barranquilla was the last straw for Myron G. Reed, the manager of the Colombian subsidiary. He and his fellow engineers were tired of repeatedly getting caught between the local complaints and the refusals of New York headquarters to release funds for Colombia. Reed himself had spent eleven years in the sweltering heat and tropical rains to try to make Barranquilla into a modern city, and now he and his fellow engineers, some of even longer service, felt that their efforts had all been wasted. They decided to cut their losses and leave an ungrateful and unrewarding country. The New York officials were normally more belligerent and would not have quit without a good fight, but paralyzed by the takeover in Cuba, headquarters just could not pull itself away to rescue a subsidiary that had rarely shown profits. The Eisenhower administration, which five years before had rapidly moved to protect U.S. interests in the Pipeline to the Pacific, was now likewise obsessed with the Cuban phenomenon. The State Department was ready to mediate, but eager to present a united front against Castro, did not want any rallying cries for anti-Americanism breaking out in the Western Hemisphere.

Without international pressures, negotiations might have concluded rapidly, but instead they dragged out for a year and a half, not over price quibbling but over a fundamental split within the Colombian elite. The fact that the U.S. company's previous offer to sell in October 1959 had been kept a closely guarded secret and had even been the focus of a cover-up scheme made the company's 1960 decision to leave the country a total surprise to many influential Colombians. Personalities such as Emilio Toro, Diego Mejía, Jorge Méndez, Vincente Pizano, and Carlos Sanclemente thought that purchasing the U.S. utilities would be nothing less than a colossal blunder. They found allies in and out of the Colombian government, such as Minister of Development Rafael Unda, who shared their concern. This group, the elite minority, sought first to keep the American and Foreign Power Company in Colombia, or failing that, to find some compromise formula that would retain at least a part of the U.S. utilities.

Nationalization meant ending any hopes of ever reducing the lag in electrification. But this was exactly what most members of the elite wanted. The short-term quick profits that could be made from the power authorities was the fundamental concern for the elite majority. A propertied class of intermediaries dependent upon handouts from the power authorities was the best way to assure internal order; at the same time, this system had the advantage of guaranteeing class control. Rapid expansion of electricity would radically change the social structures and threaten the status quo. The elite preferred to sacrifice increased wealth for the sake of greater control.

Thus was forged a strong link between the old landholding elite, the rising financiers, and the burgeoning merchant-brokers, all of whom joined ranks to block electrification as well as economic development. Early in 1961 a delegation from Barranquilla visited President Alberto Lleras Camargo, who proved sympathetic to nationalization. However, the president did not press the issue because the Barranquilla industrialists, who needed power to run their factories, began to express doubts— justifiably, as later experience showed—about whether a new public utility would supply power as efficiently and reliably as the American and Foreign Power Company had always done. The Barranquilla industrialists thus provided a breathing spell that the elite minority used to seek support abroad. All that was needed was a phone call to the Colombian government from one institution like the World Bank, the Export-Import Bank, or the U.S. State Department saying that it was in Colombia's best interests to keep the American and Foreign Power Company in place. But nobody could be found, not even in the probusiness Eisenhower administration, which had repeatedly preached the benefits that private enterprise would bring to the developing world.[13]

Curiously enough, the biggest stumbling block was the company's own insistence on getting out—an attitude that neither Electraguas nor Minister of Development Unda had been able to overcome in spite of repeated attempts. The American and Foreign Power Company would reconsider only if President Lleras himself appealed to the company. This was not an unreasonable request, especially since the president himself had made, for nationalistic propaganda, a hostile but otherwise routine speech against foreign investment in utilities. In private, the president was still not fully decided, and although he was moving gradually toward the elite majority position favoring nationalization, he proceeded gingerly. He took care not to take any independent action and left the door open to foreign suggestions until the last minute. Seeing the end closing in, the elite minority made one last desperate attempt in uncharted waters: They asked the Chemical Bank and other institutions with financial dealings in Colombia to try to convince the American and Foreign Power Company to reconsider its inflexible position, but the banks expressed little interest.

Sensing the majority behind him, President Lleras on 14 July 1961 verbally ordered the nationalization of the American and Foreign Power company assets. No public announcements were made. The decision was deliberately kept vague to give foreign interests one last chance to express their opinions. Nothing was heard in two months, so the president felt free to remove Minister of Development Unda, who had opposed nationalization. In October 1961 Lleras at last ordered prompt action. Agreement had been reached previously on a $25 million compensation figure, but many details still needed to be ironed out. Among the most significant was that the 40 percent increase in rates would take effect immediately upon nationalization so that the company could be paid in annual installments during the next twenty years out of future receipts.

The contract duly signed in late December 1961 was not the end of the matter. The government easily obtained congressional approval to eliminate much legal bickering, yet having a law did not prevent a bitter debate from raging between 1962 and 1968 over nationalization, in particular over whether the price was correct. The 1960-1961 negotiations had consumed huge amounts of time and effort, but even more wasteful were the after-the-fact debates: Electraguas saw its strength sapped by this bitter six-year controversy that only served to distract attention away from Colombia's lagging needs. The elite did not complain, since their goal was precisely to slow down the electrification of the country.[14]

Financial resources were already stretched so thinly across Colombia that retrenchment rather than advancement was the only alternative. To add responsibilities for supplying electricity to the many regions that the American and Foreign Power Company served meant nothing less than overwhelming state activity. Barranquilla, one of the largest cities in Colombia, required huge investments to meet rising demand, but where would the capital come from if future receipts were already mortgaged to pay the price of nationalization? Throughout Colombia, hydroelectric projects that were urgently needed—such as Florida II, Prado, Mayo, and Betania—had to be repeatedly postponed, and many others either canceled or not even considered. The central state tried desperately to cover the crying demands for electricity with vastly inadequate resources. Electraguas, already weakened by the struggle over the steam plants at Paipa and Zipaquirá, was reduced to nothing more than a distributor of poverty. Rather than boldly pushing gigantic projects to break the invisible barrier of underdevelopment, now it merely assigned a corresponding share of the lag to each of the provinces, all of which in the final outcome remained poor and backwards.

More consequences were also forthcoming. The managerial and technical talents of the American and Foreign Power Company proved to be irreplaceable. From a purely local perspective, the nationalization of the utilities was the one event that most clearly pointed to Barranquilla's decline in ranking among Colombia's major cities. By the 1960s the national government had revealed itself to be both unwilling and incapable of electrifying the country. The main function of the state agencies was to channel government funds to the merchant-brokers and financiers. For this role an appearance of meaningful activity had to be maintained: Some projects were concluded while most began long and complex steps toward elaboration. To provide more respectability, the central state hired French experts to compile a National Electrification Plan, which, published in English, Spanish, and French, proposed a fantastic number of projects to be carried out from 1965 to 1975.[15] No amount of publicity could hide the fact that the central state's role in electricity had ceased to be of decisive impact. Nevertheless, one small faction within the elite still refused to give up and continued to press for rapid electrification through novel proposals, as the next chapter shows.

Notes

1. René De La Pedraja, *FEDEMETAL y la industrialización de Colombia* (Bogotá: Op Gráficas, 1986), pp. 35–36.

2. *Liberal*, 23 Jan. 1948; *El Siglo*, 3, 10 July 1947; De La Pedraja, *FEDEMETAL*, pp. 36–38. This is not the place for a full evaluation of Paz del Río's performance, but the fact remains that the lack of hydroelectricity—independently of whether electricity rather than coke was used to produce steel from the iron ore—put Paz del Río at a crippling disadvantage from the very start. From a different perspective, steam plants at the steel mill had the unforeseen effect of excluding other alternatives in future expansions. Later, even when the central state wanted to build a hydroelectric dam, it could not do so because powerful private interests, including the merchant-brokers, cleverly disguised themselves behind coal workes and the owners of small mines to protect their vested stake in steam plants.

3. *El Siglo*, 27 Aug. 1953; *Industria colombiana* (Jan.–Feb. 1956), p. 35.

4. Victor Jiménez, "La termoeléctrica de Paipa, redención de Boyacá," *Industria colombiana* (Oct. 1957), pp. 9–12; René De La Pedraja, *Historia de la energía en Colombia, 1537–1930* (Bogotá: El Ancora, 1985), pp. 75–81.

5. Empresas Unidas de Energía Eléctrica de Bogotá, *Informe, 1958*, pp. 7–9; *El Tiempo*, 10 April 1958.

6. One technical reason may be mentioned as a sample: The Bogotá company pointed out that there was not enough water for cooling lakes in Paipa and that Zipaquirá, with ample water, required fewer cooling towers and hence was cheaper to build. A study by an independent Belgian firm was promptly contracted by Electraguas to refute this assertion, but even before the report was in, the Bogotá company unleashed new arguments that put the availability of water at Paipa in doubt.

7. Construction had barely started when the Bogotá company had to order a second steam plant of 37 megawatts (Zipaquirá II) to meet even higher than expected demand; Zipaquirá I came on line in 1963, and Zipaquirá II in 1964. Empresa de Energía Eléctrica de Bogotá, *Informe, 1963–1964*, p. 2.

8. Mira Wilkins, *The Maturing of Multinational Enterprise: American Business Abroad from 1914 to 1970* (Cambridge: Cambridge University Press, 1974), pp. 200–203.

9. *Liberal*, 31 July 1948; De La Pedraja, *Historia de la energía*, p. 139.

10. Compañía Colombiana de Electricidad to Minister of Development, 7 Oct. 1959, 821.2614/10-1559, Record Group (RG) 59, National Archives, Washington, D.C.; Wilkins, *Multinational Enterprise*, pp. 302–304.

11. Fidel Castro, *La experiencia cubana* (Barcelona: Editorial Blume, 1976), pp. 56–63, 104–109; 15 Oct. 1959, 821.2614/10-1559, RG 59.

12. *Fortune*, Feb. 1962, pp. 103, 220; *Boletín de la Cámara de Comercio de Barranquilla*, 28 Feb. 1961.

13. Burton I. Kaufman, *Trade and Aid: Eisenhower's Foreign Economic Policy, 1953-1961* (Baltimore: Johns Hopkins University Press, 1982), pp. 5–6, 21, 154–159, 199.

14. *New York Times*, 27 Dec. 1961, 4 Aug. 1962; *Economía Gran Colombiana* 1 (1963):420–429; *El Tiempo*, 16 Feb. 1969.

15. Electraguas, *Plan Nacional de Electrificación, 1965–1975: Informe de Electricité de France* (Vincennes: L'imprimerie H. Dridé, 1965), pp. 12–13, 121–165, 209–230.

12

Toward a National Electrical System

Three institutional changes reflected attempts to set Colombia's electric program on a sound national basis. Two of these changes occurred in 1967: the creation of an Electric Interconnection Company, ISA, and the establishment of a regional corporation, Corelca, for the Atlantic coast provinces. The next year the national government decided that Electraguas, which henceforth would be known as ICEL (Colombian Institute of Electrification), should devote itself exclusively to electric power. The Colombian Institute for Agrarian Reform would assume charge of the flood control and irrigation projects. The national government also hoped that this streamlined ICEL would be able to develop a dynamic push through the newly created ISA, but ISA failed its first major test with the Chivor project. The attempts to develop a nuclear energy program complete the picture of the government's endeavors to electrify Colombia.

The Interconnection of Colombia: ISA

Until the late 1960s, Colombia had operated with local utilities. This pattern, inherited from the late nineteenth century, meant that no provinces were ever joined by transmission lines. There were many things to worry about in Colombia's lagging electrification program, but lack of interconnection was certainly not a reason for concern. Indeed, the historical experience of Western Europe, whose interconnection only came after the development of abundant electricity, and that of the United States, which still does not have a national grid, strongly suggested that linking a country with high tension cables was not an urgent priority. This is not to deny the possibilities a grid can offer for economic development, most notably evident in the case of the Soviet Union, where gigantic power dams linked by very long transmission cables sparked that country's rapid economic growth. Thus, Colombia faced

175

two alternatives in the 1960s: either dispense with the national grid as just a luxury to be attained only after the country had joined the industrial nations, or else follow the Soviet model and include the grid within a massive plan to mobilize all resources to achieve sustained economic growth.[1]

The idea of a national electric grid gained currency in Colombia when French experts elaborated the *National Electrification Plan for 1965–1975*. Launched for publicity purposes, this idea unexpectedly caused quite a stir, and Electraguas saw no harm in convening a meeting in early 1963 to discuss the pros and cons of the plan with the CVC, the Medellín Municipal Power Company, and the Bogotá Light and Power Company. The committee met three times, but for the fourth meeting only the Electraguas officials showed up, and they concluded that the idea had died a natural death and let matters rest. Only later did Electraguas discover that in fact the other three members had continued meeting on their own, but secretly to exclude the national government. To make things more humiliating, World Bank representatives participated in these clandestine gatherings. The central state lacked any authority to enter into these discussions, much less to stop them. To the disbelief of later generations, Medellín, Bogotá, and the CVC considered it perfectly normal to decide upon a national grid without the participation of the central state; more bizarre still, it was the World Bank itself that soon realized that the conspiratorial nature of these gatherings had to end and pressed instead for the inclusion of Electraguas to legitimize them. Finally, in April 1964 the three original members invited Electraguas to join their deliberations. After a few meetings, Electraguas, still with a wounded pride, threatened to leave, but the World Bank representatives cracked the whip and told the state officials to stay.[2]

Momentum for the national grid came mainly from two sources: the merchant-brokers and the World Bank. The suggestion by the French experts to build a national electric grid was eagerly greeted by the merchant-brokers. The reason for their fervent support was quite clear: juicy contracts and rich commissions were waiting to be plucked on the sale of transmission towers, high tension cables, and supporting equipment such as transformers and installations. None of the individual utility companies had planned such large expenditures in transmission facilities, so that if this national program for interconnection was carried out, a huge and unexpected windfall profit would fall to the merchant-brokers. Each of the utilities had its own crowd of merchant-brokers, and not unexpectedly they did not want the national government to supervise and ask unwanted questions. Moving local pressures among politicians and wheeling and dealing whenever necessary, the merchant-brokers were responsible for keeping the proposal alive and finally easing its acceptance.

Most of the merchant-brokers represented foreign manufacturers of cables and transmission equipment, so that their interests neatly dovetailed with those of the World Bank, which provided the hard currency loans to buy those goods abroad. However, the World Bank had other reasons as well, and its motivation for favoring the creation of the Electric Interconnection Company, or ISA, were complex. This international financial institution was starting to realize that the existence of independent and often antagonistic utilities was hurting the electrification of Colombia. The World Bank never admitted its partial responsibility for this fragmented situation, most blatantly in the case of the CVC, where the promise of loans to the newly created regional organization was fundamental in securing independence from the central state, and indeed, later loans had kept the CVC afloat only by going from one financial crisis to another. Not surprisingly, the CVC, which had fought so hard for its independence was not about to cooperate in any type of national electrical program; the World Bank now wanted to partly remedy this situation by forcing a recalcitrant CVC, along with Medellín and Bogotá, into the new ISA.[3]

The arguments that the World Bank repeatedly expounded in favor of ISA may be summarized as follows. The first and foremost reason concerned the size of the generating plants: Each utility had built small plants to meet its foreseeable needs. But now ISA could build larger hydroelectric projects whose excess capacity, too large for any one region to absorb, would now be sent by the new transmission system to other parts of the country. Moreover, the larger plant size by itself would produce savings in construction and operation because of "economies of scale." Second, reserve capacity for emergencies would be pooled, thereby reducing the installed capacity required by at least 10 percent compared to the required capacity if each of the utilities had their own reserve because simultaneous emergencies would not be likely. Third, peak demand for electricity would not always take place at the same hour and on the same day throughout the whole system, thus making possible a savings in installed capacity while at the same time allowing the generating capacity to be used more fully all the time and not just at a peak period. A last major argument claimed that the large hydroelectric dams, by tapping different river and rainfall patterns across the country, would reduce dependence on local sources, which can dry up, thus compensating shortages of water in one region with generation from another.[4]

Without going into other details, it was sufficiently clear that the arguments of the World Bank in no way even resembled the Soviet model of rapid industrialization by means of transferring electricity from gigantic power plants via a transmission grid. Furthermore, serious objections faced each of the arguments. First, the stations were located in the same rainfall systems that had traditionally suffered droughts rather than in other areas, such as the rain-drenched Chocó. As to the benefits of having larger plants, the goal was not to have a massive impact with the simultaneous construction of many large plants, as in the Soviet model, but rather to install less national capacity than if each of the utilities had been left on its own, thereby reducing expenses. Some money could be saved in construction (actually it was not) and real savings would come from operation. These savings, however, would not benefit the country but rather served as a safeguard for the repayment of World Bank loans. In effect, the World Bank, seeing how the merchant-brokers had gutted the utilities and realizing that the Colombian elite did not want rapid electrical development, adjusted its sights to making sure the power companies had the means to repay the World Bank loans, and reducing expenses was an important way to free funds for the interest payments. As to the emergency reserves, the situation was totally different from that of industrialized countries. In practice Colombian utilities have never had a real reserve capacity. Cycles of scarcity and abundance had provided the pattern for individual utilities since the 1930s. When projects came on line, then usually an excess capacity was left idle, but as demand grew and finally caught and overtook supply, the plants ran at full steam; but demand would then remain unsatisfied until the next project came on line and the cycle repeated itself. Quite naturally, equipment cannot stand this grueling treatment without time for repairs or maintenance, so that outages and rationing characterized not only the period of insufficient capacity but also that of apparent surplus capacity. Interconnecting the whole country would only turn isolated local problems into one huge national problem—in the process making the situation worse than before, as in the case of the 1985 national blackout, the first of its kind in Colombia.[5]

The World Bank officials had already made up their minds, and the idea of creating ISA continued to advance. Mere urging did not suffice, and the World Bank had to state and back its threat—made first in late 1963—not to finance any more projects in Colombia until ISA was approved, just to keep discussions alive. Even with the sweetener of a separate World Bank loan to ISA whenever it was organized, Electraguas, CVC, the Medellín Municipal Power Authority, and the Bogotá Light and Power Company still negotiated for four years before reaching an agreement.

The controversy did not concern the merits of the proposal but rather the exact form ISA was going to assume. Each possible point was subjected to minute scrutiny and debated endlessly, yet out of the welter of details two important issues did emerge. The first was the question of how to finance the new institution: whether by a tax surcharge on retail sales of electricity, the system adopted in Brazil, or by stock subscribed by the individual utilities, the system followed in Switzerland. After much debate, the second formula won out because it reinforced the founding utilities' control over the new institution, which initially would resemble a holding company. Once its own generating plants started producing, the sale of electricity to the individual utilities would become another major source of revenue. The second important issue was more straightforward: Each of the utilities wanted to carry out one last project on its own. Thus, Bogotá secured Canoas, Medellín would take on Guatape II, and the CVC would carry the Upper Anchicayá project, so that the only project initially left for ISA was Chivor.[6]

The World Bank did not let up the pressure, and in November 1966 a first agreement between Electraguas, CVC, Bogotá, and Medellín was signed whereby each pledged to interchange electricity. This agreement was followed by the formal establishment of ISA on 14 September 1967. Although the World Bank was not fully satisfied with the arrangements, it nevertheless registered its approval by granting a loan late in 1968 to construct the "inner ring" linking the three cities of Bogotá, Medellín, and Cali. This "ring" was a "T" with a long 277-mile line of 230 kilovolts running from Cali to Medellín, and then intersected at the middle near Manizales by a shorter 180-mile line of 230 kilovolts running from Bogotá. During construction, ISA either dropped some auxiliary facilities or charged them to other projects. For many stretches the transmission towers were contracted to Colombian manufacturers for the first time. Although a cost overrun of 6 percent was incurred, in fact because of larger expenses in local currency $6 million out of the $18 million loan remained unspent when the inner ring was completed at the end of 1971. ISA obtained the approval of the World Bank to spend these leftover sums in another spur of 125 miles between Guatape in Antioquia and Barrancabermeja, but ISA had pushed its luck too far. The spur was not completed until 1975 and then at twice the cost originally budgeted.[7]

The completion of the inner ring of transmission lines in 1971 immediately opened the possibility of linking up with the Atlantic coast provinces, the largest electrical system outside of the inner ring. This was a quantum leap, because instead of linking up bordering provincial networks, the transmission line to the Atlantic coast involved crossing long distances of vast isolated spaces and required lines of 500 kilovolts for effective transfer of electricity at a time when the highest voltage used in Colombia was 230 kilovolts. Huge as the engineering challenges were, an even bigger problem was that of financing. The World Bank gradually tired of having to push, prod, and pressure, and while still interested, pruned down the offer of financing to only half of the foreign costs. This setback came as a severe shock to ISA, which had counted upon the World Bank to provide a secure foundation for carrying out the project. A somewhat frenetic rush began to find substitute financing for the other half, and many different institutions were sounded out. Finally, the German Development Bank KFW agreed to make up the difference. Difficulties continued to delay construction, and ISA was not able to complete the transmission line joining the inner ring to the Atlantic coast provinces until the early 1980s. By then the primary consideration was to provide cheap electricity from Antioquia to the nickel-mining operations at Cerromatoso controlled by multinationals.[8]

The completion of the national grid was delayed by the bitter internecine fighting over ISA. After 1967 and for as long as ISA confined itself to spending World Bank and central state funds for the inner ring of transmission lines, the confrontation remained latent, but as soon as work began on the Chivor project, bitter clashes erupted. Insufficient appropriations in the national budget had placed ICEL (as Electraguas was called after 1968) in the awkward position of not being able to buy all the shares in a new issue by ISA. The Bogotá utility exploited this opportunity to purchase the unsold shares and thus gained the power to outvote ICEL in the ISA Board of Directors meetings. A bitter fight lasting for more than two years raged over these shares, and no demands from ministers could secure their return. Only when the president of Colombia gave a direct order in person to the manager of the Bogotá utility to sell the shares did ICEL finally regain its normal position within ISA in 1974.

Longer and even more bitter was the opposition by the Medellín Municipal Power Authority. Medellín repeatedly refused to subscribe its required number of shares and bonds, leaving ISA undercapitalized. This opposition laid the groundwork for Medellín's proposal to totally change the nature of ISA. Medellín wanted ISA to serve as a banking fund to put up part of the capital for the large hydroelectric projects. A special company would be established for each dam with ISA contributing 40 percent of the capital and the local utility company providing a majority and controlling share. This proposal and others were simply a manifestation of the ongoing battle between the provinces in Colombia. Each province wanted its own project because behind each utility company or power authority stood a constituency of merchant-brokers ready to benefit from the construction and operation of the new dam. Since ISA, without its own plants, did not have a separate source of income, it was totally dependent on the wishes of the founding stockholders. This experience confirmed that ISA needed an independent base, such as the tax surcharge on retail electricity sales that had been proposed earlier. But without these mechanisms, rather than advancing to construct large hydroelectric projects, ISA became the battleground for the tug-of-war between the provinces; to placate Medellín, even the seat of the company had to be moved there from Bogotá in 1977.[9] Although the construction of the transmission lines remained a solid accomplishment, even these were only a luxury, and a harmful one at that. The money would have been better spent increasing generating capacity, and in any case, there was not the least doubt that ISA had failed to fill the huge gap left by the absence of strong central state action. The only way to end the lag in electrification and to launch the country on the road to economic growth was for the central state to mobilize rigidly all the resources. But such a strategy permanently eluded Colombia during the twentieth century.

Integrating the Provinces: Corelca

After the nationalization of the American and Foreign Power Company in 1961, electrification in the Atlantic coast provinces sank into virtual paralysis. Barranquilla faced a massive outage until the U.S. government donated three surplus generating ships in 1962. This equipment provided the breathing spell the Barranquilla Power Authority needed to finish the installation of the last steam plant unit previously ordered by the American and Foreign Power Company. As part of the purchase contract, the U.S. company had agreed to deliver this last steam unit from a factory in the United States and to facilitate its installation in every way possible. The concern for this last unit was certainly justified, as this was the last enlargement in Barranquilla's installed capacity during the 1960s. Although the surplus generating ships designed for combat conditions carried high operating costs, the power authority refused to release them because there was no money to buy replacements. Only after insistent demands did Electraguas receive at last one vessel for emergency service in the Santa Marta Power Authority, which was in even worse shape.[10]

During the 1960s, the Atlantic coast provinces were trapped in a dead end. With the earnings of the Barranquilla Power Authority mortgaged to pay off the purchase of the American and Foreign Power subsidiary, no savings were left for expansion. Electraguas, with its funds stretched thinly across the country, could provide only small sums that were quickly swallowed up by the merchant-brokers, who were now draining the power authorities in the Atlantic coast provinces. These utilities, unable to pay their bills or salaries, resorted to extensive short-term borrowing from the local banking system in order to stay afloat, thus permanently dooming themselves to paying off high-interest loans. By 1964 when Barranquilla faced power shortages, there were no funds left to finance any expansion in generating capacity. The power authority urged Electraguas to provide funds, specifically for a 44-megawatt steam turbine.

Santa Marta, Cartagena, and other cities on the Atlantic coast pressed hard for their own steam plants, and bombarded by these requests, Electraguas decided to take a regional approach. First of all, dribbling out central state funds to each power authority accomplished nothing because the voracious local members of the elite swallowed up the sums. Small plants in each city were expensive to build as well as to run, and individually, none of them offered a solution for the region as a whole. Because of these considerations, Electraguas took the lead in early 1966 to present a sweeping three-part proposal. First, the central state would construct a transmission line of 230 kilovolts between the main cities of the Atlantic coast so that deficits in one province could be covered with surplus capacity from another. Such a line had originally been proposed by the American and Foreign Power Company, and if nationalization had not intervened, would have already been in place, but now belatedly in 1966 Electraguas had to resurrect the idea. Second, for generating capacity, the Electraguas proposal called for three 100-megawatt steam units to be constructed—two in Barranquilla and another in Cartagena. Construction would be staggered, with the first one to be built in Barranquilla, the second in Cartagena, and years later, the last in Barranquilla. As the first one came on line in Barranquilla, its excess capacity would flow to Cartagena and other cities, but by the time the steam unit in Cartagena was completed its excess capacity would be needed in Barranquilla, and likewise for the third unit. Ingenious as this approach was, it nevertheless had the same implications and inevitable limitations already discussed in the previous section, which were equally valid for the Atlantic coast provinces.

The third part of the Electraguas proposal totally swept the elite members in the Atlantic coast provinces off their feet. It called for the creation of a regional power authority called Corelca. The local elites were so happy enjoying the plums they received from the provincial power authorities that they enthusiastically backed the creation of still another and bigger power authority. As a regional institution financed by the national government, the new power authority could not fail to provide juicier opportunities for many an irresistible contract. The local politicians also loved the Corelca idea, since another power authority would provide job quotas to reward their loyal supporters. Congressional approval was needed, and the bill duly presented in May 1967 became

Law 59 in December of that year. However, nearly two years had elapsed since the idea had first been broached in early 1966, and even a longer time had to pass before Corelca would start functioning on its own.[11]

The delays were caused by disagreements over the exact nature of Corelca. Its promoters hailed it as a continuation of the regional development approach pioneered in Colombia by the CVC, but Corelca was different from the CVC. The CVC had been created to take over the assets of Electraguas in the province of Cali and functioned as a regional agency independent of the national government (except for frequent subsidies), in effect permanently destroying the dream of a national electrical system. In Barranquilla the elite knew perfectly well that it could not survive without central state participation, and a key purpose of Corelca was to drag the national government even deeper into the bottomless pit of the Atlantic coast region. The provincial power authorities belonged in name only to the central state, since the local elite ran and exploited them at will, and this elite hoped that the same fate would befall Corelca. The national government, on the other hand, wanted Electraguas (newly reorganized as ICEL) to have closer control. Quite naturally, a long struggle ensued, first over the clauses of Law 59, then about the decree detailing the law, and finally over the charter issued for Corelca in accordance with the terms of the decree, so that the rest of the 1960s was spent in these costly and fruitless negotiations.[12]

Meanwhile, electricity shortages threatened the region. The Barranquilla Power Authority pressured ICEL to act on the original 1964 request for the 44-megawatt steam plant but to no avail. A compromise solution was worked out by the end of 1968 to install a gas turbine of 15 megawatts, made possible by financing from France that ICEL approved. This plan was not enough to meet the shortage, however, and thanks to an Export-Import Bank loan another gas turbine was financed for Barranquilla. Gas turbines had the advantage that they could be installed quickly but also had the disadvantage of being dependent on the availability of gas reserves in the fields. As explained in Chapter 6, most of the gas in the nearby fields had been flared. The reserves available, although adequate for a 15-megawatt turbine, soon started to falter when the capacity of the gas turbines quadrupled in Barranquilla and Cartagena. To make matters worse, the power authorities—because of their chronic shortage of funds—fell behind in their payments to the oil companies. Electric service was often suspended because of non-payment for gas. At this point the members of the Atlantic coast elite remembered that Ecopetrol existed and began pressuring the National Petroleum Company to buy controlling shares in the gas fields so that it could eventually supply Corelca with free gas. Ecopetrol dragged its feet on this proposal, but the huge political pressures wielded by the local elite eventually forced Ecopetrol into subsidizing the power authorities of the Atlantic coast provinces by the late 1970s. Obviously this arrangement worked to the benefit of the local elite.[13]

Ecopetrol also ended up providing free fuel oil for the steam generating plants, whose construction finally began in the early 1970s. The proposal for the transmission lines of 220 kilovolts had been imposed by ICEL against the bitter opposition of the merchant-brokers, who represented manufacturers of 110-kilovolt cable. Without the higher voltage, most of the advantages of sending current from one place to another would be greatly reduced. The merchant-brokers of Barranquilla, however, held firm against the three 100-megawatt steam units and demanded that the expansion begin with two 66-megawatt units in Barranquilla rather than just one of 100 megawatts. The merchant-brokers marshaled various reasons for favoring the two 66-megawatt units. The biggest unit in Colombia was in Zipaquirá with only 35 megawatts, and the merchant-brokers warned against making such a dramatic jump all at once from 35 to 100 without first acquiring some experience with the intermediate range of 66 megawatts. What clinched the argument against the 100-megawatt units was that the first installation would provide fewer megawatts than the two 66-megawatt units added together. The Barranquilla elite concluded that it was better to get 132 megawatts now than 200 in the distant future when the second 100-megawatt unit at last would be built in Barranquilla after the one in Cartagena had been completed. Actually, the motivation of the merchant-brokers remained the same as always: Since it was more costly to install and run the smaller 66-megawatt units, more commissions could be earned than from the larger 100-megawatt units.

These long and protracted battles delayed the initiation of the project, and not until 1970 was the contract to build awarded to Siemens, a German firm. This company had been chosen to install the two 66-megawatt units because the German development fund had financed most of the expenses. Indeed, without the German financing the project could not have been carried out, since an overstretched ICEL bombarded with requests from the whole country could not provide enough money. In any case, the construction proceeded much slower than planned. Work stopped whenever funds ran out, and plenty of cost overruns occurred to benefit the local merchant-brokers. The lengthy delays meant that the steam plants were too small by the time they were completed, and by the mid-1970s Barranquilla settled into its normal pattern of having very high electricity rates combined with recurrent outages.[14]

ICEL was starting to realize that it had been manipulated by the elite of the Atlantic coast provinces. Corelca, rather than breaking local control, had become just another channel to drain central state funds into the local elite. ICEL could not keep track of the provincial power authorities as well as of Corelca, so to simplify the task, the national government decided to combine them all into Corelca. ICEL wanted to fuse the power authorities in other regions as well, such as in the provinces of Boyacá, Bucaramanga, and Cúcuta, but the local elite groups in these areas forced ICEL to drop the idea immediately. In the Atlantic coast provinces, complex maneuvers ensued during the 1970s, but to no avail because the Barranquilla elite organized protests and demonstrations to defend its plums in the local power authority. Consequently, not even the original idea of having Corelca generate the electricity and sell it to the provincial power authorities for retail sale to the customers had been achieved. Rather than efficiency and division of labor, overlapping and duplication of functions became the rule, in particular in the case of the Barranquilla Power Authority. The Barranquilla elite claimed an ascendancy deeply resented by the members of the Cartagena and Santa Marta elite, and the latter two reacted violently to any suggestion that their respective provincial power authorities be abolished. Unable to agree on how to share power among themselves, the elite of the Atlantic coast decided as a first step to reduce even further what little control the central state had. Since it was precisely ICEL that was trying to curb the worst abuses on the Atlantic coast, the elite aimed their efforts at forcing ICEL to give up its shares in Corelca as well as in the provincial power authorities. This plan echoed what had happened in the CVC, but it was not exactly the same because even though ICEL was finally forced to give up its shares in the Atlantic coast power authorities during the administration of Alfonso López Michelsen (1974–1978), this loss did not mean the decline, much less the end, of central state involvement. The national government continued to be drawn into the problems, and central state funds continued to flow, always without any marked effect on the electrification of the Atlantic coast provinces. Clearly the regional development approach as exemplified by Corelca had utterly failed and had become yet another tool to enrich the local elite.

The Chivor Dam

Linking Colombia with transmission lines was a complementary but secondary function to ISA's main role of constructing the largest hydroelectric plants in the country. As explained earlier, ISA upon its creation in September 1967 embarked upon the construction of the inner ring of 230-kilovolt cables linking Bogotá, Medellín, and Cali, an action that had unsuspected implications for the Chivor project. First of all, embarking upon the inner ring precluded the initiation of the Chivor project, and the time lost later caused cost overruns. Second, utilities were starting to link up on their own. Most notably, a 115-kilovolt line joining the Bogotá Light and Power Company with the CVC via Armenia was completed in 1969, thus making the 230-kilovolt line of the inner ring less urgent. Furthermore, if a region was chronically deficient in electricity, as was the case with the CVC, specific problems of the utility were to blame, and these did not go away with either the inner ring or the Chivor dam. Lastly, the successful completion of the inner ring on schedule in 1971 at below estimated cost gave ISA an exaggerated idea about its capabilities and emboldened it to attempt the Chivor dam without having answered all the questions raised in the initial studies and surveys.[15]

Skipping over these studies did not accelerate Chivor, and in fact, only constant urgings by the World Bank during 1969 kept the proposal from dying. The World Bank approved the loan application in May 1970, with disbursements beginning in September of that year. No calls for bids were ready, and ISA did not open bids for contracts until April 1971. Even then, construction work did not really begin until early 1972. Part of the delay was certainly due to the need to negotiate a parallel loan from the Inter-American Development Bank, which did not give its approval until May 1971, but the real reason for the delays and the many problems plaguing the project lay in the very nature of ISA's structure.

ISA was a holding company whose stockholders included ICEL, CVC, the Medellín Municipal Power Company, and the Bogotá Light and Power Company. Except for ICEL, none of the others wanted to give up their own local projects, and only after much fighting had they agreed to allow ISA to construct Chivor. The Bogotá Light and Power Company had kept Canoas as its own project, but since Chivor was in its area of influence, the Bogotá utility reneged on its earlier promise and once again wanted Chivor for itself. ISA finally silenced the opposition by transferring the Mesitas hydroelectric project to the Bogotá utility and also letting Bogotá participate to some degree in the subcontracting for Chivor. This hurdle had barely been cleared when the Medellín Municipal Power Company concluded that since Chivor was so far from its sphere of influence, Medellín would not subscribe the required number of shares in ISA. Without this capital, construction, which had started in 1972, slowed down in subsequent years. To force a solution, the World Bank halted loan disbursements during 1974 and 1975. ISA was already in arrears with a number of contractors and was having to borrow short-term, high-interest credits from local banks to meet the most pressing expenses. The World Bank refused the application for a supplementary loan, and ISA had no choice but to turn to more expensive financing from foreign private banks to cover the larger than expected costs in foreign currency that were partly but far from mainly the result of the worldwide jump in prices after the 1973 energy crisis.

Chivor's potential was planned at 1,000 megawatts, but since Colombia's total installed capacity in 1970 was 2,000 megawatts, both the World Bank and ISA considered the project too big for a country whose per capita electricity consumption was below the Latin American average. The project was split into two stages, Chivor I and II, each of 500 megawatts, thus conforming to the tendency to dilute the impact of bringing a massive project on line. Even with this drastic reduction, ISA and the World Bank had underestimated the costs considerably. Although the Inter-American Development Bank in its May 1971 loan had revised the estimates upwards, when construction began big cost overruns became the rule.

The amounts that went into the construction of Chivor I will never be known exactly. Juggling the accounts of the loans from the World Bank, the Inter-American Development Bank, foreign and local private banks, as well as subsidies from the national government, ISA flashed different sets of figures to each institution in an effort to appear in the best light possible. But nothing could hide a major financial disaster. By one estimate, cost overruns were 54 percent and the payments on short-term local loans alone were 117 percent higher than expected. ISA blamed these overruns on the inflation caused by the 1973 energy crisis, but this excuse was only a handy pretext and not the real cause at all, since the problems had begun long before then. The merchant-brokers led a veritable army of contractors into Chivor to fight for contracts larger than any ever seen before in Colombia. Repeatedly, the wrong equipment and deficient services were contracted so that the procedures had to be changed, or even better, repeated. Notoriously inept contractors frequently had to be replaced in the middle of construction, and quite logically the new ones demanded to start from scratch. Whenever funds ran out, ISA, to keep work going, replenished its coffers by short-term loans from local banks at interest rates three times higher than the prevailing rates in long-term borrowing from the World Bank and the Inter-American Development Bank. For short-term loans, even the terms of New York banks were better, but intense pressures from private Colombian banks ensured that ISA turned to them instead of foreign banks, which only got bones thrown to them when extra foreign currency was indispensable.[16]

Massive engineering problems faced ISA during the construction of Chivor. The nearly five-mile long tunnel to carry water from the reservoir to the generating plant was constantly plagued with cave-ins and mistakes. The dam itself turned out to present unforeseen difficulties. Landslides complicated construction, while nearby villages entangled the access roads by demanding different routes. Chivor became an administrative, engineering, and financial nightmare. The first unit, which should have gone on line in June 1975, was not functioning until two years later. Only in September 1977 was the total 500-megawatt capacity in operation. Frequent interruptions and shutdowns for long periods became the rule because the project had been rushed to completion for political reasons: The 500 megawatts were needed to end the electricity shortage of 1976–1977, which had contributed to sparking protest movements and violent demonstrations against the tottering López Michelsen administration. Not surprisingly, many of the installations had been shoddily and poorly built, resulting in constant expenses to replace faulty equipment.

Had the repeated and constant failures of Chivor occurred in an industrialized country, they would have been the object of constant denunciations in the press as well as the focus of congressional inquiries. But Chivor was held in a death grip by the merchant-brokers and the private financial institutions that shaped elite attitudes and usually those of the national government as well. Publicity campaigns in Colombia incessantly repeated the engineering marvels but shied away from even asking the hard questions about why the delays had occurred and where all the money had gone. Even when completed, Chivor was a failure; before the reservoir could fill up, drought hit that part of Colombia and plunged the country into yet another period of electricity rationing. Furthermore, by 1977 when Chivor I was fairly functional, the 500 megawatts no longer had the same impact on the economy as would have been the case in 1970 when this project would have meant a substantial addition to installed capacity. The perennial pattern in Colombian electrical expansion manifested itself once again: Enlargements in capacity, rather than boldly pushing ahead to give a powerful boost to economic growth, instead always trailed behind apparent demand, in effect slowing down the economic development of Colombia.[17]

The Colombian elite that had so profited from Chivor I was extremely satisfied with the results and eagerly looked forward to the contracts and countless opportunities for profit represented by the second 500 megawatts of Chivor II. Not completed until the mid-1980s, Chivor II repeated the mistakes of Chivor I and, as usual, came on line without having any decisive impact on Colombia's economy. The orgy of speculation and cost overruns had set the pattern for other ISA projects. Just like the provincial power authorities, ISA had become a slush fund to subsidize the Colombian elite through the channels of the merchant-brokers and the local banks. As long as electricity continued to support the interests of the Colombian elite, the immense hydroelectric potential would never take the country out of backwardness and poverty.

Nuclear Power

The discovery of uranium ore deposits in Colombia awakened interest in the possibility of nuclear power. Prior to World War II, those conducting preliminary geologic surveys over some parts of the Colombian surface had paid scant attention to radioactive deposits, but after the war professor Nahmias in Paris obtained some reports confirming the existence of substantial deposits in undisclosed locations. The U.S. government found out about the intentions of professor Nahmias and his attorney, Jaudel, and after confused cloak-and-dagger operations, the U.S. embassy in Paris was able to foil the plans, which may well have formed part of some Cold War rivalry between Soviet and American agents.[18]

The U.S. government decided to explore for itself whether the uranium deposits were real and in the early 1950s enlisted the cooperation of the Colombian government. Several discoveries were made, such as in Antioquia, but interest soon centered on the California district in the province of Bucaramanga. A group of Colombian businessmen decided to set up a firm called the Uranium Mining Company, which was in full operation by 1959. The uranium was found among veins of gold and silver, with occasional concentrations of lead, zinc, and copper. The aim of the Uranium Mining Company was to cover operating expenses by extracting the other metals and to make its profit through the sale of uranium. Tests confirmed the abundance of uranium in the district: The richness of the uranium oxide was nine times greater than in any ore deposits then mined in other parts of the world.

The only hitch was that the 2,000 tons of ore already mined could not be processed without expensive machinery. Furthermore, neither the Colombian government nor any country in the Western Bloc was interested in buying the ore already mined, thus putting the Uranium Mining Company into dire financial straits. In early 1962 the company discovered that the state firm Techno Export of Prague, Czechoslovakia, was not only willing to supply the necessary equipment for the mining operation but would take the ore already mined in exchange as payment. The Ministry of Mines and Petroleum and the Ministry of Development, which controlled foreign commerce, granted their approval for the plan. Normally, these permits were more than sufficient, but in the case of uranium, which had been declared a strategic resource, the approval of the Ministry of Foreign Affairs was also needed. The latter rejected the proposal on the grounds that the whole operation was just a ploy to introduce Communist agents from Czechoslovakia into Colombia, which was a close ally of the United States with the Cold War then at its height. Without this equipment the Uranium Mining Company had no choice but to wind down operations, and it died a long, lingering death during the 1960s. The question of just how abundant the uranium ores were was left unanswered.[19]

The concern over uranium ores had sparked an interest in the peaceful uses of the atom, in particular atomic energy. The novelty of this unknown force struck the curiosity of some influential Colombians, such as the ambassador to the United States, who strove to get two copies of every scrap of information about atomic energy he could find to the point of causing raised eyebrows in the State Department. The distrust was misplaced, since the Colombians were just trying to return home as "experts" in a novel field to make a big splash—and to win government appointments to high positions. The United States was willing to help and in 1955 signed a nuclear assistance treaty with Colombia, one of the first of its kind. The U.S. government agreed to provide technical assistance and some aid, as well as up to six kilograms of enriched uranium; furthermore, the United States would help set up Colombia's first experimental reactor. By 1954 Colombia had created its own version of the Atomic Energy Commission in the United States, and in 1956 went ahead to also establish a separate agency called the Institute for Nuclear Matters. There was not enough work for both the commission and the institute, so in 1959 all nuclear aspects were concentrated in a reorganized Institute for Nuclear Matters under the vague jurisdiction of both the Ministry of Development and the Ministry of Mines and Petroleum, but actually with de facto autonomy.[20]

By the late 1950s the initial enthusiasm over atomic energy had faded. Preliminary calculations showed that the cost of nuclear power was at least twice that of hydroelectricity (and the price of the former has since increased even more), so that the initial investment for a capital-starved country like Colombia was prohibitive. The technology was also still beyond the reach of Colombia; for example, the experimental reactor that the United States had donated had taken years to install. Such difficulties were not surprising given the problems suffered during the construction of the coal steam plants of 33 and 66 megawatts. Yet the myth of atomic energy could not be so easily forgotten, and occasionally the national government made announcements to feed the public imagination with illusions of nuclear power plants bringing electricity to all corners of the country.[21]

More because of political and electoral reasons than anything else, the Institute for Nuclear Matters could not be closed; it had to be kept going at least as a symbol to wave before the public. The Institute's performance during the 1960s was not unusual by Colombian standards. This government agency had become a huge bureaucracy because of the job quotas each politician commanded and the large numbers of unskilled and poorly educated employees; the trained professionals received such low salaries that they resigned as soon as they landed jobs elsewhere in any other field. Each dependency of the Institute worked in a vacuum from the rest, and the individual scientists and engineers did not know what others were doing on their same floor and often even in the same office. No Ministry had shown any interest in supervising the Institute, so it operated in isolation from the rest of the government. The director of the Institute made it a point to keep other low-level bureaus from entering his bailiwick out of fear of competition. To intensify contacts with the scientific community, the Institute for Nuclear Matters appointed a steering committee of leading Colombian scientists in 1961, but after the first meeting, it was never reconvened again. The Board of Directors met infrequently, often letting months lapse between meetings. When meetings were held, they were kept short because board members left as soon as they had finished eating the free lunch served during the gathering. The director of the Institute engaged in costly travel abroad, all paid out of government funds, supposedly to attend international conferences on atomic energy, but he often overextended his travel stays to enjoy weeks of tourism at government expense. The director, in the typical manner of Colombian hierarchies, both public and private, cleverly extracted important findings from naive subordinates and presented them as his own, when in fact he was just a political bureaucrat with no concern for either science or economic growth.

The Institute for Nuclear Matters was also originally supposed to prospect and mine for uranium. This activity in the early 1970s was shifted over to still another government agency, the Uranium Institute, which henceforth would control all aspects of uranium ore extraction, either directly or by concessions. In 1973 the Ministry of Mines and Petroleum began to exercise a closer vigilance over the Institute for Nuclear Matters as well as over the Uranium Institute, but it was clear that much more compensatory work would be needed if Colombia was going to make up all the time lost in starting its nuclear program. More and more the realization grew that nuclear power had to await the twenty-first century before it could be fully developed.

Notes

1. U.S. House, Subcommittee on Energy and Power, *Centralized vs. Decentralized Energy Systems: Diverging or Parallel Roads?* (Washington, D.C.: GPO, 1979), pp. 119–129, 149–156; David Howard Davis, *Energy Politics*, 3d ed. (New York: St. Martin's Press, 1982), pp. 166–169, 192–193.

2. Electraguas, *Plan nacional de electrificación, 1965–1975: Informe de Electricité de France* (Vincennes: L'imprimerie H. Dridé, 1965), pp. 287–294, 377–409. The

findings of the French experts circulated in manuscript form from early 1963 and were published in English in 1964; ibid., pp. 12–13. A more limited interconnection had first been suggested by Gibbs & Hill, Inc., and Electricité de France in their November 1954 National Electrification Plan, but this earlier proposal found no echo.

3. Antonio J. Posada F. and Jeanne De Posada, *CVC: Un reto al subdesarrollo y al tradicionalismo* (Bogotá: Tercer Mundo, 1966), pp. 83–84, 181–186.

4. Hugh Collier, *Developing Electric Power: Thirty Years of World Bank Experience* (Baltimore: The Johns Hopkins University Press, 1984), pp. 94–95; Edward S. Mason and Robert E. Asher, *The World Bank Since Bretton Woods* (Washington, D.C.: The Brookings Institution, 1973), p. 652.

5. René De La Pedraja, *Historia de la energía en Colombia, 1537–1930* (Bogotá: El Ancora, 1985), chaps. 3, 4. A good example of cyclical behavior was provided by Medellín.

6. Collier, *Developing Electric Power*, pp. 95, 97; World Bank, *Economic Growth of Colombia: Problems and Prospects* (Baltimore: Johns Hopkins University Press, 1972), p. 210.

7. ISA, *1967–1977* (Medellín: Publi-Offset, 1978), pp. 5, 23; *El Tiempo*, 2, 10 Nov. 1966; René De La Pedraja, *FEDEMETAL y la industrialización de Colombia* (Bogotá: Op Gráficas, 1986), pp. 151–152.

8. Germán Oramas O., *Panorama de las obras hidráulicas en Colombia* (Popayán: Universidad del Cauca, 1984), pp. 31–34; ISA, *1967–1977*, pp. 23–24: *El Tiempo*, 11 Dec. 1966, 11 March 1969; ISA, *Informe anual, 1977* (Medellín: Editorial Albon, 1978), p. 11.

9. Collier, *Developing Electric Power*, pp. 95–96; ISA, *Informe anual, 1977*, pp. 4–5.

10. For the first three paragraphs, see *El Tiempo*, 29 March, 13, 25 Sept., 2 Oct. 1966; *El Siglo*, 16 April 1963; World Bank, *Economic Growth of Colombia*, pp. 209–212, 215.

11. ICEL, *Informe, 1978–1979* (Bogotá: Graficas Carmen, 1980), p. 18; *El Tiempo*, 14 Dec. 1966, 14 May 1967.

12. Besides the talks between the provinces and Bogotá, there was a parallel set of negotiations between Barranquilla and the smaller cities such as Cartagena and Santa Marta. The latter two tried, not unexpectedly, to secure the terms most favorable to the merchant-brokers in their respective provinces. Agreement was finally reached, and in this sense Corelca went beyond CVC, which had never been able to convince its bordering provinces of Caldas and Popayán to share in that first regional experiment.

13. *La República*, 27 Feb. 1970.

14. World Bank, *Economic Growth of Colombia*, pp. 211–212, 215; ISA, *Informe anual, 1976* (Bogotá: Imprenta Nacional, 1977), p. 10; *El Tiempo*, 23 Feb. 1970.

15. The first three paragraphs rely on Collier, *Developing Electric Power*, pp. 95–96; ISA, *Informe anual, 1975* (Bogotá: Lito Technion, 1976), pp. 6–7; *El Tiempo*, 10 April 1970; World Bank, *Economic Growth of Colombia*, pp. 210, 215.

16. ISA, *1967–1977* (Medellín: Publi-Offset, 1978), pp. 11–12; Collier, *Developing Electric Power*, p. 96.

17. Oramas, *Panorama de las obras hidráulicas,* pp. 38–41; Collier, *Developing Electric Power,* p. 96; ISA, *Informe anual, 1977,* pp. 7–9.

18. Robert P. Terril to Secretary of State, Paris, 31 May 1949, 821.6359/5-3149 and related documents in this file, Record Group (RG) 59, National Archives, Washington, D.C.

19. *El Espectador,* 13 Oct. 1950; *El Siglo,* 25 Jan. 1953.

20. Memorandum of 14 Sept. 1955, Henry F. Holland Files, Box 3, RG 59; 7 March 1956 report, 821.2546/3-756, RG 59; Treaty of 31 May 1955, Department of State *Bulletin.*

21. The rest of this section draws from *El Intermedio,* 19 Jan. 1957; *El Tiempo,* 6 Feb. 1972.

13

In the Provinces and the Countryside

What happened to those regions bypassed by the major electrification projects? The provincial capital of Popayán and the territory of San Andrés reveal another dimension, while the topic of rural electrification brings the reader into the countryside.

In a Provincial Capital: Popayán

Popayán was typical of those forgotten, poor, isolated provincial capitals struggling to maintain a precarious existence. Since the late 1920s, two private utility companies had served the capital city of Popayán. The provincial government had bought stock in the oldest company, La Florida (1.9 metawatts), and the city council originally had been a shareholder in the second one, Coconuco (1.2 megawatts), but by the 1940s all the shares of both utilities were in private hands. Each company owned a separate hydroelectric site and operated duplicating distribution networks; the ruinous competition finally drove both to secure a 100 percent increase in the sale price of electricity from the Colombian government in the middle of 1946, but effective only from 1 October. Actually the hike lifted Popayán only to the second lowest rank in rates charged by 472 plants throughout the country; nevertheless, it was more than enough to shock both the elite and popular groups. A protest committee appeared to plan a general strike for 5 October 1946; meanwhile, teams of 100 persons each took turns in front of the offices of the utility companies to prevent clients from entering to pay their bills. City and provincial authorities initially had been sympathetic to the strikers, but when the strike committee fell under the influence of organized labor, the mayor and the governor quickly reacted to bring the runaway movement back under elite control. Behind-the-scenes maneuvering and a partial reduction in the rate increase aborted the planned general strike, and all that a betrayed movement could do was scream for the resignation of the mayor and the governor.[1]

The stopgap measures in which the elite excelled had once again won the day, but to counter the pent-up unrest that had come to the surface in October 1946, other steps were needed to show—at least for public relations purposes—that the government planned to end the electricity shortages in this city of 40,000. After much prodding, the governor commissioned a study that in 1950 recommended that the national government construct a 10-megawatt plant (La Florida II) but that it leave distribution in the hands of the two private utilities. The La Florida II proposal both covered future demand and provided a powerful stimulus for the local economy. The private capital already invested in the two local utilities was not displaced but rather was complemented by the government funds, which would be spent only on expanding generating capacity. In spite of the many advantages, the proposal ran into difficulties. Electraguas claimed that other provinces had even more pressing needs and that La Florida II would be justified only when demand had reached 13 megawatts.

As a concession, the national government agreed to create the Popayán Power Authority in 1954 with the provincial government holding one-fourth of the shares and Electraguas the rest. Part of the investment by the central state consisted of the small hydroelectric projects that Electraguas owned throughout the province, and of these the most important was the one at Sajundí, whose 800 kilowatts supplied electricity to gold mining operations. Electraguas and the Popayán Power Authority decided to double Sajundí's capacity and to bring the excess electricity via new transmission cables to Popayán in order to reduce the chronic outages in the capital. Awarding the contracts for the Sajundí expansion proved a lucrative source of commissions for the local merchant-brokers, who were now on the prowl for more state money. The contracts and purchases for finishing the other small plants under construction in the province were only small morsels, and soon the merchant-brokers decided to speculate with the sale of the private utility companies remaining throughout the province, of which the two most important were La Florida and Coconuco, both in Popayán.[2]

The generators and the distribution network of Coconuco were obsolete and had deteriorated after thirty years of constant use, so to get the state to buy the utility the merchant-brokers had to pull strings with politicians. The sale of the smaller Coconuco utility was quietly arranged in 1963. But to get the national government to release funds for the purchase of the more expensive La Florida, the speculators orchestrated a tangled transaction whereby the city government was supposed to first subscribe shares in the Popayán Power Authority before Electraguas would purchase the private utility. Electraguas paid a high price for the private shares, only to discover afterward that the distribution network of La Florida was unusable and had to be replaced. Many a juicy contract was forthcoming for the local merchant-brokers, who rushed to supply equipment and cables. This was just the beginning: When the city needed electric posts, the power authority ordered them first in wood, then in steel, and finally in reinforced concrete, but even most of the latter had to be discarded. In another strange twist, the Popayán Power Authority acquired and maintained at huge expense a fleet of trucks and cars capable of transporting all the inhabitants of the city, yet the vehicles were put at the disposal of privileged members of the local elite. The Popayán Power Authority had institutionalized a way for the elite to live off the state.

Not surprisingly, funds vanished so rapidly that the Popayán Power Authority had to abandon expansion plans until electricity rates could be raised. When the state regulatory commission authorized the increase in August 1961, the news provoked an outcry in Popayán because the majority of the inhabitants did not understand why they had to pay more for an irregular and scarce service. To try to head off the rising wave of unrest, the governor proposed nothing less than turning over the Popayán Power Authority to the CVC. During the 1950s, Popayán had vehemently rejected any idea of joining the Cali-dominated CVC, but now, so real was the threat of disorder that the governor felt that extreme measures were required. The rest of the members of the Popayán elite did not agree with the governor, and before the fusion with CVC went into effect, they joined forces with Electraguas to block the proposed merger. Meanwhile, the protest movement continued to gain force and was fully organized by May 1962. A general strike in June 1962 enjoyed the support of the labor unions, and the elite realized that partial concessions were needed. The Popayán city council now negotiated through political channels with Bogotá and obtained the repeal of the August 1961 rate increase. The repeal came as a shock both to Electraguas, which deeply resented having been bypassed, and the manager of the Popayán Power Authority, who resigned in protest.

The general strike, which was on the point of becoming an armed insurrection, now disintegrated. Popayán remained in a situation all too common for Colombia of mounting or "repressed" demand, and current was unavailable at any price. The merchant-brokers milked away state funds, and the low rates prevented accumulating any capital reserve for expansion during the 1960s. Political pressures occasionally required installing diesel plants in isolated towns, but their high operating costs only made the financial strains worse. Another alternative was no less ruinous. To dispose of occasional amounts of surplus electricity, the CVC had built transmission lines southward into the northern part of Popayán province. As a result, the power authority purchased the CVC electricity at high prices for resale at the local low rates.

Officials in Popayán repeatedly clamored for the hydroelectric plant at La Florida II as the best way to cover the power shortages. But to head off this reasonable request, the National Planning Department came up with a delaying tactic: that the Popayán Power Authority buy electricity from the 21-megawatt dam under construction in the Mayo river in the province of Nariño to the south. Unable to convince larger provinces like Barranquilla to accept these "pooling" arrangements, the national government now wanted to impose them on weaker provinces like Popayán and Huila. These pools followed their usual cycle: By the time the project was finished, the host required most if not all of its capacity, leaving nothing to share with the neighbor.[3]

Still another solution created many illusions during 1963–1964. Since the 1950s proposals had surfaced to build a dam in Popayán province at Salvajina that would be larger than any other dam in Colombia at that time. Its expected capacity of 300 megawatts was larger than that of either Bogotá or Medellín and dwarfed the 8.8 megawatts the Popayán Power Authority had during the late 1960s. The cost of the dam was astronomical for the province and even for the national government, but the election in 1962 of Guillermo León Valencia, a native of Popayán, to the presidency of Colombia provided a unique opportunity. The financial problems miraculously disappeared when the World Bank, in a very rare gesture, offered president Valencia favorable financing. Soon, however, a struggle erupted over who would build and control Salvajina— the CVC, which had jurisdiction over this part of the Cauca river and its tributaries, or Electraguas, which also had jurisdiction through the Popayán Power Authority. The latter was the choice of the Popayán elite, but Electraguas was reluctant to challenge the powerful Cali elite, which stood behind the CVC. President Valencia agreed that Electraguas should construct the dam, but in spite of his repeated urgings, the CVC and lower officials of the World Bank managed to delay action. The CVC also monopolized the information on Salvajina. By the time the Popayán Power Authority began to repeat the measurements and observations, too much time had elapsed and the World Bank lost interest.[4]

Short-term emergency solutions became the order of the day. To avoid a repetition of the 1962 general strike, the Popayán Power Authority bought or borrowed mobile diesel power plants, but even these did not come on line before 1970. But because the high cost of running diesel plants was a sure formula for total bankruptcy, work finally began in 1967 on the 24-megawatt La Florida II. Completed ten years later, La Florida II (proposed in the 1940s) was by then too small to cover demand.[5] The Popayán Power Authority had failed to overcome the lag in electricity of a province that remained poor and backwards, yet it had succeeded in its primary mission of serving the local elite.

The Territories: San Andrés

Six hundred miles to the northwest of the Caribbean coast of Colombia but only 200 miles east of Nicaragua lies the archipelago of San Andrés and Providencia. Originally settled by the English, during the eighteenth century the islands had become an outpost for the Spanish naval base at Cartagena and had played an important role in the Anglo-Hispanic struggle over the Mosquito coast of Nicaragua. Independence from Spain brought Colombian authorities to the islands who succeeded in keeping control—more because of repeated good luck than any particular strivings. The English-speaking inhabitants, descendants of the black slaves introduced by the British, seemed content with Colombian rule. In 1934, they repulsed an expedition that Nicaragua had sent to annex the islands.[6]

The national government undertook various measures to bolster the inhabitants' loyalty toward Colombia. In this effort, electrification assumed a crucial role. In the late 1930s the State Agency for Territories had placed a very small (50-kilowatt) generator in San Andrés. In 1944, the Ministry of Public Works assumed the responsibility for building a larger plant, but the equipment it brought to the island turned out to be useless. A 100-kilowatt generator was finally inaugurated in 1948, but the other aspects of the service remained badly deficient. The Ministry of Public Works sent another engineer to the island in an attempt to remedy some of the problems, but this engineer did not help matters when after some "tests" he burned out the transformers and the control panels. Meanwhile, the rudimentary distribution network had collapsed under the tropical weather, and even more disturbing, the posts had to be purchased in Nicaragua.[7]

By 1956 the idea of transforming the island into a trade and tourist center had emerged. To meet the demand for electricity in the airport, stores, and hotels, the national government recommended a 1,000-kilowatt plant. This capacity was considered insufficient by some engineers, but in any case it was not built. the 100-kilowatt generator was by now only producing 50, and a second 150-kilowatt plant that the territorial government had set up with funds originally ear-marked for the water supply soon broke down, leaving the island with neither light nor fresh water. Electraguas sent the parts to repair the diesel engine in time for a presidential visit to the island by General Gustavo Rojas Pinilla in June 1956, but soon both plants resumed their fitful operation that left the island largely in the dark.

Part of the problem was due to the fact that although half a dozen state agencies dabbled with power projects in San Andrés, the one with final responsibility—the State Agency for Territories—lacked the technical capability. Long and complex negotiations culminated on 10 February 1960 when the State Agency for Territories agreed to transfer jurisdiction over power to Electraguas, which delegated the daily running to a subsidiary, the Barranquilla Power Authority. The streamlined institutional arrangement was supposed to hasten electrification but instead provoked an unexpected complication.

Only later was it discovered that the real reason for the reorganization had been to give merchant-brokers another chance to win the contracts. The territorial government had called for bids prior to the 10 February 1960 agreement, and the parties not favored now hoped to have Electraguas award them the contracts. To dislodge the winners of the original bid (Brown-Boveri, the Swiss manufacturer of generators, and Blackstone, the English manufacturer of diesel engines), rival merchant-brokers waged a determined campaign. But the two firms fought back just as strongly and even had their embassies press their cases in a blatant form of diplomatic intervention. The Ministry of Foreign Affairs and the Ministry of Defense were particularly worried about England, which still retained some lingering claims to the poorly defended archipelago. After heated nationalistic discussions within the Colombian government, the Ministry of Foreign Affairs finally imposed its view that Colombia should capitulate rather than risk losing the islands over a couple of engines. Electraguas ratified the original awards, and after a round of soothing correspondence had reassured everyone that no improper pressure had ever been intended by the foreign embassies, the Colombian government declared the episode closed.

Work began just in time, because by 1960 the only remaining 150-kilowatt plant on the island barely generated 100 kilowatts, as no machinery could long survive the standard treatment of bad weather, improper use, and poor maintenance. Fortunately a new plant of 800 kilowatts was on line by 1962, but already in 1964 the inhabitants were complaining about shortages and recurrent breakdowns even with the new equipment. The national government listened carefully to the petitions because of an event in 1964 that had revived the worst fears about the future of Colombian rule over the archipelago of San Andrés and Providencia. A group of natives had proclaimed their annexation to the United States, but when ignored by the U.S. government, had instead proclaimed their independence.[8] No significant local support materialized and the Colombian forces on the islands remained in control, but the military feared the independence movement was a pretext to spark a foreign intervention in the same manner as the 1903 loss of Panama.

To reduce the likelihood of another rebellion, the Colombian government began to cultivate the elite of the island more carefully; henceforth, the territorial utility concentrated more on trying to tie the islands closer to Colombia rather than simply providing electricity. The Colombian government sent larger amounts of funds, transforming the utility into the single largest business on the island. Most of the money was supposed to increase generating capacity, but the territorial governor had instead spent the funds to erect distribution lines in an isolated part of the island where he was also constructing his own luxurious mansion. An idealistic state engineer denounced this misuse, but the national government, rather than take remedial action, proceeded with plans to make sure that in the future the local elite could enjoy the plums of the utility business without any need to worry about the prying eyes of other state agencies.

The local elite particularly resented the indirect dependence via the Barranquilla Power Authority and instead had always wanted its own institution, but Electraguas had very little to build upon. The islands lacked native talent for even the simplest tasks, and several companies set up to distribute the electricity were total failures. Nevertheless, the local elite staged protest demonstrations to press for cheaper rates and to keep alive the demands for an institution under its control. The national government finally agreed in 1974 to surrender its plants, equipment, and distribution network to the newly constituted power authority for San Andrés and Providencia, which combined the by then standard pattern in the Colombian provinces as well as the territories of national ownership with local control. Less confident of its abilities, the San Andrés elite requested technical assistance from the national government on a permanent basis just to keep the plants going. Clearly the struggle to introduce modern electric service into these islands still had a long way to go, but the more immediate goal of tying the local elite to Colombia had been attained—at least for a time.[9]

Rural Electrification

Rural electrification began in Colombia in 1900. The first hydroelectric plant on the Bogotá river was situated at El Charquito (Map 3), twenty miles from the capital city. The owners of the intervening estates demanded light as a condition for allowing the erection of transmission posts through their properties and thus, in this very accidental way, electricity first came to the countryside. The utilities in Medellín, Bucaramanga, and other cities likewise extended services to rural areas in exchange

202

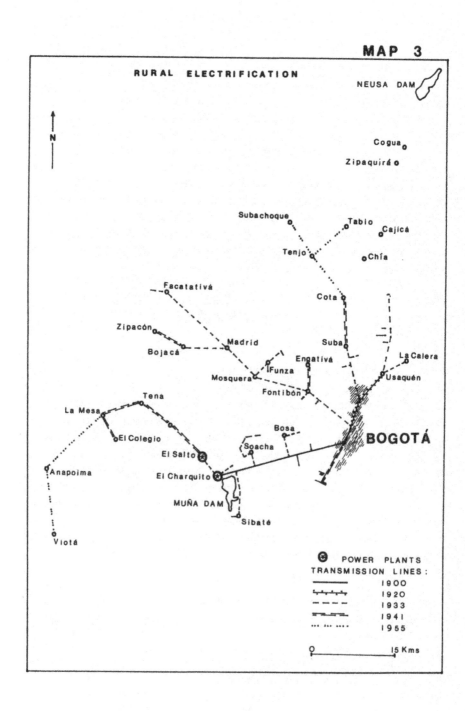

MAP 3

RURAL ELECTRIFICATION

NEUSA DAM

N

Cogua

Zipaquirá

Subachoque   Tabio   Cajicá

Tenjo   Chía

Facatativá   Cota

Zipacón   Suba   La Calera

Bojacá   Madrid

Engativá

Mosquera   Funza   Usaquén

Fontibón

Tena   BOGOTÁ

La Mesa   Bosa

El Colegio   Soacha

El Salto

Anapoima   El Charquito

MUÑA DAM   Sibaté

Viotá

POWER PLANTS
TRANSMISSION LINES:
1900
1920
1933
1941
1955

0   15 Kms

for right of way for their transmission lines. This situation occurred whenever a substantial distance separated a utility's generating plants from the urban consumption centers.[10]

None of the private utilities wanted any deeper involvement in the countryside, and they preferred to postpone this task until the twenty-first century. Nonetheless, isolated factories like the Industrial Corporation of Garzón appeared in the countryside. Such factories had no noticeable impact, however, since the overwhelming majority of industries preferred the cities. Landlords in the estates surrounding Bogotá had begun to use electric pumps for irrigation by 1915 in order to more fully exploit their fields, which were otherwise limited to an average of six months of rainfall each year. In effect, the landlords were responding to the increasing demand for food in Bogotá, whose population had increased from 100,000 in 1900 to over 400,000 by the end of World War II. The owners of the landed estates reached agreement in 1924 with the Bogotá Light and Power Company to receive power seven months of the year from 6:00 A.M. to 6:00 P.M. for a flat monthly fee. Because of fluctuations in the rainfall, this arrangement was not quite satisfactory. In practice, the electric pumps were not utilized every day during a specific month but rather on a number of days throughout the year that was equivalent to seven months. The Bogotá Light and Power Company installed meters in 1931 so that the farm estates could use power from 6:00 A.M. to 6:00 P.M. any day of the year and pay only for what was actually consumed.

The Bogotá Light and Power Company continued to serve the landed estates only because the owners were influential members of the elite who, if antagonized, could create difficulties for the company. Because of the wear and tear on the vehicles struggling through the impassable farm roads, just reading the meters cost more than the rates paid by these landlords. As a stopgap measure, the company decided in 1941 to take readings only twice a year and to estimate from those two readings the probable monthly consumption for billing purposes. As a consequence of such difficulties, utility companies throughout Colombia tried to put as much distance as possible between themselves and the countryside.

By 1940 the task of electrifiying the towns of Cundinamarca (the province that surrounds Bogotá) had become too big for the provincial government to handle, so it now pressed the Bogotá Light and Power Company to bring current to many of the isolated communities. The provincial government paid the company to build the transmission lines, which remained company property. But even with this inducement the company incurred losses because the extremely low income of most inhabitants of the towns did not allow them to subscribe to electric service. The only hope of covering expenses was to install additional distribution lines so that the company could gradually add clients who could pay—namely, the owners of the large landed estates. Political pressures had forced the Bogotá Light and Power Company to extend its transmission lines gradually during the 1940s to towns like Engativá, La Mesa, Tena, and others (Map 3). In the wake of this advance, the radius of rural distribution lines widened, more as an accidental byproduct than a deliberate goal, but service was always limited to the landlords.[11]

The Bogotá Light and Power Company steadfastly declined to participate, both as a private and later as a municipal firm, in the project to electrify the vast area that began from the northernmost lines of the company and stretched into the southern part of the bordering province of Boyacá. This refusal did not deter the proponents of such a plan, who instead managed to convince the Central State Bank to buy the Zipaquirá utility from the American and Foreign Power Company in 1947 and to build a large dam at the Neusa river. Investing scarce national capital to displace foreign investment was bad enough, but in addition, it was not even clear who would consume the electricity from the proposed hydroelectric plant. The real value of the dam was in the much needed flood control it could provide, but as a generating plant, it was too small for Bogotá and too large for the isolated towns in the Zipaquirá area. The sodium compound factory under construction could absorb some of the current, and any surplus capacity could go into rural electrification. But once again, it was not the peasants who would benefit, but rather the landlords who could use cheap electricity for irrigation.[12]

The Central State Bank proceeded with the Neusa dam and also poured large sums of money into creating distribution systems to reach the landed estates, but problems plagued the project. Strange leaks appeared in the foundations of the dam in 1954, and to prevent public panic out of fear the reservoir would break and cause massive flooding, expensive repairs were carried out in secret. When put in operation, drought hit the region and the reduced output of the plant provoked a political outcry from the inhabitants, who had been promised cheap and abundant electricity. The dam, which at first had seemed too large for the isolated communities, in fact turned out to be too small because the supply of water for generation was more unreliable than originally believed.[13]

By the 1950s the whole Neusa operation should have been turned over to either the Bogotá Light and Power Company or at least to Electraguas, but instead still another central state agency, the Autonomous Regional Corporation, was created in 1961 to handle the electric service as well as to protect the wildlife and natural resources of the area. With ample state subsidies, this Autonomous Regional Corporation went one step further and erected a distribution network that for the first time brought low-priced current to the peasants. The success was short-lived, because soon the Neusa dam faded into the background and became valuable more for its recreational attraction, and instead the Autonomous Regional Corporation had no choice but to buy almost all the electricity at high prices from the municipal Bogotá Light and Power Company for resale at subsidized low rates to rural consumers. A rate increase in 1966 met bitter opposition and made the corporation reluctant to risk another confrontation over hikes in the future. Finally, in 1970, not able to withstand buying high and selling low any longer, the Autonomous Regional Corporation handed the electricity business over to the Bogotá Light and Power Company. Only by means of transferring income from the city could the municipal company permanently subsidize electric service to the rural districts, which, groaning in poverty, otherwise would have remained in the dark.[14]

The economic system reigning in Colombia made it not only unprofitable but simply ruinous to provide electricity to peasants, yet this proven fact did not stop the Agency for International Development (AID). As a matter of fact, AID first popularized the idea of providing electricity to the peasants and even coined the expression "rural electrification," which previously was not heard in Colombia. According to the original AID formula, U.S. funds would go to newly created Electric Cooperatives in which the inhabitants of small towns and rural areas would pool their resources. Supposedly, as individual consumption rose, a snowballing effect would cause the whole countryside to become covered with these Electric Cooperatives and the communities would soon be able to repay the subsidized loans which had originally triggered electrification. Needless to say, such a logical but idyllic formula totally ignored the abject poverty and lack of skills in the Colombian countryside: When AID itself set up fifteen small plants on a trial basis, after a few months they broke down because of faulty maintenance. When the U.S. agency channeled the funds via other institutions, such as CVC, they were often sidetracked into the hands of the elite. As a matter of fact, CVC saw rural electrification more as a slush fund: Repayment of the AID loans for rural electrification was charged off to Electraguas, while CVC made no commitments about the final disposition of the loans.

However, at times the central state showed that it could electrify a rural area, as in the case of Marquetalia, a center of guerrilla activity in the Huila and Tolima provinces. The Colombian government was always afraid that this region might ignite a revolution modeled on Cuba. As part of a campaign on all fronts to eradicate the guerrillas, the central state agencies backed the army in the task of bringing electricity to the bulk of the population in the rebel districts. Because fighting was heavy and continuous in Marquetalia, the power authorities of Huila and Tolima, besides providing the equipment, had to train the army personnel who provided the service while fully armed. Several thousand soldiers were tied down for years in Marquetalia, but as the campaign gradually turned to success, the army became convinced that aspects like electrification had to be stressed in the coming pacification campaigns.[15] The National Federation of Coffee Growers went one step further and realized that electricity helped to prevent revolts from breaking out and turning regions into havens for guerrillas. Beginning in the 1960s, the National Federation of Coffee Growers financed projects to bring electricity to agricultural districts, but the sums invested were always dwarfed by the needs.

The growing popularity of rural electrification led to its use for public relations purposes, since at last here was a goal on which all could agree—particularly because nobody knew exactly what it meant. In July 1970 ICEL and the Bogotá Light and Power Company hosted the First National Congress of Rural Electrification, which was a complete publicity success. However, a real understanding of the true nature of rural poverty was still a long way off. No numerical definition for "rural" existed, and the main reason cited for electrifying the countryside was to keep the peasants on the land so that they would not come into urban areas and complicate "the problems of the city."[16] In any case, after this First Congress, the national government created a special bureau in ICEL to push programs for rural electrification.

The honeymoon for rural electrification quickly ended, and already by 1970 these programs had fallen prey to the permanent battle for contracts between rival factions of merchant-brokers. What little electricity was installed in the countryside was done mainly as a reward to bolster the position of the local bosses who delivered the votes on election day. By 1973 the much publicized concern over the fate of the 7 million peasants without electricity gave way to the goal of replacing the imported fuels consumed in the countryside with hydroelectricity. Out of a total of 1.5 million rural households, a very small minority of 25,000 generated a total of 25 megawatts in their own diesel or gasoline plants. These engines, which had appeared since the 1950s, testified to the inability of the central state to bring electricity to even all the wealthy residents in the countryside. In any case, nothing could change the fact that after nearly a century of experimenting with different formulas, rural electrification remained a prerogative of the elite.[17]

Notes

1. René De La Pedraja, *Historia de la energía en Colombia, 1537–1930* (Bogotá: El Ancora, 1985), pp. 121–123; *Popayán Liberal*, 10 Oct. 1946; *El Tiempo*, 14 Sept. 1946; *El Espectador*, 13 Oct. 1946; *El Siglo*, 6 Oct. 1946.

2. ICEL, *La electrificación en Colombia* (Bogota: Gráficas Carman, 1979), p. 20. Of the other small private companies, only Asnazú (400 kilowatts) did not require money for its purchase: The plant belonged to the gold mining concession, which reverted to the central state with all its equipment when the lease expired in 1956.

3. Antonio J. Posada and Jeanne de Posada, *CVC: Un reto al subdesarrollo y al tradicionalismo* (Bogotá: Tercer Mundo, 1966), pp. 163, 167; *El Tiempo*, 10 June, 4 July 1966.

4. *El Tiempo*, 16 Feb. 1963. For the CVC's "official account," see Posada and de Posada, *CVC*, pp. 83–85.

5. Germán Oramas O., *Panorama de las obras hidráulicas en Colombia* (Popayán: Universidad del Cauca, 1984), pp. 107, 122; *El Tiempo*, 11 Jan. 1964; *La República*, 12 Feb. 1970.

6. James J. Parsons, *San Andrés and Providencia: English-Speaking Islands in the Western Caribbean* (Berkeley: University of California Press, 1956), pp. 1–43; Robert H. Davis, *Historical Dictionary of Colombia* (Metuchen, N.J.: The Scarecrow Press, 1977), p. 198.

7. *El Siglo*, 7 Nov. 1947; *El Tiempo*, 16 Oct. 1948.

8. "Declaration of Sovereignty," 1964, White House Central Files, CO 51, Lyndon B. Johnson Library.

9. *El Tiempo*, 8 Aug. 1972; ICEL, *La electrificación en Colombia*, p. 22.

10. De La Pedraja, *Historia de la energía*, pp. 71–73, 130–131.

11. Empresas Unidas de Energía Eléctrica, *Informe*, 1940, p. 2; *El Siglo*, 10 Jan. 1946; *El Espectador*, 28 July 1946.

12. *El Espectador*, 27 July, 11 Dec. 1948.

13. Preliminary observations were enough to convince engineers of the Bogotá Light and Power Company that Neusa was not suitable for the company's power goals, and they quickly moved on to other more promising sites. As a goodwill gesture, the company handed these preliminary reports over to the Central State Bank, where without further surveys or measurements they were copied and turned around to prove that the Neusa hydroelectric dam was a desirable project.

14. Davis, *Historical Dictionary of Colombia*, p. 97; *El Siglo*, 30 July 1963; *El Tiempo*, 15 June, 19 Nov. 1966; *La República*, 10 April 1970.

15. Richard C. Maulin, *Soldiers, Guerrillas, and Politics in Colombia* (Lexington, Mass.: D.C. Heath and Co., 1973), pp. 30, 77. These pacification campaigns have become self-perpetuating in the 1970s and 1980s because of built-in momentum. Irrespective of the huge loss of life, the army can justify its role, and the rural populations, by revolting, finally get electricity and other much needed services.

16. World Bank, *Economic Growth of Colombia: Problems and Prospects* (Baltimore: Johns Hopkins University Press, 1972), pp. 216–217; *La República*, 18, 20 Feb., 27 July, 9 Oct. 1970; *El Tiempo*, 1 March 1970.

17. *La República*, 2 Aug. 1970; ICEL, *Plan Nacional de Electrificación Rural, 1973*, pp. 0-1-0-2, 138–141.

PART THREE

Coal

14

Coal: Ebb and Flow

Petroleum and electricity monopolized almost all of the attention the Colombian government could afford to provide for energy policies, leaving scant time for coal. Furthermore, petroleum and electricity replaced coal as the main fuel in many traditional uses. However, coal output did not decline and on the contrary continued to rise because of the appearance of a new type of consumer. The interplay between private investors and the national government over coal thus provides some final revealing glances into the shaping of energy policies in Colombia. The first section of this chapter offers a broad overview; of the many aspects of coal policy, three have been chosen for a more detailed presentation: the supply of coal to Bogotá, which constituted one of the few times this fuel attained public prominence, and attempts to export from the province of Cali as well as from Cerrejón on the Atlantic coast.

Coal in Colombia: A Global View

National policies toward coal were lacking partly because regional priorities have generally predominated in coal policies. Each region in Colombia had traditionally exploited its coal deposits in accordance with its own capabilities and perceived needs. Mining has been important in provinces such as Boyacá, Caldas, and Popayán, but production has been concentrated in the areas surrounding the three largest cities in Colombia, namely Bogotá, Cali, and Medellín. As a matter of fact, the abundance of nearby coal deposits was instrumental in the rise to prominence of those three cities. Conversely, the lack of coal deposits within close distance to the urban centers of the Atlantic coast provinces had placed another obstacle in their path blocking their ability to develop at the same pace as the cities of the interior.

The inadequate transportation system within Colombia made it easier for the Atlantic coast provinces to import coal from England and the United States than to transport it from the interior of Colombia. Con-

211

sequently, starting from the last decade of the nineteenth century, the Atlantic coast provinces imported increasing annual amounts of coal. In 1935, however, the impact of fuel oil as a substitute had sharply reduced coal imports, which henceforth hovered around 500 tons annually. The outbreak of World War II in 1939 halted coal deliveries from abroad, and to fill the gap, mines from Antioquia sent coal by railroad across the mountains to the Magdalena river for shipment downstream on barges to Barranquilla. Although temporarily workable, this system was very costly and only hastened the conversion from coal to fuel oil and other petroleum products for most Atlantic coast consumers.[1]

Fuel oil, because of its abundance and low prices, has been a strong rival of coal in Colombia since the 1930s. This abundance was a result of the type of oil deposits in Barrancabermeja and along the Magdalena river valley; the crude found underground, when subjected to normal refining processes, yielded unusually large amounts of fuel oil and, conversely, less gasoline. Expensive ways to extract more gasoline out of the crude existed, but generally at the Barrancabermeja refinery, if enough crude was refined to cover the domestic demand for gasoline, a surplus of fuel oil normally resulted. Traditionally Colombia has been unable to consume all this surplus. Even when Ecopetrol had to import gasoline in the 1970s and 1980s, it still exported excess fuel oil. Quite naturally, with this cheap fuel so easily available, the temptation for many consumers to abandon coal has been great.[2]

Although fuel oil could not replace coal in all areas, mine owners began to fear a sudden drop in their incomes. They had become accustomed to rising levels of coal output, which had surpassed 500,000 tons in 1940 and reached 1 million in 1949. The mine owners, who belonged to the Colombian elite, could not stop industrialists and other elite members from switching to fuel oil, but they could pressure the Colombian government to slow down the transition in the state railroads. A national railroad network did not exist; instead, small trunk lines isolated from one another served each region, at most only linking with the Magdalena river. The locomotives of each trunk line consumed the coal from their respective region. The Barranquilla railroad, which consumed imported coal, was the first to convert to fuel oil in 1935. This switch was the main reason for the sharp drop in coal imports in that year. The shortage of foreign currency and the lack of an organized group of local mine owners had allowed Barranquilla to convert quickly, but this was not the case in the Cali-Buenaventura trunk line, called the Railroad to the Pacific.

The Ministry of Public Works (in charge of the state railroads), had wanted to convert the Buenaventura-Cali line to fuel oil since the late 1920s. At that time, controversy over granting storage facilities in the port of Buenaventura to either Exxon or Shell had allowed the mine owners to halt the conversion to fuel oil. When in 1939 the Railroad to the Pacific announced the planned acquisition of eight fuel oil locomotives out of a total of seventy-seven in operation, the debate flared up again. The railroad needed the fuel oil locomotives to improve its passenger service because the high ash content of the local coal was covering the riders in soot. But none of this convinced the mine owners, who began to wage a campaign supposedly to defend regional interests against orders from the central government in Bogotá. The mine owners had traditionally exploited their labor force to the maximum, but now they paraded their workers as the victims who would suffer unemployment and hardships if the state railroads stopped purchasing coal. In 1940 the pressure mounted to the point that the Railroad to the Pacific decided to convert only 6 of the locomotives to fuel oil and to begin a very slow transition for the rest of the coal-burning locomotives that would not be completed until the late 1960s.[3]

Running old and wasteful locomotives caused state railroad services to deteriorate. The problems were not due to any inherent inefficiency in state organizations but rather to the fact that, between the 1930s and the 1950s, the state railroads were drained to subsidize the private mine owners, always on the pretext of saving the thousands of workers who were being brutally exploited in the mines. The strong protests in Cali had convinced the central state not to risk similar confrontations with the miners in the Bogotá area who had clearly expressed their opposition to converting the railroad lines to fuel oil. In Bogotá, the mine owners had overestimated their capabilities and soon discovered that the real problem was mining enough coal to supply the growing consumption in the capital city. Unable to supply all the coal needed, the local owners softened their insistence for coal in the Bogotá railroads. In 1951 the Colombian government ordered brand-new diesel locomotives with an Export-Import Bank loan.[4] These measures came too late to save the state railway system: By the time the opposition of the mine owners had disappeared, a new and even more formidable enemy had appeared in those members of the elite who, in order to safeguard the monopoly profits in their new truck companies, had to keep the state railroads in near bankruptcy.

As the railroads declined in importance for coal consumption (but not in their role as coal carriers), the mines found new markets that more than adequately absorbed their capacity, making any serious search for export markets unnecessary. Indeed, a situation of near scarcity prevailed with respect to coal, since mine owners were reluctant (with a handful of exceptions) to invest heavily in modern mining techniques and equipment. As a result, many corporations, both private and state, had to exploit their own deposits in order to cover their coal needs. In some cases conversion to fuel oil was not feasible; for example, certain technological processes specifically required coal. As a matter of fact, fuel oil remained an alternative mainly for small and medium-sized factories and shops.

The new markets for coal within Colombia can be classified under the principal headings of steam-generating plants, cement factories, and steel (including metal smelting), but there are also other important consumers, such as breweries and chemical plants. Steam plants to generate electricity had appeared in Colombia as early as the 1890s, but their impact upon coal consumption did not become significant until the 1940s. The pressure to mount steam plants increased as the utilities became state-owned. Once again, powerful influences forced Electraguas to buy coal from the private mines, in effect repeating the procedure used with the state railroads by making the utilities, such as Paipa, subsidize mine owners who were mostly members of the elite. This practice has not occurred in all cases, however; for example, the Bogotá Light and Power Company discovered that even after buying the available coal from private owners, it could only complete the supply it needed for the Zipaquirá steam plants by exploiting its own deep mines.[5]

Coal has been an indispensable energy source for the production of cement, and as construction increased throughout Colombia, cement factories have become important coal customers for the miners. The Samper family established Colombia's first cement factory in Bogotá in the 1900s, and a second factory appeared in Antioquia during the 1910s. Total coal consumption for the production of cement had already reached 37,500 tons by 1938. The inauguration of the cement factory in Cali in 1940 provided an important outlet for the coal of that region, and this factory was instrumental in easing the pressures that had kept the Railroad to the Pacific from switching to fuel oil.[6]

The metal shops of Colombia had consumed coal for their small smelters for decades, but the inauguration of the modern Paz del Río steel mill in 1955 had repercussions on energy consumption throughout Colombia. Up to the start of production in Paz del Río, Colombia had imported virtually all its iron and steel. But now the metal industries became major coal consumers. They needed large amounts of coal, beginning with the need to produce the coke consumed in the blast furnace and proceeding through the shops that elaborated the steel into finished products. To assure the supply of coal, Paz del Río has exploited its own mines, but here again a delicate balancing act has taken place between the large company and the many private mine owners: For its own coal mining operations, Paz del Río has preferred the deep veins, which is hard to find and expensive to extract, in order to avoid antagonizing the mine owners who can bring powerful political pressures to bear when not enough of their more easily mined coal is purchased.[7]

Other branches of industry, like the Bavarian breweries and the tire plants, have also been important consumers of coal. Chemical industries became large purchasers of coal in the 1950s, most notably the sodium compound plant near the salt mines at Zipaquirá, which branched out of its traditional activity (extraction of salt from the underground deposits). Coal has been used as an energy source but not as a raw material for the chemical industry—an intriguing possibility that because of lack of capital seems beyond the reach of the country.[8]

The Supply Crisis in Bogotá

In the 1910s coal became the main fuel for Bogotá, a city whose population rapidly grew from 100,000 inhabitants in 1900 to more than 400,000 by the end of World War II. Easily mined surface deposits of coal had displaced firewood and charcoal, whose output could not be increased because of the pressure upon agricultural land to grow food. Coal deposits were abundant; the proven reserves could supply Bogotá at the very least for the rest of the twentieth century.

This abundance had the private mine owners worried about lack of sufficient markets to sell the coal during the 1930s, which was why they did not want the state railroads near Bogotá to switch from coal to fuel oil. Their lobbying was so successful that the locomotives near Bogotá continued to use coal until the late 1940s. Yet the main consumers remained the individual households that burned the coal primarily for cooking but also for heating water and ironing. Because of Bogota's high altitude (8,500 feet above sea level), the coal did not burn properly and the abnormally high soot emissions soon enveloped the city in dense smog clouds. It only took a few hours for soot to accumulate around shirt collars. Besides, coal had the usual disadvantages of messiness in handling, the need for storage space, and higher transportation costs.[9]

The elite in Bogotá tolerated the many inconveniences of coal burning stoves for nearly half a century, partly to protect the mine owners, who were also members of the elite. The bargaining position of the mine owners was somewhat weak since they were handling an inferior product with possible substitutes. Yet the availability of coal tied in well with a larger elite goal. Because of coal, the elite could put off enlarging the generating capacity of the Bogotá Light and Power Company. Thus, coal in effect not only enabled the elite to postpone the introduction of electric stoves, but even more important, prevented rapid economic expansion. This situation served elite purposes well. Bogotá tolerated occasional interruptions in coal supply, as in 1933 when excessive rains flooded the mines, because once normal operations returned, the price of coal was still cheaper than electricity. In large measure, such price differences could be traced back to the elite's opposition to large hydroelectric expansions that could have lowered the price of the electric current. At the very least, the coal mine owners had to be very careful not to antagonize the other members of the Bogotá elite. Nevertheless, they eventually forgot how dependent they really were on these elite members.[10]

The break came in 1942, when the mine owners confronted Bogotá with sharp price rises. Coal suddenly became so scarce that the railroads had to seize their coal cargoes in order to reach the city. Wartime shortages had caused price increases in other articles as well, and the Colombian government established an office to put price ceilings on a variety of products. But the coal shortage in the Bogotá area could not be easily attributed to World War II because the region neither exported abroad nor imported this fuel. More to blame were the backwards mining methods then in use. Geologists had detected the problem as early as the 1920s, but without preventive measures the situation became worse: As mine shafts went down deeper, costs increased and underground water flooded the tunnels. Rather than install pumps and modern machinery for deep mining, the owners had grown accustomed to the mining equivalent of slash-and-burn agriculture in order to exploit their cheap labor force more intensively. The mine owners preferred to abandon a shaft and open another one nearer the surface into which they could send their masses of laborers to work effectively and profitably without any further investment. But in 1943 the dividing line was at last crossed when the coal output from easily mined surface deposits could no longer keep up with rising demand in Bogotá.

From the end of 1942 to the end of 1943, the price of coal rose 80 percent in Bogotá. The coal mining companies and retailers reaped windfall profits during this shortage because coal was still a basic necessity for cooking. The coal miners could not resist letting the prices float upwards, and to partake even more directly in the profits, now entered more deeply than before into the retailing of coal for homes. This bid by the mine owners to make fat profits out of a shortage caused by their own inability to assure an adequate supply of coal in the end became their own ruin, and the elite in Bogotá was quick to express its outrage at the exorbitant prices and to demand redress. The mine owners sensed that it was time to relent, yet the only way they knew how to push down prices was to impose cutbacks in workers' wages. In 1944, their normally submissive workers erupted into a wave of strikes with more than 2,000 workers in protest; not until 1946 did the labor agitation subside after the unions had won most of their demands.[11]

Under this crossfire between the unions, which wanted higher wages, and the Bogotá elite, which wanted lower prices for coal, the mine owners still did not back down but instead engaged in questionable means to stretch their profits. Since there was not enough coal to go around, the owners used their control over distribution to sell the consumers larger amounts of coal than what was actually delivered. Housewives protested against these unscrupulous practices; yet the temptation for profits was so great that in spite of numerous sanctions imposed by the price office, the violations continued.

The Bogotá elite concluded that clearly the time had come for stronger measures to deal with the mine owners. In spite of the cost and scarcity of electric stoves, they spread among upper class homes in Bogotá in the late 1940s. Many small factories that consumed coal converted to petroleum, and the railroads began their shift to fuel oil. Most significant, bottled gas became widespread for cooking and even reached into many lower class households. The gas previously flared at Barrancabermeja now at last reached urban consumers in Bogotá. Shortages of bottles, stoves, and auxiliary equipment kept gas from immediately displacing coal, but already in July 1947 coal prices took an unexpected nose dive. The drop had been motivated by a mine owner who, with unusual foresight, realized that unless all mining companies lowered their prices, they would soon lose their customers.[12]

The rest of the mine owners failed to follow suit, and coal prices resumed their upward rise again in 1948. The price office still did not approve raises high enough for most mine owners, and the national government tried vainly to curb another round of speculation and unscrupulous practices in the sale of coal to households. But the mine owners soon pointed to the strong labor unions as the perfect excuse to gradually abandon their mines or sell them to factories that needed the coal and would directly manage the operations. The households in Bogotá were not vulnerable to fluctuations in coal supply by this time, since during the 1950s and 1960s most housewives had turned to gas and electric stoves, which were later complemented by white gasoline.[13]

Coal Exports from Cali

The mines in the province of Cali, connected by road and rail with the Pacific coast port of Buenaventura 40 miles to the west, had exported modest amounts of coal during World War I and World War II. Shortages caused by wartime disruptions were responsible for these exports, but could Cali become a permanent coal exporter during peacetime market conditions? The question was irrelevant to a group of merchant-brokers in Cali headed by an influential member of the elite. These merchant-brokers concluded that the opportunity for large profits existed but not from the difficult coal mining operations. Rather, their profits would come from the commissions and kickbacks that would ensue if a complex for exporting the coal was built.

Europe's coal shortages did not end with peace in 1945 but continued into the postwar years. Playing upon fears of renewed scarcity, the Colombian merchant-brokers convinced the normally tightfisted French to grant a $3 million loan in 1949 to install an export capability for coal in the province of Cali. According to normal European practice, the loan from the Banque de Paris et des Pays Bas was conditioned upon the purchase of equipment from French manufacturers. But in this case France's need for a guaranteed supply of coal, rather than the desire to sell goods abroad, remained uppermost in French thinking.

With the French loan and Colombian state funds and under the prodding of the merchant-brokers of Cali, the Colombian government organized the Colombian Coal Company in 1950. In theory the shares would be held in equal parts by the state railroads, a consortium of private miners, and the Institute for Industrial Development, but in fact the latter was the real owner. The shares contributed by the state railroads represented the value of their coal mines, which they gladly turned over to the new company so that the Railroad to the Pacific could start to convert to fuel oil and at the same time stop subsidizing the private mine owners. The merchant-brokers found enthusiastic allies in the private mine owners, who eagerly supported the new coal complex as another way to channel public funds to their own pockets.[14]

The core of the export complex was the Coal Washing Plant imported from France. The merchant-brokers justified this expensive equipment on the grounds that in order to export large quantities, the coal had to be washed to reduce its high ash and sulphur content. Otherwise, foreign consumers could not mix it with other coals to produce coke. The Institute for Industrial Development also earmarked funds to modernize mining techniques with new equipment, while to improve transportation, the Institute spent part of the French loan to buy coal-carrying wagons for the Railroad to the Pacific. Each of these purchases generated profits for the insatiable merchant-brokers. Not surprisingly, the Coal Washing Plant overspent its budget, which forced the national government to postpone the inauguration of the plant that was supposed to have taken place early in 1955. The Coal Washing Plant required its own steam turbine to generate electricity, but lacking funds, Colombian Coal Company officials asked Electraguas to give them an electricity plant left from the Asnazú gold mining operations on the argument that the plant was supposed to remain within the mining sector. Electraguas turned down the request, and it was only after the Institute for Industrial Development invested larger capital sums that the Coal Washing Plant could at last begin production at the end of 1956.[15]

The operations of the Coal Washing Plant soon provided answers to the question of whether Cali could become a permanent coal exporter. The plant had the capacity to wash 125 tons of coal per hour, although it never reached that volume because of insufficient amounts of coal. The mine owners would only sell to the plant if it paid substantially higher prices than other customers. As to sales, local consumers were not convinced that the washed coal was inherently superior to the raw product and hence were not willing to pay more for it. Thus, the Colombian Coal Company could only produce coal for export. But since it had to pay high prices for its raw coal, from the very first the firm priced itself out of the world market. Shipments of washed coal caused disruptions for the Railroad to the Pacific, which was not used to handling these large amounts even with the new wagons. The port of Buenaventura lacked storage and loading facilities, so the coal piled up at one end of an open air dock for ten months. Only after 10,000 tons of coal had accumulated did the company finally, in October 1957, sell the coal to France for shipment aboard French vessels.[16]

These difficulties had gone beyond those normally expected in a new operation and in fact reflected deep underlying structural weaknesses within the very idea of the Coal Washing Plant, which gradually the Institute for Industrial Development came to regard as a white elephant. After careful studies of different reports and geologic surveys, the Institute finally untangled the contradiction that had appeared between the large proven reserves in the area and the small mining output. Abundant as the coal was, the deposits were located in narrow, twisting veins that were widely scattered, often vertical, and that frequently vanished. Small-scale extraction of modest amounts rather than large-scale operations were advisable. In the Cali area only a few mines were suitable for mechanization (unlike in Boyacá and near Bogotá), and almost all the shafts faced flooding problems from underground water. Earlier chemical analysis had also failed to detect the true magnitude of the composition: Ash content in the coal had originally been calculated at 15 percent, but later tests raised the figure to 27 and then 35 percent for the average deposits; finally, some geologists concluded that instead of talking about ash content, they should be referring to ash with coal sprinkled in! A Coal Washing Plant that could be profitable when using coal with 15 percent ash content could hardly expect to be so with a raw material of 35 percent and even more ash. As to sulphur, whose percentage content must be low in order for the coal to be suitable for making coke for blast furnaces, the Coal Washing Plant had little if any effect.

Too late, the Institute for Industrial Development realized that it had fallen into a cleverly prepared trap of the Cali merchant-brokers, who now hid behind provincial aspirations to keep the Coal Washing Plant in operation as a source of procurement and supply contracts as well as replacement parts. Early in 1958 the Institute put the Coal Washing Plant (the main asset of the Colombian Coal Company) up for sale in the hope of luring private investors. By now, however, news of the impending ruin of the Coal Washing Plant had spread throughout Colombian business circles and nobody had the least interest in taking over the bankrupt operation. Nevertheless, one foreign firm concluded that this plant was just right for its needs. This was the Dade Petroleum Company of Miami, Florida, the owner of coal-consuming industrial operations throughout the Caribbean and the Gulf of Mexico. This U.S. firm preferred to have its own supply of coal instead of depending on the uncertainties of the international market. The company made a good offer for the installations, and the Institute for Industrial Development, which by now was stuck with another 10,000 tons of coal piling up at the open air wharves at the port of Buenaventura, was all too glad to close the deal. The government moved fast but not quickly enough: Private mine owners in the Cali area felt that the efficient operations of the U.S. coal company would put them out of business—a groundless fear since the U.S. firm's primary concern was to export to its subsidiaries, not to supply local markets. These disgruntled mine owners teamed up with the merchant-brokers, who wanted the flow of central state funds via the Coal Washing Plant to continue undisturbed. Since no economic grounds existed for blocking the entry of the U.S. company, the mine owners and the merchant-brokers waved the flag of provincial interests and denounced the Bogotá government for selling away the Coal Washing Plant. In this way, they succeeded in stopping the deal with the U.S. firm.[17]

The money-losing Coal Washing Plant remained the property of the Institute for Industrial Development, which, with its hands tied, could do very little during the 1960s. The Institute did dissolve the Colombian Coal Company and put a new debt-free entity in charge of the holdings. Operations gradually ground to a halt, but expenses continued, since the upkeep alone on the installations was quite costly. The Institute for Industrial Development hit upon another idea in the 1960s: to dismantle and transfer the idle Coal Washing Plant to Boyacá or Bogotá to process the coal deposits of these regions. As soon as word of this move leaked out, the local politicians had a field day denouncing the national government for draining the province to favor the capitol, conveniently overlooking the fact that the plant had been totally financed out of the French loan and central state funds.[18] The provincial public outcry blocked the move. As a result, during the 1970s the Coal Washing Plant was left stranded and gradually deteriorated until it was unusable, thus bringing to an end this first major attempt of Colombia to become a permanent exporter of coal. By then, however, the attention of the Institute for Industrial Development had shifted to other coal deposits—this time on the Atlantic coast, as those were most likely to offer the best prospects for large-scale mining for export.

The Cerrejón Coal Deposits

In 1865 the engineer John May, in the service of the Colombian government, discovered the coal deposits of Cerrejón 42 miles from the Atlantic coast. May correctly estimated huge amounts of reserves, and he urged the Colombian government to exploit the deposits, claiming that they could become the center of a vast industrial complex. A bankrupt Colombian government, torn by civil wars and unable to obtain foreign financing, could do nothing, and by 1883 the Cerrejón project was dead.[19]

A few other inspections were carried out, but gradually the Cerrejón project disappeared from sight and was almost forgotten, in spite of the fact that the national government had published some of the geologic reports. Not until the outbreak of World War II did interest in Cerrejón revive. Because of the wartime demand for all the coal Colombia could export, the national government, looking for ways to increase its foreign exchange earnings, sent a geologic mission to the region around Cerrejón under Victor Oppenheim in 1941. The researchers reported back favorably to the Institute for Industrial Development, which then took the Cerrejón project under study. Strong international interest was evident: The U.S. government followed events closely, while Brazilian and English firms wished to invest in the project; however, World War II ended without any action or even commitments.[20]

Cerrejón remained the responsibility of the Institute for Industrial Development, which continued to examine the issue; but its attention was distracted by other projects, in particular the Paz del Río steel mill. In 1951 the Institute was ready to exploit the coal deposits by itself, since the cost of the machinery and equipment for the mining operations was not very high for a modest output. On closer analysis, however, the Institute dropped the endeavor as prohibitive in cost when it realized that a railroad as well as a harbor (not just a wharf) had to be constructed to export the coal. Since the national government was not willing to budget additional sums for the railroad and the harbor, the Institute had no choice but to turn to direct foreign investment as the only way to raise enough capital for the enterprise.[21]

To make sure no possible investor was ignored, the Ministry of Mines and Petroleum made an international call for bids closing in January 1958. The Germans were particularly interested in the Cerrejón coal deposits, but not the French, who had already been burned with the Coal Washing Plant in Cali. A number of U.S. companies had taken the first steps toward possible future exploitation by undertaking field surveys and hiring merchant-brokers as agents to handle the preliminary permits, and one investment banking firm, Smith, Barney & Company, claimed to have obtained property rights to the Cerrejón lands from local Indian tribes. Several U.S. coal companies wanted to participate, in particular Peabody Coal Co., but there were others as well, such as the Kentucky River Coal Corporation.[22]

The Colombian merchant-brokers pressed enthusiastically for these proposals as a sure way to make windfall profits by securing the mining concessions for the foreign firms, but the maneuver failed because none of the foreign companies took the bait. In addition to the bitter taste left by the Coal Washing Plant episode, the sums required to make Cerrejón productive were so large that any likely investor wanted all questions answered before pouring money into the project. Second, the coal in the deposits raised major marketing problems: Its low ash content (2 to 5 percent) made it ideal for steam boilers in electric generating plants but unsuitable for producing the coke used in blast furnaces. World demand for coal during the 1950s and 1960s leaned heavily toward coke rather than fuel for the steam generating plants, so that unless the Cerrejón deposits could be mixed with other types of coal to obtain a mixture suitable to produce coke, its export possibilities were severely limited. No solution could be found for this marketing problem, and by 1963 the Cerrejón mining project returned to the study stage, not to come out into the open again until the early 1970s when exciting international developments totally changed the perspectives for Cerrejón coal.[23]

Notes

1. René De La Pedraja, *Historia de la energía en Colombia, 1537–1930* (Bogotá: El Ancora, 1985), pp. 145–156, 166–170; República de Colombia, *Anuarios de Comercio Exterior, 1935–1945* (Bogotá: Imprenta Nacional, 1937–1949).

2. Luis Carlos Galán, *Los carbones de El Cerrejón* (Bogotá: La Oveja Negra, 1982), pp. 121–123, 139. From the late 1960s on Ecopetrol had wanted to install a new unit in the Barrancabermeja refinery to extract more than the usual 67 percent gasoline from a barrel of crude in order to reap foreign exchange benefits

greater than those gained from exporting the surplus fuel oil. The Colombian elite once again delayed and entangled the project so that when finally completed in 1979, it was too small for the refinery volume, and fuel oil remained in surplus.

3. 14 May 1929, 821.6362/17, Record Group (RG) 59, National Archives, Washington, D.C.; De La Pedraja, *Historia de la energía*, pp. 162–164; *El Siglo*, 22 Feb., 27 March 1939; *Boletín de minas y petróleo*, no. 154 (1950), pp. 67–68.

4. *El Tiempo*, 31 Oct. 1944; *Boletín de minas y petróleo*, no. 154 (1950), p. 63.

5. De La Pedraja, *Historia de la energía*, chap. 4; Empresa de Energía Eléctrica de Bogotá, *Informe y balance, 1975* (Bogotá: Cromos, 1970), pp. 49–50.

6. René De La Pedraja, *FEDEMETAL y la industrialización de Colombia* (Bogotá: Op Gráficas, 1986), pp. 28–30; E. Livardo Ospina, *Una vida, una lucha, una victoria* (Medellín: Empresas Públicas, 1966), pp. 82–84.

7. De La Pedraja, *FEDEMETAL*, pp. 35–38, 47–54.

8. Departamento Nacional de Planeación, *Plan de Integración Nacional, 1978–1982*; Kaiser Engineers, "Colombia Coal Deposits. Export Program Study," 20 April 1955.

9. D. Jaramillo to Alfredo Lozano, 24 Aug. 1931, Academia Colombiana de Historia; De La Pedraja, *Historia de la energía*, pp. 149–151; *Liberal*, 16 March 1946.

10. *El Tiempo*, 15, 19 Nov. 1933, 9, 10 June 1936, 15 Sept. 1941; *La Razón*, 4 March 1937.

11. *El Tiempo*, 28 Sept. 1937, 26 Feb., 27 March, 5 June, 22 Dec. 1943, 26 May 1944, 21 Jan. 1946; *El Siglo*, 9 June 1944, 17 March 1946.

12. *El Tiempo*, 22 June, 5 July 1946, 2 July 1947; *Liberal*, 16 March 1945.

13. *El Tiempo*, 15 June 1948, 21 May 1949; *El Siglo*, 23 May 1949; *El Espectador*, 16 Sept. 1950.

14. De La Pedraja, *Historia de la energía*, pp. 161–163; *El Siglo*, 5 July 1949, 24 April 1950; *El Tiempo*, 17 Nov. 1948, 23 May 1950; *El Espectador*, 16 Sept. 1950.

15. Kaiser Engineers, "Colombia Coal Deposits. Export Program Study," 20 April 1955; Oscar Iragorri, "Los carbones del Valle y del Valle del Cauca," *Industria colombiana*, no. 11 (Nov. 1954), pp. 41–43.

16. 22 April 1957, 10 Oct. 1957, 821.2552/4-2257, 10-1057, RG 59.

17. J. Phillip Rourck Report, 26 Aug. 1958, 821.2552/8-2658, RG 59.

18. Instituto de Fomento Industrial, *Informe 1970*.

19. René De La Pedraja, "La Guajira en el siglo XIX: Indígenas, contrabando y carbón," *Desarrollo y sociedad*, no. 6 (1981), pp. 353–354.

20. Sumner Welles telegram, 2 May 1941, 821.6362/19A, RG 59; *El Tiempo*, 16 Dec. 1944, 7 Dec. 1970.

21. Bureau of Mines letter, 9 Jan. 1950, 821.25A/1-950, RG 59; *El Tiempo*, 12 June 1951.

22. Memorandum of Conversation, 29 July 1959, 821.2552/7-2959, RG 59; Harvey F. Kline, *The Coal of El Cerrejón: Dependent Bargaining and Colombian*

Policy Making (University Park: Pennsylvania State University Press, 1987), pp. 52–53.

23. For subsequent developments, see Kline, *Coal of El Cerrejón*, pp. 55–177. I am not at liberty to discuss the Cerrejón crisis that rocked Colombia during the 1970s.

Epilogue

A survey of events from World War II to the present reveals how the Colombian elite has continued to manipulate energy policies to the detriment of the rest of the population. World War II convinced the ruling class to soften its opposition to economic growth. The export of agricultural products to pay for manufactured imports no longer guaranteed sufficient consumer goods to an upper class facing wartime supply shortages due to disruptions in shipping and foreign production. Colombia could not remain a purely agricultural country but had to attain a minimal industrial base to guarantee a good life for the elite. Scarcities of tires, steel, gasoline, and other items had inconvenienced many who could not understand why these shortages existed when Colombia was stockpiling unusually large foreign exchange reserves during the war.

The creation of Ecopetrol in 1951 was part of the process of industrialization that began in 1940 with the establishment of the Institute for Industrial Development. Later steps included the founding of additional industries, like the tire factory, the organization of the Flota Gran Colombiana shipping line, and the inauguration of the Paz del Río steel mill in 1955. These steps did not constitute true industrialization, much less "modernization," but were conscious and deliberate attempts by upper class members to guarantee a minimal supply of those goods and services considered vital to maintaining their quality of life. Since all these endeavors encountered bottlenecks because of insufficient electrical capacity, the Colombian elite accepted the creation of Electraguas in 1946 to reduce the lag in electrification.

By the mid-1950s Ecopetrol, Electraguas, the steel mill, the shipping and aviation companies, and other enterprises had all grown so rapidly that the mechanisms by which the Colombian elite had ruled a formerly agrarian society were no longer sufficient. This danger became clearly evident in the late 1940s during the outbreak of *La Violencia*, which resulted in tens of thousands of deaths. Thus, from the mid-1950s the Colombian elite, by means of a delicate balancing act, placed the brakes on economic growth and was successful in blocking expansion in sectors like electricity and steel, as well as others. In the case of petroleum, the same goal was achieved by the foreign oil companies that shackled Ecopetrol during the 1950s.

Before the Colombian elite could tighten the lid securely on further economic growth, a revolutionary movement came to power in Cuba in 1959. For the upper class, the timing of the Cuban Revolution could not have been worse; it totally upset their plans to slow down economic growth in Colombia. Guerrilla movements inspired by the Cuban Revolution appeared in Colombia, and the ruling class, much to its dislike, had no choice but to tolerate another burst of runaway economic growth during the 1960s as the only stopgap measure likely to check the armed insurgencies. While the Alliance for Progress was spending U.S. funds to prove that economic growth and political reform were possible within the system, the Colombian elite was looking for the first opportunity to bring a halt to the renewed economic expansion of the 1960s. Rather than serving the interests of the elite, the growth was unduly benefiting a middle class that was rising rapidly out of the lower class.

Guerrilla insurgency ceased to be a real danger during 1965–1970, and without this constraint, the elite slowly regained its freedom of maneuver to restore full control. Yet an event was needed to silence a faction within the elite that still clamored for more economic growth, and the proof came with the presidential election of 1970. The opposition candidate, none other than General Gustavo Rojas Pinilla back from exile, had mobilized considerable support among the middle class to the point that he weakened the control the elite had over lower-class voters. Rojas Pinilla won the election by an overwhelming majority, but he was not ratified by the government, which instead imposed the defeated candidate Misael Pastrana Borrero for a four-year term (1970–1974). The minority faction of the elite had been convinced that in order to prevent a repetition of the 1970 electoral disaster, they would have to halt economic expansion, the real threat to elite control.

Measures were swift in coming during the Pastrana Borrero administration, a turning point in Colombian history. Ecopetrol was permanently saddled with subsidizing the bus fares of the lower class, an impossible task that only served to perpetuate the country's bleak poverty. The Pastrana administration also terminated the Agrarian Reform and introduced a Housing "Reform" directed against the middle class, which henceforth was crushed with usurious loans whenever attempting to purchase a home. Not only was the middle class heavily penalized, but Colombia was trapped into crushing poverty for the remainder of the twentieth century. Yet a return to the quiet days of the 1920s was an impossibility, since economic and social forces had been released that deprived the Colombian elite of the privilege of acting with impunity. As a direct result of the 1970 imposition of the defeated candidate

Pastrana Borrero and his repressive measures, newly formed guerrilla groups emerged to perpetuate fluctuating levels of violent resistance.

The onset of the energy crisis of 1973 dealt another shock to Colombia. The sudden rise in world oil prices hit the country just as its own output was declining, so that in order to cover domestic consumption Ecopetrol had to import crude at prices that eventually reached the highest of the twentieth century. Colombia's cupboard of proven reserves was bare because during the previous decades the government had deliberately and consistently allowed foreign companies to drain away Colombian oil for export at rock-bottom prices. In 1973, there were still other fields waiting to be discovered, and accumulating evidence pointed toward the existence of large lakes of oil under the Llanos, but the Colombian government, rather than intensifying exploratory activity to find substitute fields, embarked upon a different strategy of importing large amounts of crude.

Two windfall opportunities gave Colombia time to experiment with alternate solutions to the foreign exchange crisis unleashed by the world energy crisis. First of all, frosts in Brazil pushed coffee prices upward from the mid-1970s until the early 1980s. Second, after 1976 the first stage of drug trafficking, characterized by the export of marijuana grown mainly in Guajira, brought large amounts of dollars into Colombia. By the time the market for Colombian marijuana crashed in the early 1980s, drug dealers had established an infinitely more profitable trade in cocaine, both as middlemen and refiners, and to a lesser degree as a source of coca leaves. By 1980 the drug business was bringing at least $2 billion into the country annually. The administrations of Alfonso López Michelsen (1974–1978) and Julio César Turbay Ayala (1978–1982), swimming in drug and coffee dollars, claimed to have permanently ended Colombia's foreign exchange scarcity. They had no hesitation about purchasing foreign crude with these earnings to cover domestic consumption; as a matter of fact, their economic advisers, under International Monetary Fund and World Bank influence, considered such a policy necessary to keep inflation at "acceptable" levels.

Few realized that the precious opportunity to invest Colombia's windfall coffee profits into long-term investments had been lost and that only the morally objectionable drug money now could foot the growing fuel bill. Even the López Michelsen and Turbay Ayala administrations tried to find a solution more acceptable in moral terms. Under the assumption that Colombia would always need to import oil, the López Michelsen administration pushed the idea that alternative ways of earning foreign exchange were the answer to the question of how to pay for foreign crude. The government placed great hopes on two big projects, both in the Atlantic coast provinces: the Cerrejón coal mines and the Cerromatoso nickel mill. Exxon received the concession to Cerrejón, whose deposits supposedly guaranteed massive exports far into the twenty-first century. At the same time, this project made the country a "net exporter of energy" because the exported coal amounted to more energy than the imported petroleum. Just in case coal prices fluctuated during the coming decades, the export from Cerromatoso of nickel ingots, a strategic metal, would compensate with additional foreign currency.

The rise of oil prices after 1973 likewise renewed interest in coal. Mines were reopened or expanded throughout Colombia by both private and state agencies to reduce their fuel costs. Strangely enough, the central state made no concerted effort to pursue this third alternative and neglected to replace oil- and gas-burning power plants with those fired by coal. The National Planning Department, ICEL, and most utilities throughout the country opted instead for launching vast hydroelectric projects that would make oil-burning power plants unnecessary. With so much money floating around, financing was no problem, and soon an impressive list of dams were on order across the country and in varying stages of work. The Colombian Ministry of Treasury decided to rely on traditional sources of financing, such as the World Bank, the Inter-American Development Bank, and the government export banks of individual foreign countries rather than obtaining private commercial loans from overseas. Thus, Colombia has the dubious honor of being one of the very few if not the only country in Latin America that cannot blame the foreign debt for its predicaments of the 1990s. While the central state kept the foreign debt to manageable proportions, the utilities ran up huge domestic debts as part of the traditional policy of subsidizing the elite through high-interest, short-term loans from local banks. As the different projects moved slowly from drawing board to the initial stages of construction, huge cost overruns enriched the merchant-brokers who benefited from an endless stream of contracts.

All the projects, including Cerrejón, Cerromatoso, the hydroelectric dams, and the few coal-burning steam plants, had assumed the indefinite continuation of high oil prices. When the prices started tumbling down after 1981, the whole economic policy program of the Colombian government had to be overhauled, a task that fell to the Belisario Betancur administration (1982–1986), which also faced declining coffee prices. The foreign exchange reserves accumulated during the second half of the 1970s started to evaporate as if they had never existed, and Colombia drifted once again into its normal pattern of recurrent foreign exchange crises. The country had thrown away the precious opportunity during the 1970s to escape underdevelopment. In the final analysis, drug money from cocaine dealers bailed out the country. But the failure of the government to come to grips with this reality forced the Belisario Betancur administration to search anywhere for a solution free of the moral drawbacks associated with the drug dealers.

Cerromatoso and the Colombian side of El Cerrejón ran up considerable debts of their own, and rather than foreign exchange earners became additional drains on the government. The foreign oil companies, however, had a convenient solution: In 1983 the press announced to an utterly surprised Colombian public the discovery of huge oil deposits in the Llanos by Occidental Petroleum Company. The fact that this oil company had not been prominent before in Colombia gave substance to the government's claim that its policy of incentives to new oil companies had at last, and for the first and only time, borne favorable fruits. Three years later it was finally disclosed that Occidental had merely acted as a partner for Shell, which now wanted to return to Colombia to exploit the oil fields that its geologists, working under Trompy, had discovered in the late 1930s. Shell obtained a 50 percent share of this venture, and Occidental transferred operations to a subsidiary (Cities Service). The Colombian government rushed to construct and pay for a pipeline that would carry the Llanos oil not to the teeming Colombian cities in desperate need of the energy source but once again to the coast for export as another "incentive" to the foreign oil companies.

Thus Colombian oil policy resumed its inevitable cycle: exporting crude when prices were lowest, and importing crude during periods of highest world prices. The oil company strategy for Colombia was clear: When prices were low, only very cheap fields like Llanos oil could be tapped for export, while during periods of higher prices, the more expensive fields were drained. A grateful Colombian elite cheered on the oil companies, who had loyally prevented any runaway economic growth that might threaten the privileged position of the ruling class. And the fears of the elite were far from groundless: The overthrow of the Shah of Iran in 1979 had shown that a rapid process of economic growth could lead to massive political upheavals.

Not all of Colombian society agreed with the elite's policy toward oil. Guerrilla units, always lurking in the background since the early 1970s, found in the Llanos oil deal a propitious opportunity to revive their activities. Beginning in 1984, guerrillas began hit-and-run attacks against oil camps and the newly constructed pipeline, causing huge monetary losses as well as large oil spills. Not even the combination of intense military patrolling and protection payments could fully halt the attacks. The guerrillas claimed that this oil belonged to all the Colombian people, but their message was lost in those isolated regions after the sensational seizure and burning of the Palace of Justice at Bogotá in 1985 monopolized world media attention. In spite of repeated negotiations, the Belisario Betancur administration failed to reach a meaningful truce with the guerrillas, who in larger groups attacked not just the Llanos pipeline but also an ever increasing number of targets throughout the country.

The Virgilio Barco administration (1986–1990) certainly did not inherit a very favorable panorama, but lacking original ideas, its only solution was to turn to the United States for a sloppy copying of some of the clichés then popularized under the Ronald Reagan presidency. Ignoring advice to drastically strengthen state institutions, the Barco administration preached a return to free-market mechanisms and proceeded to curtail state intervention whenever possible. No more public funds were invested in new enterprises, and numerous attempts were made to partially or totally sell the central state's shares in mining projects like El Cerrejón and Cerromatoso as well as in a whole range of economic activities, such as the Renault automobile assembly plant. Typical of the bills the Barco administration presented to the congress was a new mining code that attempted once again to revive the nineteenth-century precedent of recognizing subsoil rights as private property. Multinationals received concessions over the new gold discoveries near the Brazilian and Venezuelan borders. The draining of Llanos oil for export continued unabated—although Ecopetrol was still required to import crude to meet domestic demand.

The looting of natural resources has traditionally evoked little concern from the Colombian elite, but cutting back state enterprises was another matter. Members of the minority group that defended state intervention suddenly found themselves joined by powerful allies in the elite who realized that the private sector could only survive as a parasite draining funds from state agencies. Ample confirmation of this parasitic behavior could be found in the electrification projects, which by 1986 faced the worst possible scenario. The numerous projects begun in the flush years of the 1970s had not been finished even though their original budgets had been overspent, in some cases several times over. Government advisers worried incessantly about how to sell the electricity from this allegedly excess capacity, as Colombia's consumption in per capita terms has historically been among the lowest in Latin America. But in reality, shortages and rationing continued to plague many cities. Emergency measures such as costly diesel plants only increased the state's expenses, but since the merchant-brokers continued to reap profits from the bottomless pit of power plant expansions and operations, the elite necessarily had to oppose any drastic cuts in government subsidies to the utilities as well as to the other state enterprises.

The foreign debt crisis had blacklisted Colombia unjustly, so that the belated attempts in the 1980s to secure foreign commercial financing failed. Moreover, borrowing from local banks at high-interest rates had been stretched to its limit. The Barco administration was bankrupt of both funds and ideas by 1989, and the economy was left to limp along. The small middle class, reeling from repeated blows since the early 1970s, was virtually wiped out, and the lower class sank into levels of even more horrifying misery. The only bright spot was a slackening of population growth, but this trend did not have any impact on unemployment, which under its different forms climbed to the highest levels ever known in Colombia.

Guerrilla activity increased and was countered by death squads. An open civil war inflicted a growing number of casualties throughout the country on a daily basis, and the warfare drove Colombia to a situation similar to El Salvador's. In 1988 the guerrillas added power facilities to their list of targets, and one of their attacks left Bogotá without electricity for two days. Yet towering above all, the Colombian elite had so far managed to perform its balancing act and to survive in power by keeping the remaining classes poor, even at the cost of reducing the country to ruins. As Colombia enters the 1990s, an important question remains: For how long can the elite continue to waste natural resources and sacrifice the welfare of the majority of Colombians for the sake of maintaining its privileged position? Cracks and strains appear in the tottering structure, and although the ever ingenious elite may still be able to plug the gaps, there is no denying that unless a clean sweep is made during the 1990s, the failure to take the Colombian masses out of the grinding misery of the twentieth century will once again be repeated in the twenty-first century.

Index

www.ingramcontent.com/pod-product-compliance
Ingram Content Group UK Ltd.
Pitfield, Milton Keynes, MK11 3LW, UK
UKHW020432010325
455677UK00029B/1119